RORY
...

Also by Alan Shipnuck

LIV and Let Die: The Inside Story of the War Between the PGA Tour and LIV Golf

Phil: The Rip-Roaring (and Unauthorized!) Biography of Golf's Most Colorful Superstar

Like a River to the Sea: Heartbreak and Hope in the Wake of United 93 (with Jack Grandcolas)

The Best Is Yet to Come (with Harriet Diamond)

Monterey Peninsula Country Club: A Complete History

The Swinger (with Michael Bamberger)

Swinging from My Heels: Confessions of an LPGA Star (with Christina Kim)

The Battle for Augusta National: Hootie, Martha, and the Masters of the Universe

Bud, Sweat & Tees: Rich Beem's Walk on the Wild Side of the PGA Tour

RORY

The Heartache and Triumph of Golf's Most Human Superstar

ALAN SHIPNUCK

SIMON & SCHUSTER

London · New York · Amsterdam/Antwerp · Sydney/Melbourne · Toronto · New Delhi

First published in the United States by Avid Reader Press, an imprint of Simon & Schuster, LLC, 2026
First published in Great Britain by Simon & Schuster UK Ltd, 2026

Copyright © Alan Shipnuck, 2026

The right of Alan Shipnuck to be identified as the author of this work has been asserted in accordance with the Copyright, Designs and Patents Act, 1988.

3 5 7 9 10 8 6 4 2

Simon & Schuster UK Ltd
1st Floor
222 Gray's Inn Road
London WC1X 8HB

For more than 100 years, Simon & Schuster has championed authors and the stories they create. By respecting the copyright of an author's intellectual property, you enable Simon & Schuster and the author to continue publishing exceptional books for years to come. We thank you for supporting the author's copyright by purchasing an authorised edition of this book.

No amount of this book may be reproduced or stored in any format, nor may it be uploaded to any website, database, language-learning model, or other repository, retrieval, or artificial intelligence system without express permission. All rights reserved. Enquiries may be directed to Simon & Schuster, 222 Gray's Inn Road, London WC1X 8HB or RightsMailbox@simonandschuster.co.uk

Simon & Schuster strongly believes in freedom of expression and stands against censorship in all its forms. For more information, visit BooksBelong.com.

www.simonandschuster.co.uk
www.simonandschuster.com.au
www.simonandschuster.co.in

Simon & Schuster Australia, Sydney
Simon & Schuster India, New Delhi

The authorised representative in the EEA is Simon & Schuster Netherlands BV, Herculesplein 96, 3584 AA Utrecht, Netherlands. info@simonandschuster.nl

The author and publishers have made all reasonable efforts to contact copyright-holders for permission, and apologise for any omissions or errors in the form of credits given. Corrections may be made to future printings.

A CIP catalogue record for this book is available from the British Library

Hardback ISBN: 978-1-3985-5259-3
Trade Paperback ISBN: 978-1-3985-5260-9
eBook ISBN: 978-1-3985-5261-6

Interior design by Silverglass

Printed and Bound in the UK using 100% Renewable Electricity at CPI Group (UK) Ltd

For Diana Horowitz and Ann Hill, the strongest women I know

RORY

Foreword

The thick-cut steaks were long gone and the remnants of the ice cream sundaes had been cleared away, too. Rory McIlroy leaned in from his cushy leather seat in the Bombardier jet and finally asked me a question he had been stewing on for most of his life: "What's he really like?"

The man in question was, of course, Tiger Woods. The magnetic presence on a grainy TV screen who had inspired McIlroy to chase his golf dreams when he was a wee lad in Northern Ireland. The living legend who set a standard of excellence against which every great player coming up would forever be measured. The cautionary tale whose tawdry self-immolation terrified all the young studs just getting their first, succulent taste of fame and fortune. Rory had studied Tiger, venerated him, modeled himself after him, pitied him. Now McIlroy was the anointed successor: the Bombardier was whooshing from Shanghai to Zhengzhou, where Rory would face Tiger in an eighteen-hole exhibition match. It was a glorified way to pimp real estate at a gaudy new development catering to Chinese robber barons, but, for McIlroy, the day had a deeper meaning. Woods never had a real rival or even a reliable foil. David Duval was too aloof to connect with the public; Vijay Singh, too misanthropic. Ernie Els didn't want that smoke. Phil Mickelson had more game than any of them, and he slowly warmed to the challenge, but Tiger wouldn't deign to legitimize him as a worthy adversary—he couldn't stand Phil's bluster and bullshittery. Woods also felt Mickelson had committed the original sin of not working hard enough to maximize his awesome talent. Then McIlroy came along and won the 2011 U.S. Open by eight strokes at age twenty-two and then the '12 PGA Championship by another eight shots. Woods recognized the kid's immense physical gifts and, more to the point, detected a familiar hunger.

McIlroy ascended to number one for the first time by dusting a resurgent post-scandal Woods in a shootout at the Honda Classic in March 2012. Afterward, he said with a laugh, "It had to be Tiger." Eight months later, McIlroy found himself alongside Woods in Zhengzhou for this orchestrated passing of the baton.

The opening ceremony was over-the-top even by the standards of Chinese new money: a drum corps, fireworks, a confetti shower, stunt planes, a ceremonial gong. McIlroy and Woods kept stealing deadpan glances at each other, trying to hold in their laughter. On the course, the scene was barely contained chaos. Three thousand fans streamed across the fairways, with soldiers locking arms to form a human fence to keep perfectly coiffed female fans from aerating the greens with their stilettos. On the tee boxes, there were so many camera clicks that it sounded like machine-gun fire. McIlroy and Woods chatted and laughed throughout the early going, their chemistry palpable. It got a little quieter after Woods missed a short birdie putt on the ninth hole, leaving him two shots behind McIlroy in their stroke-play match. Woods continued to brood, dropping a couple of f-bombs that weren't translated for the audience watching live on CCTV. He chipped in for birdie on the twelfth hole but could not run down McIlroy, who was flawless tee to green while shooting a 67 to win the match by a stroke. "When he gets things rolling it's impressive," said Woods. "He's really, really hard to beat."

McIlroy was gracious in victory. He had enjoyed immensely being welcomed as an equal by Woods but still found him unknowable. What had he learned about Tiger during their mano a mano?

"Nothing," McIlroy said. "We talked a lot, but he gave away nothing. It's not like I didn't try."

Despite dozens of ensuing biographies and an HBO documentary, Woods's inner self remains a well-guarded fortress. Yet somehow, McIlroy has maintained his open, engaging, intellectually curious manner. That was part of the problem: lacking the asshole gene that is prominent in so many great golfers, McIlroy spent a full decade as a semi-tragic figure, serially failing in the tournaments that meant the most. The outpouring of emotion around McIlroy's triumph at the 2025 Masters was not really about golf—it was more about the affection that fans (and reporters) have for him as a person and the shared admiration for how he has handled himself growing up in the spotlight. McIlroy's completion of the career Grand Slam at Augusta cemented his status as the most important figure of the post-Woods epoch; no other player can match his consistent excellence, massive media presence, and transcontinental impact. McIlroy has often been celebrated as Tiger's antithesis thanks to a (mostly) squeaky-clean image, but in fact Rory has had more than his share of tabloid romance, bitter business disputes, and divisive politicking. Once universally liked and admired, McIlroy has become more polarizing in his mid-thirties.

"He's a lovely person," says Chris Peel, McIlroy's old headmaster at Sullivan Upper School in Holywood, Northern Ireland. "Heroes sometimes become fallen heroes . . . That's never going to happen to Rory. I would bet my house on that—because of his upbringing."

Lee Westwood has a different take: "He's a fucking drama queen."

McIlroy contains multitudes. He has always been the undisputed pressroom MVP because of his candor, thoughtfulness, and capriciousness. He is both a stately ambassador and trash-talking troll, often in the same monologue. "I'm ignorant and naive and don't give things much thought," he says, in what is actually an admirable bit of self-reflection.

I have experienced the different sides of McIlroy. In 2017, I wrote a cheeky, purposefully over-the-top obituary for the Ryder Cup, forecasting a decade of U.S. dominance that would kill interest in the event.

This became bulletin board material for Team Europe in the run-up to the '18 Ryder Cup. When the American team laid an egg in Paris, I had plenty of yolk on my face, too. I knew the victors' press conference was going to be rough when, as the players were arriving on the dais, Sergio García winked at me and Ian Poulter raised his champagne glass and blew me a kiss. But it was McIlroy who brought it all home, saying to a global audience, "I think collectively we all have one question: Where is Alan Shipnuck? Heeeyyyyyyy!" Fair play. If you dish it out you gotta take it, too. Three years later, after Europe lost the Ryder Cup, I asked McIlroy a golfy question, and at the end of a long answer, he added, "Have you seen the name of the seventh hole this week? It's Shipwreck for the people in the back!" That's a nickname a few Tour players have tagged me with through the years. It was an amusing moment in an otherwise downbeat press conference.

But McIlroy also has "pointy elbows," in the words of Paul McGinley, his onetime Ryder Cup captain. McIlroy and his manager, Sean O'Flaherty, didn't pretend to be thrilled when I told them I was writing this book. Said O'Flaherty, "If it's not *our* book, there's not much incentive for Rory to participate." I parried that Jack Nicklaus and Arnold Palmer had been the subjects of dozens of books, and they always sat for interviews with their biographers because they understood the value of burnishing their own legends and telling their side of every story. O'Flaherty said he'd pass that sentiment along. I got McIlroy one-on-one after his victory at the 2025 Pebble Beach Pro-Am, and I thought I detected a détente in his thoughtful answers. I pitched O'Flaherty on an interview pegged to McIlroy's burgeoning business empire, which would have value for both of them, as the agent looks quite clever for taking a 20 percent stake in their investment firm, Symphony Ventures. I wanted the opportunity for the book, of course, but I also had a contract to write up the story for *Bloomberg Businessweek*, which I knew would make the idea more attractive to McIlroy, as former Mayor Mike Bloomberg is an occasional golf buddy. O'Flaherty loved the idea; we started going back and forth about putting the interview on the calendar. The conversation continued into the '25 U.S. Open. As McIlroy warmed up on the driving range for his second round, I found O'Flaherty where he always is, twenty-five yards behind his man, leaning against a metal railing. We were chatting quietly when I heard "Hey, Alan . . ." in a familiar lilt.

I looked up and McIlroy was staring me down. His eyes were slits and his face twisted into a scowl. As soon as we made eye contact, he growled, "Fuck off."

O'Flaherty and I froze. *Wait, did he just say what I think he said?* McIlroy took a couple of steps toward us and pointed his driver at me.

"Seriously, fuck off." There was no mirth.

I asked O'Flaherty if he knew why his man was upset. "No idea," he said.

In that split second, I had to make a decision. My USGA-issued press credential granted me access to the range—no player has the authority to revoke that. But McIlroy had been in a weird headspace ever since his life-changing Masters victory two months earlier. Now he had the puffed-up body language of a matador, and a constructive conversation seemed unlikely; I was disinclined to provoke more profane misbehavior a half hour before his second-round tee time, in full view of a packed grandstand and the NBC cameras. I walked away. McIlroy marched to Oakmont's first tee and promptly suffered a double bogey, making it clear that this would be another lost week during his post-Masters ennui. In the ensuing hours, he tomahawked a club down the fairway and eviscerated a tee marker in fits of pique. (As a consummate professional, I allowed myself only a tiny bit of pleasure in McIlroy's crashout.) Afterward, he stormed past waiting reporters, continuing a sudden and mystifying churlishness.

With some trepidation, I waited by McIlroy's courtesy car in the Oakmont parking lot following the final round, hoping to clear the air. He frowned when he saw me. I raised my hands and said, "I come in peace." McIlroy stopped short of apologizing for his driving range outburst but did allow he "could have used different language." I said I still didn't understand why he had been so angry. "I was trying to get ready for my round," he said, "and when I saw you talking to Sean, I couldn't concentrate." It was a bizarre admission from one of only six men in golf history to win the career Grand Slam.

But we were practically whispering—could he even hear our voices?

"No," Rory said, "but just your presence was bothering me."

Well, there goes the sit-down interview! That was fine. Collaborative biographies skew toward the bland and sanitized, and McIlroy has enjoyed such a public life that there was already a wealth of material for me to draw upon, including over a thousand press conference transcripts, to say nothing of our various conversations through the years. Still, I asked him why, exactly, the idea of this book had gotten in his head. McIlroy said, "It pisses me off that you're making money off my name." This seemed utterly ridiculous coming from a man on his way to becoming a billionaire, but Tiger Woods, whose earnings topped out at $120 million a year, always conveyed the same beef to the many would-be biographers he blew off. I assured McIlroy that book money is a tiny fraction of Grand Slam lucre and that he wasn't missing out on much. Beyond that, he's a serious student of golf history and an avid reader—didn't he want to be part of the game's rich literary tradition? I mean, when you're one of the most compelling golfers ever, *someone* is going to write a book about you.

"You can do what you want," McIlroy said, "but don't expect me to be excited about it."

I'm pretty sure the issue isn't money—it's control. McIlroy was the first golfer whose superstardom was born during the social media age, which upended the dynamic between reporters and athletes; the jocks quickly sussed out that they didn't need old-fashioned scribes to tell their story. In 2019, McIlroy cut a groundbreaking deal with Golf

Channel and its parent company, NBC, to cofound GolfPass and monetize his media: for $99 annually, subscribers have access to a wealth of exclusive McIlroy-centric content (among other things). Throw in his 8 million social media followers and the slick ad campaigns of his many blue-chip sponsors, and McIlroy has near-total dominion over his image. He would have no such control over this book. In the Oakmont parking lot, he referenced my 2022 biography of Phil Mickelson; Lefty got himself in very hot water due to impertinent and deeply cynical remarks in the book about his soon-to-be masters at LIV Golf.

"You fucked Phil," McIlroy said.

"Actually," I replied, "Phil fucked himself."

"I'm not going to make the same mistake."

It was a good walk-off line. We shook hands, wished each other happy Father's Day, and then McIlroy drove off to catch a ride home in his $60 million G-VI jet. (Authors fly coach, sometimes in a middle seat.)

McIlroy need not be so concerned. The only goal for this book is to provide an unvarnished answer to an old question as McIlroy enters the final act of a highly eventful career: What's he really like?

1.

Bobby Fischer's brilliance was nurtured on the chess tables in Washington Square Park, Mozart's gifts were fine-tuned on the piano in the family flat in Salzburg, Rimbaud's poems informed by the seedier corners of the Left Bank. Rory McIlroy's genius first became evident on the cramped practice area adjacent to the seventeenth hole of Holywood Golf Club, in the hills outside of Belfast. Holywood is a little bandbox of a course lacking the land for a proper driving range; the modest hitting area was where members could smack balls late in the day, as Gerry McIlroy often did before his shifts as a bartender. He would park his only child in a stroller on the practice tee to watch. This wouldn't fly at a stuffy joint like Royal Belfast, but Holywood has always been a low-key, workingman's golf club. (There is a sign in the men's locker room that reads: *The washing of Golf Shoes & Clubs is strictly prohibited in the Toilets, Wash Hand Basins and the Showers. By order of Management Committee.*) Watching his father, little Rory delighted in observing the *whoosh* of the golf club and the *thwack* of a well-struck shot. He was barely a year old when Gerry gave him a set of toy clubs. "He was holding a golf club before he could walk," says Rory's mother, Rosie. "He'd be sitting in the pram with a plastic golf club in his hand. That's the way we were woken up in the morning: banged over the head with a plastic golf club!"

When the boy was old enough to wriggle out of his stroller, he duly imitated his dad. The pint-sized Tiger Woods had a strikingly similar initiation to the game, watching his father, Earl, smash balls into a net in the garage of the family home in Cypress, California. At ten months old, Tiger took his first swings, and Earl shouted to his wife, Tida, "We have a genius on our hands!"

Gerry McIlroy had none of Earl's bombast but possessed a similarly keen eye for golfing talent, as he grew up competing against three brothers who were strong players, including Colm, who long held the Holywood course record with a 63. Colm was not even the best athlete in Rory's family tree, as his maternal uncle, Mickey McDonald, played semipro soccer and high-level Gaelic football. A scratch golfer in his heyday, Gerry was awed by his young son's hand-eye coordination and the smooth, efficient way he coiled his body into the golf swing. The plastic clubs were swiftly replaced with a cut-down 5-wood. Gerry imbued a few basic fundamentals and let Rory have at it. The boy's precocity soon became the talk of Holywood. "As soon as Rory was able to get out of the buggy, he had plastic clubs and was knocking it around the club," says Paul Gray, a fixture at Holywood G.C. for decades as the general manager and, before that, head professional. "It wasn't too long after, when he was 3, that he had this little proper golf swing." Gray, who used to caddie for Gerry McIlroy in club championships, became an occasional dispenser of counsel for young Rory.

The McIlroy home, at 43 Belfast Road, was a simple brick structure attached to the house next door. Rory turned it into a homemade golf course, hitting plastic balls from room to room. With Rosie's grudging assent, he began chipping real golf balls from the hallway through the kitchen and into the washing machine. Gerry installed a synthetic putting green in the yard, and Rory spent so much time there that floodlights were eventually installed. Rather than cartoons, the kid was transfixed by *Nick Faldo's Masterclass*, a VHS tape filled with old-school wisdom imparted with Faldo's voice-of-God assuredness.

Rory also began tagging along for rounds at Holywood G.C. with his father and a rotating cast of uncles and their friends. The club had rules legislating access to the course for junior golfers, but they were not strictly enforced for Rory because he was a well-mannered kid from one of the club's most popular families. It certainly helped that Rory's game was advanced enough for him to keep up with the adults. He would have been eligible for a junior membership at age ten, but recognizing a special talent in their midst, Holywood stewards allowed the kid to join the club three years early. "At seven he had a complete game," says Gray. "You never know how far someone is really going to go but it was all there in terms of technique, how he hit certain shots and how he could see the game." It fell upon an old-timer named Eddie Harper to conduct McIlroy's admission interview. Speaking generally of the role golf can play in helping youngsters grow up, Harper says, "You could see them progressing from some of them thinking they are Jack the Lad until they were told: 'You do what you are told.'" Already displaying a high emotional intelligence, McIlroy appealed to Harper's old-school worldview during his interview. "He assured me he knew all the rules of golf," says Harper, "and would not annoy people."

As a boy, McIlroy already had a vision of his future. He would amble into the pro shop, grab a scorecard and pencil, and, in careful script, write his destiny into existence. In the scorecard box titled "Competition," he would jot, *Open Championship*. "And then he'd fill out his score," says Gray. "And it was always like 6 under, 9 under. It was always something ridiculous and then he'd sign it at the bottom: *Rory McIlroy*. And then in the marker's box he would sign, *Nick Faldo* or some other great player. At the time I didn't think anything of it. But he was really stirring the dreams in his own mind."

McIlroy turned seven in 1996, the year Tiger Woods left Stanford and immediately reshaped the pro game in his image. Highlights of Woods's brooding intensity, lusty fist pumps, ferocious swings, and spectacular recoveries were beamed all the way to Holywood. Woods's panache and creativity were starkly different from Faldo's plodding, meticulous, anodyne precision. A poster of Woods quickly found a place on the wall in McIlroy's bedroom.

The 1997 Masters remains a core memory for McIlroy. He already enjoyed a Sunday tradition of watching the final round of European Tour events with his father and then, after dinner, being allowed to stay up past his bedtime to catch the PGA Tour telecasts. But the Masters was a four-day holiday in the McIlroy household, as Gerry and his son would cram in as many hours of viewing as possible. "I watched it all," Rory says of Woods's march to history in '97. "He shot 40 on the front nine on Thursday, came back in 30, and then just completely blitzed the field after that. I remember him hitting wedge like into 15 both days on Friday and Saturday. Yeah, it was just a complete masterclass." He adds, "I certainly tried to model part of my game off him." In a later interview, Rory admitted, "Ever since then all I wanted to do was be like him. I was a cocky and arrogant kid, I told anybody who would listen I'd be the best golfer in the world."

It was also when he was seven that McIlroy began one of the foundational relationships of his life, with Holywood's young teaching pro, Michael Bannon. It was a comfortable pairing: Bannon attended Gerry and Rosie's wedding and had lived across the street from the McIlroys for three years. (He eventually left Holywood to become the head pro at Bangor Golf Club, fifteen minutes down the A2.) Bannon understood that he had been entrusted with a weighty responsibility. His philosophy was to let Rory be Rory. He eschewed overly technical talk and focused on feel. "I would never stand there and say, 'Do this, do that,'" Bannon says. "I'd give him a little something, he'd go away with it and make it his own." Bannon has thousands of McIlroy's swings on video, meticulously cataloged by year; they started out on DVD and now live on hard drives. He still possesses a DVD on which is scrawled, *Rory: 8 years old*. The kid is wearing a yellow Nike sweatshirt and a black Nike hat in the manner of his new god, Tiger. (As defending champ, Faldo helped Woods wriggle into his green jacket.) "Bend your knees a wee tiny bit," Bannon says on the video in a gentle voice. "Hold your balance. Hit it when you're ready." Little Rory absorbs the instruction effortlessly and makes a fluid, rhythmic swing; the ball disappears to the horizon. Within a year, Bannon could ask McIlroy to hit a draw or a fade on command. "Just like a Seve," Bannon says, a reference to the high priest of shotmaking, Severiano Ballesteros of Spain, whose youthful brilliance reinvigorated European golf in the late 1970s. "He could feel the ball with his hands," Bannon says of McIlroy. "He could feel the club. 'Hit it high. Hit it low.' He could just do it."

Gerry and Rosie had long talks about what to do with their young prodigy. They may or may not have been aware of the most famous line from the Irish writer James Joyce's classic *A Portrait of the Artist as a Young Man*: "When the soul of a man is born in this country there are nets flung at it to hold it back from flight." The McIlroys decided to do all they could to give their child wings; they were haunted by the feeling that their son's talent came with an obligation, even a burden. Gerry embraced a rigorous work schedule to fund Rory's golf: from 8:00 a.m. to noon he cleaned toilets and locker rooms and vacuumed hallways at a rugby club—it doesn't get any more blue collar than that. From noon until 6:00 p.m., Gerry tended bar at Holywood Golf Club; after racing home for supper and a spot of tea, Gerry returned to the rugby club at 7:00 p.m. and worked as a bartender until midnight. As soon as he walked in the door, Rosie would leave for the graveyard shift at a nearby 3M factory, assigned the mind-numbing task of filling shipping crates with packing tape. One day, Rory asked his parents, "Why are we not like a normal family?" Gerry had a ready answer: "Sometimes, you might get a bit browned off or tired but Rosie would always cheer me up. 'Gerry,' she'd say, 'one day this could be all worthwhile.' . . . We wanted to give our child a chance—after all, he was the only one we have."

Of his parents, Rory says, "They basically never saw each other." Yet he learned much from observing them. Rosie was a tower of strength—

loyal, loving, steadfast, wary of outsiders. Both of her parents died young; she dropped out of school at sixteen to work on an assembly line. Gerry came from a slightly more prosperous clan. He could light up any room with his warm and open manner. Rory absorbed his father's favorite saying: "It's nice to be nice and it doesn't cost you a penny." His parents had high standards for his comportment. Gerry did not brook any displays of petulance or anger on the golf course. Rosie kept Rory in line everywhere else. Seamus O'Connor was a regular presence at Holywood Golf Club during Rory's youth and would later become club captain; his wife was Rory's elementary school teacher. "Rosie would ask how he was doing and, if there was ever a problem, just to let her know," says O'Connor. "There was no messing about. By that time he was obviously very good at golf but there was no question of special treatment."

Rosie's sleepless nights and Gerry's endless workweeks funded their son's golf dreams. In 1997, when Rory was eight, the family traveled to San Diego for the Junior Worlds—Tiger Woods launched his legend by winning his age group six times—and Hawaii for the World Junior Masters. Seeing the wider world inspired Rory to dream big. In a 1998 interview with BBC Sports, the young, shy boy first told the world about his most outlandish dream: "I want to win all the majors." Later that year, when Rory was nine, the McIlroys journeyed to Florida for the Junior Orange Bowl International Golf Championship, played at Doral's Blue Monster, a longtime PGA Tour venue. Rory competed in the 9–10 age division, cutting a distinctive figure. "He had a little swagger and a big head of curls," says Wally Uihlein, then the CEO of Titleist and FootJoy's parent company, Acushnet; his son, Peter, played in the same age group as McIlroy. "His swing then doesn't look much different than now, with this wonderful full shoulder turn. From there, he dropped it in the slot and just let the club go. In the under-fourteens, there are always a few big kids who can bomb it but have no short game. What stands out is the kid who has all the shots. Rory wasn't big, but he had so much polish. You could tell he had been playing a lot of golf with adults who were good players."

Uihlein chatted with Gerry and Rosie in the crowd, forming a lasting impression. "I thought it was a really neat story," he says. "They were very well-grounded, no pretense—just good people from pretty humble backgrounds, and they were sacrificing everything because their son was a prodigy. They were memorable because they were different from many of the other parents."

McIlroy was starstruck in this brave new world: "I remember being on the 18th fairway of the 'Blue Monster' thinking: 'Wow! Tiger has been here. He's been on the same fairway!' That sort of stuff." McIlroy won his age group, cementing his belief in himself and beginning his notoriety. News of his victory made its way back home to Gerry Kelly, who hosted an eponymous television variety show in Northern Ireland. He invited McIlroy to appear on the show in a case of art imitating life, as Tiger Woods's star turn on *The Mike Douglas Show* when he was only two years old has always been part of his lore. But it was Rosie who had orchestrated the TV appearance: on the eve of the trip to Miami, she buttonholed Kelly during a chance encounter in Belfast. The McIlroys understood the power of mass media; they had already begun leaning into their working-class origin story.

On the appointed evening, Rory came to the TV studio in his snazziest Nike polo, black with white trim. He shyly answered a couple of questions from the host with a winning, gap-toothed smile. Then Kelly asked Rory to bounce a ball on the face of his wedge, and he did it effortlessly. With a showman's flair, Rory kept bouncing the ball while putting the club between his legs. The audience's approving cheers filled the soundstage. Then came the good stuff: an actual washing machine had been set up for Rory to chip balls into. He came oh-so-close on the first three attempts and then hooped the fourth. The crowd whooped. With the cameras still rolling, Kelly then sauntered over to the audience to ask Rosie about her son's recent victory in Miami. Channeling Tida Woods, she replied, "Well, he didn't go over there to lose." Kelly mentioned that Gerry was missing out on a dinner that night at Holywood Golf Club, as he had been part of a team from the club that won the Belfast Industry Cup, a spirited event that brought together players from all over the city. In a cute scripted touch, Rory presented his dad with the medal he had earned for the victory. Kelly brought it all home to close the segment, saying, "Look out for this guy. If the Americans have Tiger Woods, we have young Rory."

The McIlroys continued to make annual pilgrimages to South Florida and San Diego to expose their son to better competition. Along the way, Rory became good friends with a fellow competitor, Scott Pinckney of Orem, Utah. When Rory was eleven, Gerry and Rosie put him on a plane, alone, to spend the summer with the Pinckney family. "I cried for days," says Rosie. Tony Finau lived about half an hour from Orem and saw a lot of McIlroy at Utah junior tournaments during that summer. "The hair, the freckles—he was a funny-looking kid with a wild accent," says Finau. McIlroy amused the other players by mimicking Woods's outfits, including rocking trousers in the searing heat while everyone else wore shorts. McIlroy reunited with his parents in San Diego at the end of the summer, and they were shocked by his American slang. Also, he had bleached his hair blond.

The McIlroys spared no expense on their son's golf game. One of Rory's contemporaries, Gareth Shaw, says, "I'll never forget the day he showed up at Greenacres Golf Course [in Northern Ireland] with a brand-new Callaway ERC driver that had been cut down to size, literally custom-fit before custom-fitting was invented. It cost 450 sterling, a hefty investment for Gerry. But he knew how good Rory was going to be and was obviously willing to pay any price to help him." Rory was twelve years old at the time.

Northern Ireland did not have the same infrastructure for junior golfers as California or Florida, so McIlroy often competed against adults. When he was twelve, he played in a Senior Cup event at Holywood Golf Club, which featured a fancy dinner to announce the matches on the eve of the competition. Gerry topped out at five foot seven, and the prepubescent Rory stood barely five feet tall. "They called out this big guy from the club first and then they announced, 'Rory McIlroy,' and Rory walks out and the guy starts laughing," says Gabby Maguire, who was managing the club restaurant in those days. "[The match the next day] was all over on the 13th [hole]. The guy obviously didn't know about Rory back then. I guarantee you that guy's not laughing anymore." McIlroy posted a 63 in another club competition that year. He had intuited how to squeeze every extra yard out of his small frame. "I think all of us have thought about how Rory could hit it so far at a young age," says Shaw. "He put a load of pressure into his front side and would spring off the ground, and then he had that unique double hip action, too. It was a sequence of moves that was unique and I'm not even sure could be taught. He just figured it out, and he had the athleticism to make it work."

Bannon puts it another way: "His swing is him—it has personality. It has flair."

Rory's status as a top prospect was cemented when he was thirteen and Darren Clarke invited him to be part of a small gathering of elite Northern Irish junior golfers hosted by Clarke's charitable foundation. By then, Clarke had established himself as the best golfer ever to come out of Northern Ireland, with nine European Tour victories and a memorable beatdown of Woods in the championship match of the 2000 WGC Match Play Championship. Clarke spent a couple of days offering tutelage at Portmarnock Golf Club, outside Dublin. He invited Dermot Gilleece, the dean of Irish golf writers, to observe. "It was a miserable winter's day," says Gilleece, "and we went out to the par-3 seventh hole.

Darren says, 'C'mon, Rory, show us what you have.' There was a hard wind blowing off the right, and Rory held up a 7-iron that landed next to the flag. Just a beautifully executed shot. Darren looked at me and smiled but said nothing. That spoke volumes."

Clarke warmed to the role of mentor. As McIlroy later recalled, "He says, 'Rory, come here. Anything you want or need, just give me a call.' And he handed me his number. A 13 year old with Clarke's number! It was quite special."

McIlroy finally caught a growth spurt at the outset of his teenage years, profoundly changing his game. "He was always miles behind us off the tee, obviously just a wee small fellow," says his uncle Colm. "Then one day, when he got to be 13, all of a sudden we're walking up to our drives and there were a couple bunched together and there was one 10 yards ahead. And we're going, 'God, that's Rory.' He got to his ball, looked back and said, 'Everything all right back there, guys?'"

Nothing would ever be the same.

•

THE ISLAND OF IRELAND had been the site of bloody conflict since at least the ninth century, when Vikings began raiding seaside villages. The Anglo-Norman invasions of 1169 led to centuries of conflict with the native Irish, who spoke Gaelic and were overwhelmingly Catholic. In 1542, Henry VIII of England was named king of Ireland by the Crown of Ireland Act. The British dominion was cemented in the early seventeenth century, when half a million acres in the northern reaches of the island were colonized under the Plantation of Ulster. By law, the settlers had to be Protestant, English-speaking, and loyal to the king. The ensuing sectarian tension exploded in 1641, when an uprising by the native Irish led to the killing of thousands of Protestants, touching off a decade of civil war; conservative estimates put the death toll at a quarter million, more than 10 percent of the island's population. For the next 150 years, outbreaks of fighting were followed by exhausted, tenuous peace.

After the Irish Rebellion of 1798 was quelled by British forces, the Irish parliament was abolished and the island subsumed into the United Kingdom of Great Britain and Ireland. Catholics were legislated into second-class citizens by the Protestant minority, ensuring the inevitability of more violence. The infamous Easter Rising of 1916, followed by the Irish War of Independence, resulted in the Anglo-Irish Treaty of 1921. It required that all of Ireland swear allegiance to the British Crown, which, of course, begat more violence. The bloody Irish Civil War (1922–23) finally cleaved the island. Fierce fighting by the Irish Republican Army and widespread civil disobedience, including the refusal of Irish railway workers to transport British troops, led to the creation of the Irish Free State. It comprised twenty-six counties, while six other counties opted out of the new state and remained under British rule as Northern Ireland. The partition stranded half a million Catholics in Northern Ireland, including the forebears of Gerry and Rosie McIlroy. This disenfranchised minority often felt discriminated against in the job and housing markets and was denied political representation; the term "gerrymandering" became popular during this period in Ireland to describe the insidious manipulation of political boundaries. Northern Irish unionists, aligned with the United Kingdom, "saw themselves as a frontier community facing wily and violent enemies, and backed by only half-hearted friends," David McKittrick and David McVea write in their expansive history *Making Sense of the Troubles*. "Unionists were for the most part inward-looking people, conservative, cautious and suspicious of change."

Discontent and discord simmered for decades before finally exploding in the summer of 1969. The spark was a civil rights campaign to end discrimination against Catholics in Northern Ireland. A demonstration in Derry, inspired in part by Martin Luther King Jr.'s march on Selma, turned into a riot, with protesters battling the notoriously brutal Royal

Ulster Constabulary. The violence spread to Belfast, and British troops were swiftly deployed. More than 750 injuries were reported, including 133 gunshot wounds. The Troubles had begun. The Irish Republican Army began a bombing campaign of terror or liberation, depending on your point of view. The British Army meted out its own violence; in 1972, soldiers fired on unarmed protesters during another civil rights march. Thirteen died on this bloody Sunday, an atrocity that would later be memorialized in song by U2. Rosie McIlroy's hometown of Lurgan was the scene of so many bombings and assassinations that it earned the grim nickname "Murder Town."

The simmering civil war directly impacted the McIlroy clan. Rory's paternal grandfather, Jimmy, painted and repaired the towering cranes on the Belfast docks but was banned from better-paying jobs in the shipyards, as those were given exclusively to Protestants. (The *Titanic* had been built in Belfast.) The McIlroy family strove to be apolitical, and it took a deep optimism for Jimmy's brother Joe McIlroy to move his Catholic family into Orangefield, a Protestant stronghold in East Belfast. (The neighborhood name is a dog whistle, an ode to King William III, aka William of Orange, a hero of Protestant rule.) Joe worked as a computer technician and was seeking a quiet place to raise four daughters, but the family's very presence became a provocation. On the evening of November 21, 1972, Joe was in his home fiddling with a broken washing machine when a torrent of bullets ripped through the back door. Joe, thirty-two, was shot in the stomach and died in front of his wife and daughters. Mary McIlroy was covered in her husband's blood. "I'll never forget it as long as I live," a neighbor was quoted in the book *Lost Lives*. "Mrs. McIlroy ran out of the house and stood on the step shouting." Decades later, intelligence files would be made public; accounts vary as to whether the killers were members of the Ulster Volunteer Force (motto: "For God and Ulster") or the Ulster Defence Association's paramilitary unit, known as the Baker/McCreery gang (motto: *Quis Separabit?*—Latin for "Who will separate us?"). Joe McIlroy was the seventy-fourth victim of the Troubles that year.

Political violence continued to roil the Irish island until a lasting ceasefire finally arrived in 1998 with the Good Friday Agreement. The deal was struck on what happened to be the day of the second round of the Masters. Gilleece was in Augusta covering the tournament. "By way of emphasizing how prepossessed golfing people are about their own activities," Gilleece says, "the only mention of the agreement that I can recall was from my sports editor at *The Irish Times*, who referred to it as a 'remarkable happening.' This was probably his way of warning me to keep my copy tight!" It felt like kismet when, two days later, Irish American Mark O'Meara claimed the green jacket.

Rory was eight when the Good Friday Agreement was signed, becoming part of the first generation of Northern Irish youth to know peace. Rather than send their son to Holywood Primary, the town's secular elementary school, Rosie and Gerry chose St. Patrick's Catholic elementary school, where Rory's first Holy Communion photograph still hangs on the wall. He then matriculated to the nondenominational Sullivan Upper School, where he was compelled to wear a blazer emblazoned with the Gaelic motto *Lámh Foisdineach An Uachtar*: "With the Gentle Hand Foremost." It was an aspirational notion for kids who finally had a chance to remake their homeland after centuries of bloodshed.

Golf played a small but meaningful role.

The Golfing Union of Ireland (GUI) was founded in 1891, three years before the United States Golf Association (USGA). The GUI remained a beacon of neutrality throughout the political tumult. "The Golfing Union predated partition," says Pat Finn, who ran the GUI from 2011 to 2020, "and it has always represented the thirty-two counties equally. Thankfully, nothing was ever done to change that." Kids of all backgrounds were thrown together with golf as their shared religion, competing not under the Republic of Ireland's tricolor but the Four Provinces flag, which represents the entire island, including Ulster in the north; the logo on the GUI clothing was a noncontroversial shamrock. McIlroy played out of the GUI's Ulster branch, which received money from the Sports Council for Northern Ireland, financed by the National Lottery of Britain. "Protestant, Catholic—we didn't care about any of that," says Shaw. "We just wanted to play golf and try to chase our dreams." The GUI's mandate was to nurture the best young talent on the island. McIlroy was invited to train with other top prospects beginning when he was thirteen, and the GUI's apolitical values dovetailed with what he had been taught at home.

As always, McIlroy stood out among his peers. "He always wanted to show off—hit it higher, hit it lower, curve it more," says Shaw. "He always had that swagger, which he needed because he was younger and smaller. He got thrown into the deep end, and either he had to sink or swim." The GUI occasionally brought in top teachers for clinics, including Pete Cowen, who across the decades would minister to practically every top European pro. "Sometimes you can tell if a kid is going to make it just by looking in his eyes," says Cowen.

And what did he see when he met young Rory's gaze?

"Determination."

Like everyone else, Cowen was wowed by the pipsqueak's power. In trying to explain how the wee lad generated such unlikely clubhead speed, Cowen eschews technical mumbo jumbo and cites school recess. "You watch the boys run around," he says, "and there are slow ones and fast ones and always a fastest one. Why is he the fastest? It's the musculature and coordination he was born with, it's the biomechanics he figured out intuitively. And there's one more thing: he wants to be the fastest. That was Rory with a driver in his hands."

It was through the GUI that McIlroy first became friendly with a big, garrulous kid who was two years older, a head taller, and possessed a magical short game: Shane Lowry. Cowen has vivid memories of their first encounter. "There were a lot of talented players at that first session but two of them stood out," he says, "a curly-headed little kid from Holywood and a fat kid with glasses." It was a stroke of good fortune that McIlroy had another world-class talent to train alongside. "They pushed and pulled each other," says Cowen. "It was a friendly rivalry. Very friendly, but still a rivalry."

Lowry's first impressions of the young McIlroy? "He swung the club better than anyone else, even at that age, and always looked the part," Lowry says. "I know Gerry was working his nuts off [to pay for it] but he had all the gear. He was this cocky little fooker from the North, that's how I would have seen it."

With the material support of the GUI, McIlroy began to travel beyond the invisible border of Northern Ireland to face stouter competition. He arrived at the 2004 West of Ireland Championship to considerable fanfare. "He was already big news on the scene," says Stephen Moloney, a fellow competitor sixteen years McIlroy's senior. "He had been on the TV show, he had the Darren [Clarke] connection. He was a kid everyone was keeping their eye on." During the second round at Rosses Point, Moloney played a match versus Paddy Devine one hole ahead of McIlroy. "We stood on the second tee watching the crowd walk up the first fairway, about two hundred people strong," says Moloney. "In the early stages of an amateur tournament, it's usually only the birds watching. It was like, *Holy shit!* That was when we all realized Rory was going to be a star. Or maybe he was one already and the rest of us just hadn't realized it. Anyway, Paddy and I looked at each other and kind of shook our heads: one of us was going to have to deal with that the next day. I was working in a bank then. Imagine going back to Limerick after having my ass handed to me by a fourteen-year-old who is barely taller than his golf bag!"

Moloney and McIlroy both won their matches, setting up a showdown in the round of sixteen. "I'm not a short hitter, and on the sixth hole I crunched one," says Moloney. "Rory hit his drive right next to mine. That was another holy shit moment. This kid had effortless power." But McIlroy missed a couple of short putts in the middle of the round and got beaten by a wily veteran. "It's fun to look back and say I got him one time," says Moloney. "I get to hold on to that."

As well he should, because McIlroy was about to go to a whole different level. In 2004, at age fifteen, he became the first player to win the Irish Youths' Open and Irish Boys championship in the same year. McIlroy was already beginning to wear a cloak of inevitability. Pat Finn bumped into the McIlroys exiting the clubhouse after Rory's victory in the Irish Youths'. The kid was holding a shiny trophy but wearing a sullen expression. "It almost felt like it didn't matter to him," says Finn. "I said to Rory, 'Why aren't you smiling? Don't you realize what you've just done?' He looked at me like, *What are you on about? This is what I do*. He wasn't mean about it, just matter-of-fact. This was just another step on a long journey he knew he was making."

McIlroy's fine play earned him a spot on two prestigious squads in the summer of '04: representing Ireland at the European Boys' Team Championship and Team Europe at the Junior Ryder Cup. The Cup was played at Westfield Country Club, outside of Akron, Ohio. McIlroy went 1-0-1 during Europe's lopsided win. Along the way, he reunited with Tony Finau, who couldn't stop laughing at McIlroy's elaborate new hairdo, as the Ulsterman's long curls glistened with gel. "I was like, *Dang, Rory has Jheri curl now!*" says Finau. "*With blond tips!*"

McIlroy's ascent accelerated on Easter weekend of 2005, a few weeks before his sixteenth birthday, when he became the youngest winner in the history of the West of Ireland Championship, one of the island's most prestigious events. Shortly thereafter, McIlroy became the youngest winner of the Irish Amateur Close Championship (the old-fashioned name means "closed to professionals"). Gerry had seen enough. He marched to the local betting parlor and put down £200 on his son to win an Open Championship by the time he was twenty-five, having been granted 500–1 odds by the somewhat mystified bookies. Two friends placed similar but smaller bets.

Gerry and his pals were hardly alone in suddenly recognizing that there was money to be made on McIlroy's future.

2.

In the autumn of 1983, a corpulent Scot lit out of Roswell, New Mexico, with his head shaved and his tail between his legs. Colin Montgomerie had traveled from Troon, Scotland, to attend the New Mexico Military Institute. His wavy locks were shorn upon arrival. The reigning Scottish Boys champion looked around at his fellow grim-faced cadets and realized that he had made a terrible mistake. He caught the first bus out of town and eventually wound up in Houston, where he made a desperate phone call home to his father, James, the secretary of the Royal Troon Golf Club. James rang a well-connected priest in England, who called a friend in Houston who happened to know the head coach of the golf team at Houston Baptist University (now Houston Christian University). Just like that, Monty was granted a walk-on spot on the team.

A prissy, proper graduate of a leading Scottish boarding school, Montgomerie strode the Houston Baptist campus in his golf trousers. "And no girl in the U.S. is going to talk to you if you're getting around in golf pants," recalls his roommate Glenn Joyner. "I finally got fed up and took him out to buy jeans." Montgomerie had been forbidden by his stern father from wearing denim; unchaperoned, he chose a pair of Jordache with a white cotton frill down the leg. "Looked bloody ridiculous," Joyner says.

This small Christian college similarly became a place of self-discovery for Montgomerie the golfer. He turned himself into a two-time All-American and led the Huskies to three straight conference championships. "People think that because I had my first experience of golf at

Troon, I should have become a great links player," Montgomerie says. "But it was on American courses that I learned my craft. The strengths of my game were developed here. As a student, I found the weather and the facilities were so good that I wanted to practice seven days a week. I put in a hell of a lot of effort in college."

In 1998, as Montgomerie was lording over the European Tour on his way to the World Golf Hall of Fame, a lad from Portrush, Northern Ireland, followed Monty's footsteps from the linksland to the Bible Belt. The language barrier was the biggest challenge when Graeme McDowell enrolled at the University of Alabama at Birmingham. "Between their accent and my accent, every conversation was an adventure," he says. "Sometimes it was hard to believe we were all speaking English." According to McDowell, he was merely a "pretty good amateur golfer" when he arrived in Birmingham, but he, too, thrived in the college ranks: he won six tournaments during his senior year and claimed the Fred Haskins Award as the nation's top collegiate golfer. The transatlantic talent kept flowing, including Englishman Luke Donald's star turn at Northwestern and Alex Norén, of Sweden, earning All–Big 12 honors at Oklahoma State.

Taking note of all of this was Fred Warren, the head coach at East Tennessee State University (ETSU). "You know why Texas and Florida are so good every year?" Warren asks. "They get the best players in the state to stay home. We're a mid-major, kids don't grow up dreaming of playing here. We have to cast a wider net. I decided I would try to get the best players from Ireland, Scotland, Wales, and England. If we could do that, I figured we'd be pretty good."

His first overseas recruit was a gadfly Irishman named J. P. Fitzgerald. Warren made many phone calls to the Fitzgerald home but could never reach J.P.; his mom always said he was at the driving range, practicing. This impressed Warren, but, in fact, J.P. was usually at the track betting on horses. "I just told my mum to say that," Fitzgerald ultimately confided in Warren. At one of his first practices at ETSU, Fitzgerald spent more time schmoozing than hitting balls. When Warren gently admonished him, J.P. shot back, "Eh, Coach, has your name and Hitler's ever been used in the same sentence before?"

For all the grief that Fitzgerald caused his coach, his outsized presence helped create a pipeline of talent between the Emerald Isle and the Volunteer State. In the early aughts, Warren nabbed two strong players from the Irish island, Gareth Shaw and Cian McNamara. Both told tall tales of a mega-talent back home named Rory McIlroy, who was about four years younger than them. Warren was intrigued enough to fly to the 2004 European Boys' Team Championship in Finland to watch the fifteen-year-old McIlroy compete. "I'd seen outlying talent before," says Warren. "I saw Tiger for the first time when he was thirteen, I saw Sergio [García] when he was fourteen. Something about Rory just sucked you in. I was gonna watch him for only a couple of holes, but that's like trying to eat just one potato chip—you can't do it! I went all eighteen. I was in awe of his charisma and his talent. He was really long off the tee and could hit shots that took your breath away, but what stood out was the look in his eye. He knew he was good. I came home and told someone how great this kid was going to be, and they didn't believe me."

The coach recruited McIlroy hard, knowing he could forever alter the trajectory of the ETSU program. Warren made another trip overseas, to Dublin, to woo McIlroy at the Boys Home Internationals. Warren buttonholed Rory's dad in the parking lot of Portmarnock Golf Club. Gerry had been doing his due diligence, including some long talks with Gareth Shaw's father, an old friend. He knew how important American colleges had been in the development of Monty, McDowell, and Donald. Even Tiger Woods, after a record-setting amateur career, had resisted the siren song of the pro game and enrolled at Stanford.

"Would Rory be interested in playing college golf?" Warren asked.

Gerry replied, "Yeah, he'd like to play at ETSU."

All these years later, Warren says, "My heart skipped a couple of beats."

At the age of fifteen, Rory took the SAT with minimal preparation and scored 1170. A few months later, in November 2004, he signed his letter of intent to play for ETSU beginning in the fall of '05. (In Northern Ireland, compulsory education ends on the June 30 following a student's sixteenth birthday.) But in college recruiting it ain't over till it's over, so coaches continued to ring the McIlroy household. Rosie would usually answer and shout upstairs to her son, who wouldn't bother coming to the phone, instead bellowing, "Tell them not to bother, I'm going to ETSU."

The plot thickened when McIlroy won the West of Ireland and Irish Close in the spring of 2005, cementing his reputation as one of the brightest prospects in European golf. "I thought I only had to worry about the other college coaches," says Warren. Turns out there were bigger sharks circling.

ANDREW CHANDLER WASN'T MUCH of a student growing up in Cheshire, England. "I was smart but lazy," he says. "I earned a degree in common sense." He became a professional golfer, but not a very good one. "I never had the necessary focus and dedication to be a really top player, although I probably had the talent to be one," Chandler says. Still, he had a helluva time playing the wild and woolly European Tour of the 1970s and '80s. A raconteur whose waistline betrayed his love of food and wine, Chandler earned a nickname that only hinted at his outsized presence: Chubby. In just one of his endless number of colorful stories, Chandler was playing in South Africa when he gave an off-duty caddie ten bucks to buy, as Chubby puts it, "ganja." The caddie came back with a messenger bag stuffed with marijuana and handed it to Chandler mid-round. "It lasted for a good while," Chandler says of his stash, "but perhaps not as long as you'd think."

Chandler's playing career was going up in smoke by the late '80s, and he began ruminating on life after golf. A friend offered a little sponsorship money for the 1989 season, but Chubby felt he'd be a bad investment, so he asked if he could broker a deal to redirect the money to another player. Just like that, he became an agent. He started scrounging up small endorsement deals for his mates on tour. In 1990, Chubby was contacted by folks close to Darren Clarke, who was then a blue-chip amateur trying to decide when to turn pro. They played a round of golf to get to know each other, and Chubby was awestruck by Clarke's ball-striking and charmed by his outsized personality. "I knew then I had a business," he says.

Clarke swiftly turned pro and enlisted Chubby's services. Chandler knew that Mark McCormack, who invented the role of the dashing, dealmaking superagent, had launched his business with nothing more than a handshake with Arnold Palmer, so Chubby did the same thing with Clarke. The Northern Irishman won his first important tournament in 1993, the year the talented Englishman Lee Westwood turned pro. He, too, joined Chubby's stable, which had been christened International Sports Management (ISM). Clarke and Westwood quickly became best friends, and Chandler was an omnipresent part of the fun: pints after the round, decadent dinners, forays to the track to bet on horses. In 1997, Westwood emerged as one of the best players in the world, winning tournaments in Japan, Malaysia, and Spain, as well as beating Greg Norman in a playoff to take the prestigious Australian Open. The globe-trotting success put Chubby at the forefront of the game. He served as his own publicist, charming reporters with wry observations and refreshing candor. More and more top international players flocked to ISM: Ernie Els, Charl Schwartzel, Louis Oosthuizen. Chubby cornered the Northern Irish market by signing Graeme McDowell to go along with Clarke. Both began whispering in Chandler's ear about this prodigy out of Holywood. At thirteen and fourteen, McIlroy had been hosted by Clarke for a weekend of mentorship through Clarke's charitable foundation. Chubby made the scene and was struck by McIlroy's composure. "He was the only kid there who wasn't scared shitless," he says. "There were seventeen-year-olds there, sixteen-year-olds. Everybody else was too scared to ask a question or say anything, and this little kid wanted to show Darren how to play certain shots! He just took over." Chandler knew star quality when he saw it; he slid his card to Gerry McIlroy, telling him, "Things are going to get interesting for you. If you get stressed about anything, give me a call."

Other folks were also beginning to cozy up to the McIlroys. In 2005, on a sojourn to Florida, Rory was eating lunch with his dad at PGA National when Louis Wellen, the sports marketing manager for Oakley, sidled up and gave them a handful of sunglasses, on the house. "Rory, you don't know it yet, but you're going to be a big part of Oakley's history," Wellen told him. The McIlroys were flattered but baffled.

ISM had begun dabbling in event management; among the tournaments it ran was the British Masters, one of the better stops on the European Tour schedule. In 2005, following McIlroy's double-dip at the West of Ireland and Irish Close, the sixteen-year-old received a sponsor's invitation to compete in his first professional event at . . . the British Masters. "Funny how that happened," Chandler says, cleaning the blood and feathers from his whiskers.

The first round—played at the Forest of Arden course outside of Birmingham, England—featured cold temperatures and high winds. Fewer than twenty players broke par, which adds a little context to McIlroy's dispiriting 82. Still, a well-traveled pro named Damien McGrane had kind words for his baby-faced playing partner, saying, "Rory is a fantastically talented golfer and it's like a breath of fresh air to see someone as young and as talented and enthusiastic as he is. He is a superb player and can hit shots that I cannot certainly hit. He didn't have the best of days in the conditions but he showed his class out there."

McIlroy went on to miss the cut, calling the tournament "an experience and a learning curve." Rather than feeling discouraged by his scores, McIlroy left his pro debut rather buoyant. "The kid saw with his own bloody eyes that he was already better than many of the players on tour," says Chubby.

As McIlroy's star continued to rise, Fred Warren began to get a little nervous back at ETSU. "There was a story in one of the Irish papers," he says, "where Rory talked about his future, but he didn't mention college golf." Chandler was a factor in McIlroy's waning interest in undergrad life. "Gerry called me," says Chandler, "and he goes, 'You said to call if we got stressed out, and we're stressed out because seventy-eight colleges want Rory and we don't know what to do. We don't even know if he should go at all.' And I told him that some kids are too good for college golf. You know what I mean? And that's why the guys following Rory, like Jordan [Spieth] and Justin [Thomas], they only spent one year there. They wanted to learn how to drink and how to shag, and then they got out of there and started chasing the money. And so I told Gerry that Rory would get bored of college golf and likely regress. And he said, 'Yeah, that sounds right.'"

Warren rang Rory after the publication of the newspaper story in which McIlroy didn't express even a token interest in ETSU. "I said, 'Rory, there's no hard feelings. I know you have lots of options, but I'm giving you a full scholarship, which is pretty rare in our program. If you know you're not coming but don't want to tell me, it's okay, just let me know now so I can use that scholarship on other players.' He said, 'Coach, I'm still coming, but don't worry about the scholarship, I'll pay my own way.' My heart sank. I knew at that moment he wasn't coming." (The scholarship went in part to Irishman Séamus Power, who would go on to win tournaments at ETSU and then on the PGA Tour.)

After the McIlroy recruitment fizzled, the athletic secretary at ETSU was going to shred his signed letter of intent, but Warren stopped her. He had a hunch. The framed document now hangs in Warren's office, a forlorn reminder of what might have been.

3.

Rory McIlroy played in three professional events in the spring and summer of 2005, missing cuts (badly!) and raising the hackles of the stewards of the amateur game in Europe, who were trying to finalize their Walker Cup team. From 1947 to '97, the U.S. had won the biennial team competition all but three times. Great Britain & Ireland (GB&I) turned the tide around the turn of the century, winning three in a row beginning in '99. The quest for a historic four-peat in 2005 would play out at Chicago Golf Club, one of the five founding clubs of the USGA. Team USA would be anchored by future PGA Tour winners Brian Harman, J. B. Holmes, Anthony Kim, and Jeff Overton. GB&I was a scrappier lot.

Oliver Fisher, a baby-faced sixteen-year-old from England, had already locked up a spot on the ten-person squad as the selection process wound down. Peter McEvoy, the GB&I captain in 1999 and '01, chaired the selection process in '05. Garth McGimpsey, who would captain the team in Chicago, had a prominent voice in the proceedings, which seemed to favor McIlroy, as McGimpsey also hailed from Northern Ireland. The group of men who presided over the Walker Cup—and in those days it was pretty much only men—evoked Skull and Bones or even the Illuminati: an all-powerful, shadowy cabal that met in secret to alter the future. "You sit around and talk about it, and the first six or seven spots are always easy," McEvoy said. "When you get down to the end, it gets to be a bit of a problem for us as selectors."

McEvoy had been tracking McIlroy for years. "There was an unusual amount of enthusiasm for him beginning when he was twelve or thirteen," he said. "In his mid-teens, Rory was already a fantastic driver of the ball. But his putting could be dodgy, and people were already talking about him being a weak wedge player."

After much discussion, presumably over cigars and brandy, the final spot for the GB&I team came down to McIlroy and an Irish lad named Brian McElhinney, then twenty-two. They were diametrically different players. McIlroy oozed talent and insouciance, while McElhinney was a gritty, grindy, short-hitting junkyard dog of a player. In match play he was known for wearing down opponents with a cold-blooded short game and relentless competitiveness. While McIlroy spent the summer of 2005 gallivanting at professional events, McElhinney played a full slate of amateur events, including a victory at the august British Amateur Championship.

"The fact is, when you looked at their records, it was terribly difficult to justify picking Rory ahead of Brian," McEvoy said. "And we already had another sixteen-year-old on the team in Ollie Fisher. It's a brave group of selectors who would take two sixteen-year-olds, especially playing away [in the U.S.]." Still, just as McEvoy was about to write down McElhinney's name on the ballot, ending the selection process, his pen hovered over the paper. He looked around at Captain McGimpsey and the tweedy gents who served as gatekeepers for the amateur game in Europe. "Are we sure about this, lads?" McEvoy said to the room. "I think this chap McIlroy is something special." McElhinney got the nod.

Chubby Chandler, in his role as McIlroy family adviser, saw the snub as part of a larger war that Rory and his parents were quietly fighting. "They did things their own way," Chandler says, "and the powers that be didn't like it. They wanted to punish Rory for playing in those pro events. They wanted to rap him on the knuckles for breaking tradition."

McIlroy took the news hard. "I was certainly peeved at the time," he says. "I had gotten to know Garth McGimpsey pretty well, and it was tough to take that maybe he wasn't in my corner."

Exactly one week after the team was announced, McIlroy delivered a thunderbolt from the edge of the world. With a sigh, McEvoy said, "That's when he went to Portrush and did what he did."

FOR MOST OF ITS history, the Royal Portrush Golf Club held a kind of mystical place in the imagination of golfers. This spectacular links, on the northern coast of Northern Ireland, was first envisioned by Old Tom Morris in 1892 and finally brought to life by Harry Colt forty years later. The great old-timey golf writer Bernard Darwin declared, "Mr. H.S. Colt . . . has thereby built himself a monument more enduring than brass. The course does not disdain the spectacular . . . Altogether I find it hard to imagine a more admirable test of golf." Proving that he's one of us, Darwin added, "The temptation to play three rounds a day is very hard to overcome."

Portrush hosted the 1951 Open Championship, exposing the wider golf world to its heaving dunes, serpentine fairways, treacherous bunkers, and well-fortified greens. Max Faulkner summoned a shot for the ages on the final hole of the championship, a slicing 4-wood that flirted with out-of-bounds down the left but bounced and rolled and trickled near the flag, securing his victory. Playing partner Frank Stranahan called it "the greatest shot I've ever seen." But Royal Portrush receded from view once the Troubles began in Northern Ireland. Professional tournaments stopped coming, and tourist golfers didn't dare make the pilgrimage. Portrush came to feel as far away and fabled as Shivas Irons's Burningbush Links.

In July 2005, Royal Portrush hosted the provincial North of Ireland amateur championship. McIlroy was in the middle of the pack after the first of two rounds of qualifying. On day two, he turned up in white trousers, a hot-pink belt, a white mock turtleneck with a raspberry-colored stripe on the back, and a light pink hat. You had better play well if you dress like that. McIlroy toured the first eight holes in 2 under par. "Steady enough but nothing special," recalls playing partner Stephen Crowe. "Then he went birdie-eagle-birdie and all of a sudden we were standing on the 11th tee and he was six under from nowhere. At that stage you start to think something special might happen because he had momentum."

Says McIlroy, "Honestly, there are not many rounds where I remember every shot, but that day I do. There was a funny moment on the eleventh tee, the par-3 down the hill. We were waiting on the group ahead of us to finish out, and I saw the guy in front of us fist pump when he holed a putt. And I said to my playing partners, 'Why would you be fist-pumping on the second day of qualifying in the North of Ireland?' Then I holed a putt on the eleventh green to go 6 under, and out of nowhere, I give it a fist pump. And I remember one of my playing partners said on the twelfth tee, 'What was that you said about fist-pumping?!'"

Says Crowe, "The crowds were getting bigger so word was filtering back but Rory always had a crowd anyway. Even as a teenager, no matter where he played, he had a crowd because everyone wanted to watch him and knew who he was. That had never happened to an amateur until he came on the scene."

After pars at twelve and thirteen, McIlroy stepped to the tee of Calamity Corner, which rates as one of the most fearsome par-3s in the world, demanding an uphill, all-carry tee shot of at least two hundred yards, with a green surrounded by death and despair. (When upgrades were made to Portrush ahead of the 2019 Open, Calamity became the sixteenth hole.) Wielding a long iron, McIlroy unleashed a towering draw that never left the flagstick. It was the kind of shot "that you can only dream of hitting," says Crowe. The birdie pushed McIlroy to 7-under on a par-72. For years, Pádraig Harrington held the Portrush course record at 65, until Randal

Evans, a strong amateur from Northern Ireland, lowered it to 64, a number that was very much on McIlroy's mind after he birdied the par-4 fifteenth hole (nicknamed "Purgatory" by Portrush's understated stewards).

At sixteen, McIlroy faced a twenty-five-foot birdie putt. "You could see the look in his eye. That putt was going in before he reached the green," says another playing partner, Aaron O'Callaghan. "At that point I thought, *Holy shit, this is some round.*" Giddy disbelief filled the air as the crowd continued to swell with McIlroy nearing the clubhouse. "The more the people appeared, the better he got," says O'Callaghan. "It was very obvious that he was a show-off, almost, where he thrived on the energy of the people. By the time we got to 17 it felt, to me, like the whole country was out there; I had never seen that many people at an amateur event."

There was a wait on the tee of the par-5 seventeenth. McIlroy drifted away from the crowd and his playing partners, gathering his thoughts. He needed to par the last two holes to own the course record. He could have hit a 5-iron off the tee to avoid the seventeenth fairway's many boobytraps, but where's the fun in playing it safe? He pulled driver and smashed a perfect tee shot, then reached the green with a long iron, setting up a two-putt birdie. "I got to 10-under and said, *Just don't screw this up at the last,*" says McIlroy. Instead, two textbook shots followed, leaving him with a final birdie putt from twenty feet. "Honestly, I was just trying to two-putt," he says. Then the hole got in the way. Birdie. And the most momentous 61 this side of Roger Maris.

"It lit up the golfing world," says McIlroy's swing coach, Michael Bannon. "A member of the golf club phoned me and told me, and I thought it was a joke. No one can shoot 61 around Royal Portrush."

News traveled at the speed of light to the Home of Golf, as July 12, 2005, was Tuesday of Open Championship week at St. Andrews. When Darren Clarke completed his practice round on the Old Course, one of the first questions was about McIlroy's 61. Clarke immediately dashed off a congratulatory text message.

Says Graeme McDowell, "You hear about the next great thing. 'We've got this kid, he's playing at plus-7 (handicap) and blah, blah, blah.' Then [Rory] shot 61 … and I'm like, 'Really? OK. Hold on. Now I have to pay a little more attention to this.' That was probably the first time that I realized we had something pretty special on our hands."

Poor Pete McEvoy.

"If I had known he was going to shoot 61 a couple of days later, we definitely would have picked him," he says. At the Walker Cup, McElhinney played poorly in a singles loss on the opening day and was benched for the rest of the competition. Team GB&I lost the Walker Cup by a single point. "If we had Rory on our side, we would have won, there's no question about that," McEvoy said. (McElhinney went bust playing professional golf's minor leagues and now works, contentedly, as a teaching pro at North West Golf Club in Donegal.)

With the benefit of hindsight, McIlroy is at peace with the snub. "Maybe if I had made the team, things would have panned out differently," he says. "If I made that team, I might not have waited for '07 to turn pro and maybe I would have struggled for a couple of years on the Challenge Tour [the feeder to the European Tour]. Who knows, anything could have happened."

Meanwhile, McEvoy's decision haunted him for more than two decades. In June 2024, ten months before his death, he said in a tone drier than melba toast, "There were issues of timing and circumstance, but suffice to say, leaving Rory McIlroy off the Walker Cup team was not a highlight of my selectorial career."

4.

Rory McIlroy's 61 quickly became folklore and launched the next phase of his amateur career—as a full-time golfer. McIlroy had left Sullivan Upper School a couple of months before torching Royal Portrush. He was fifteen when he ended his schooling, a year younger than Bobby Fischer had been when he dropped out of high school to obsessively focus on chess. McIlroy's apparent disinterest in education would later launch a variety of angsty headlines, like this one from the *Irish Independent*: "Why Rory McIlroy Is the Wrong Role Model for Young Irish Golfers." For the whiz kid, it was a pretty straightforward choice. "All I wanted to do was play golf and I knew by the time I was 15 or 16 that that was the path I was going to take," he says. "Leaving school was a big decision, and a lot of thought and talk went into it. It was a tough one, tougher probably for my parents than me, and they had a number of meetings with the school principal." He later explained, "I was away quite a lot [playing tournaments] so every time I came back I was always trying to catch up. It was very tough to try to balance everything, but I tried my best."

One of McIlroy's uncles would later say his nephew's impetuous decision-making—in business, romance, launching press conference barbs, and sundry other topics—could all be traced to a lack of higher education, a strong opinion that Rory himself doesn't entirely dispute. "The only thing I regret is not having the thirst for knowledge back then that I do now," McIlroy said at the ripe age of thirty. "For whatever reason, when I got into my mid-twenties, I started to get more curious about different things and started to read more. I don't regret missing out on the experience [of university], but I regret not being as curious as I am now."

Unlike Seve Ballesteros, who turned pro at sixteen, McIlroy elected to remain an amateur after he left school. McIlroy set his sights on the 2007 Walker Cup, which was to be played for the first time in Northern Ireland, at Royal County Down. The way forward became crystal clear: he would spend the two years between Walker Cups doing a kind of work-study, playing as many big-time events as possible to prepare for a professional career, which would commence after a triumphant swan song to amateur golf at Royal County Down. McIlroy fell into the warm embrace of the GUI, which now had as its headliner the kid whose name was on the lips of the golf cognoscenti. McIlroy began building a global brand, playing in the Dubai Desert Classic in January 2006. (He shot 72-72 to miss the cut by one stroke.) "For two years they sent me all over the world," he says of the GUI. "I was playing golf virtually full-time, and all at their expense. You couldn't afford to do that yourself."

It was during his teens that McIlroy cemented one of the foundational friendships in his life, with Harry Diamond. He was five years older than McIlroy and more cosmopolitan, as his family owned popular bars and nightclubs in Belfast. During his amateur playing days, Diamond displayed none of McIlroy's firepower off the tee but was renowned for his wizardry with a wedge. "You could put him up against Phil [Mickelson] in a flop contest and it would've been a good battle," says Gareth Shaw, a contemporary. Diamond would win the prestigious West of Ireland Championship in 2012, six years after McIlroy had taken the title for a second time. They first met on the putting green at Holywood Golf Club when Rory was seven; by his teen years McIlroy habitually referred to Diamond as his best friend. "I was an only child and Harry was a big brother," he says. "That's sort of how it felt growing up—a big brother's influence on a little brother. He was the one that introduced me to alcohol; the one that introduced me to girls."

For all of McIlroy's wanderings with the GUI, his home base remained sleepy Holywood. How does a sixteen-year-old fill every day when school is no longer in the way? In McIlroy's case, the answer was Holly Sweeney, a buxom blonde who towered over her boyfriend whenever she wore heels, which was often. Sweeney grew up in a Protestant family in Holywood. She and Rory met cute on the practice putting green at the golf club. The romance began during his final year in school. "She knows me better than basically anyone else in this world does, apart from my parents," McIlroy said a few years later. Gerry came up with a nickname for his son's glamorous girlfriend: "Holly Hot Lips."

Sweeney gave young Rory his first taste of normalcy detached from his identity as a prodigy. In the summer of 2006, McIlroy had his first (but hardly last) existential crisis. After winning in a playoff at the Mullingar Scratch Trophy, a noteworthy Irish amateur event, Rory was overcome with emotion. "It was a weird one," he says. "We were driving home, and I had this real sense that doing what I was doing wasn't making me happy. It wasn't making me feel how I thought it would feel. I was probably the best amateur in the world at the time, but I think I maybe built it up in my head too much. I thought it was going to feel better than it did. And I started thinking, *Well, if this isn't making me happy and I'm missing out on summers with friends and doing things they're doing—getting drunk on beaches and meeting girls and that stuff—what's the point?*" McIlroy "started to punch the window and just had this complete outburst . . . My dad was driving, and he said, 'Son, if it really bothers you that much, your mom and I are not going to put pressure on you to play the game. Why don't you take a few days off and see how you feel?' It was a great piece of advice, because literally four days later I couldn't wait to get back on the golf course. It was just a teenage, stroppy, petulant thing."

Just a couple of weeks later, a rejuvenated McIlroy enjoyed the biggest win of his career to date, at the European Amateur, played outside of Milan. He joined a roll call of winners that included Sergio García (and Walker Cupper Brian McElhinney!), but more to the point, the victory came with an exemption into the 2007 Open Championship. The Rory McIlroy show was headed to the big time.

ON FEBRUARY 6, 2007, the World Amateur Golf Ranking made official what golf obsessives already knew: McIlroy was the number one amateur in the world. His professional debut was still months away, but, in the background, you could already hear the cash registers ringing. Chubby Chandler had continued to advise the family, and he was now deputized to begin lining up deals for when McIlroy turned pro. Rory was already spending the money in his mind. He had become increasingly close to Chandler's client Darren Clarke—a dandy, a hedonist, and a profligate spender. Just before he summited the World Amateur Ranking, McIlroy sat down with Brian Keogh of *Irish Golf Desk* and raved about a recent flight on Clarke's jet and a visit to his palatial manor on the outskirts of London: "The plane is amazing. It can take ten and [Clarke] was telling me he was getting speakers on it for his iPod. We went to his house and he'd just got a new Lamborghini Murcielago with a new sports exhaust on it, new wheels. DVD player in the front. Unbelievable ... He started playing Scissor Sisters on it in the car when we went for a spin. The Lamborghini is a silver-gray six litre, V12. He's redoing his house as well and some of the new stuff he's got in his house is amazing as well ... He's got seven cars in the house. Bentley, Lamborghini. Range Rover Sport, he got a BMW M6 convertible the week after I saw him, two Jags and a BMW X3."

Paul McGinley ran in the same circles as Clarke, and he grew tired of hearing him talk about the teenage McIlroy. "Darren likes to associate with success, and he saw this guy was going to the top," says McGinley. "It was a big deal for Darren to give somebody a lot of praise. He didn't do that lightly. Having Darren for a mentor was very important for Rory. I'm a big believer in culture. On tour, you're like a gypsy, you're like in a circus. Who you hang around with is going to determine, to a large extent, how successful you'll be, and my experience tells me that. Because when I came on the scene, I was not a particularly good player, but I was lucky because Darren Clarke was my friend. He dreamed big and talked big, and he had the fancy cars, and the fancy house, and the fancy girlfriends on his arm, and he lived like a superstar before he *was* a superstar. I fed into that culture, Lee [Westwood] fed into that culture, and they dragged me along. They ignited my belief in myself. Rory was much farther along than me, but Darren showed him that, if he stayed on his path, if he honored the gift he had and became the player he was supposed to be, the world was in the palm of his hand."

Clarke had the good fortune to be a touring pro in the Tiger Woods era. The PGA Tour was negotiating a new slate of TV contracts when Woods changed the sports landscape with his epic win at the 1997 Masters. The revamped TV deals kicked in for the '99 season, and, overnight, the Tour's purses doubled. The revenue streams became gushers as Woods turned himself into perhaps the most dominant and marketable athlete in the world. Suddenly, a very-good-but-not-great player like Clarke was making more money than he ever dreamed possible. McIlroy's talent—nurtured in the humble precincts of Holywood—had become a golden ticket. That he would prosper among the pros became even more evident at the 2007 Dubai Desert Classic, when McIlroy, seventeen, opened with rounds of 69-69 to make the cut at a European Tour event for the first time. He went on to finish fifty-second but had to forgo €7,600 in prize money due to his amateur status.

McIlroy continued his preparations for the Open Championship at the 2007 European Amateur Team Championship, where he and Shane Lowry led Ireland to its first gold medal since 1987. A week later, McIlroy blew into Carnoustie, the most fearsome course in the Open rota. The hype machine was already humming. "He was known to us before the Open because of his amateur record," said Peter Dawson, then chief executive of the Royal and Ancient Golf Club of St. Andrews (R&A). "He was a very exciting young man, a real prodigy. Every year there are good amateurs who come through but very few of them have star quality. He clearly had star quality. He had a swagger."

Having seen plenty of tantalizing prospects flame out, Dawson remained circumspect about McIlroy. "He was recognised as the most likely lad to rise to stardom, but you can never be sure about these things," he said. "Many have looked good but never made it."

McIlroy began his Open week with a practice round with his hero, Nick Faldo. The persnickety Brit called it quits after four holes. "It was a bit wet for him so he went in," McIlroy said. That afternoon, the kid set up shop on the driving range. It was pissing rain and McIlroy was the only golfer there, though he did have company in Holly Sweeney, who huddled under an umbrella and heroically worked on her high school math homework. Swing coach Sean Foley had just begun his teaching career, and he found himself drawn to this solitary figure smashing balls through the storm. "I introduced myself and sat behind him for thirty minutes or so and just took it in," says Foley. "Wind's off the left and he's hitting these towering 4-irons. I went back to my bed-and-breakfast and said to my wife and my dad, 'I've never seen anyone this good.'"

But what was McIlroy's "it factor"?

"As it relates to that, it's strength and flexibility," says Foley. "What is the it factor for [NBA legend] Vince Carter? It's a fifty-inch vert. The 'it' for me was seeing this kid from Northern Ireland hitting it to the moon in a pounding rain."

But Vince Carter was 6'6" and a shredded freak of nature. McIlroy stood 5'8" and was still encased in baby fat. How did he do it? "I remember in high school football," Foley says, "there were a couple of guys who never went to the gym, but they just destroyed people. It's the same thing that Rory did to a golf ball—a combination of strength, speed, mobility, attitude. Think about a slingshot. Give me some thick tubing, and if I can pull that thing back ten feet, the elastic energy being created is immense. That was Rory's swing and still is: elastic recoil that's off the charts."

It was a measure of the R&A's respect for the young prodigy that it gave him a plum first-round pairing alongside two stalwarts of European golf, Henrik Stenson and Miguel Ángel Jiménez. McIlroy turned up in a Titleist hat, Puma jumper, and pants rakishly flared at the cuff. He had a bag full of Titleist gear, including a 907 D2 driver. McIlroy looked jumpy on the first tee and the tension showed in his swing as he missed the first four fairways, though he saved par each time. On the par-4 fifth hole, he played two textbook shots and rolled in a midrange birdie putt. After that, McIlroy played with a more typical insouciance. A birdie on the tenth hole propelled him to −2 and a spot on the leaderboard, and then he stuffed his tee shot on the par-3 thirteenth hole to get within one of the lead. The TV announcers lavished him with the highest praise imaginable, comparing his youthful brilliance with that of swashbuckling Seve Ballesteros, who finished tied for second at the 1976 Open at the age of nineteen. The great man was top of mind because Ballesteros had announced that the 2007 Open would be his last as a competitor. This passing of the baton from one generational talent to another would become obvious only in hindsight.

Rory channeled Seve on his final swing of the day on Carnoustie's dastardly eighteenth hole: from 230 yards out, into the wind, he ripped a 2-iron pin-high to set up a stress-free par. McIlroy was the only player in the field without a bogey, and his 68 left him tied for third, three strokes behind leader Sergio García. The large galleries instantly fell in love with the kid. "It was just like a chill down the back of my spine with the ovation I got [on eighteen]," McIlroy said. "I soaked up the atmosphere and really enjoyed it."

He had no trouble charming the assembled scribes. "I've sort of grown up around the media, I suppose, in the last few years," McIlroy said. "I sort of learned how to handle it. I think I've been getting interviewed since I was about seven or eight years old. I'm pretty good at this talking thing, I think." That last line drew a laugh from otherwise crusty reporters. Chandler watched all of this with an almost paternal pride. It was an open secret in the golf world that he would be representing McIlroy the day he turned pro. "He wasn't fazed at all by what was going on around him," Chandler says. "He relished the attention. He had been born for that."

The second round brought much tougher playing conditions, and McIlroy had to fight hard for a 76 that dropped him to thirty-first place. No other amateurs had made the cut, assuring McIlroy the coveted Silver Medal. For the third round, he played alongside Arron Oberholser, a young American who a year earlier had enjoyed a breakthrough victory at Pebble Beach. McIlroy matched him shot for shot but didn't putt as well as his playing partner, shooting 73 to Oberholser's 72. "I watched him hit his opening tee shot and thought: 'Man, who is this kid?' We didn't know about him in America. I didn't even know how he got into the tournament," says Oberholser. "I remember the fourth hole specifically. I hit a driver and seven-iron into the green. He hit driver and I thought: 'That's a different flight that I haven't seen from many guys before.' Then we get up there and he is 15 to 20 yards past my drive. He was 145 yards out. It was grey, it was cold, it was windy. It was into the wind. He took the nine[-iron], put the ball back in his stance and the shot made a sound I'll never forget. At that point I'd only ever heard one player make that sound with their irons: Tiger Woods. He just hit it so clean, so crisp[,] and there was so much effortless speed at the bottom of the swing. The way he compressed the ball was unlike anything I'd ever seen apart from Tiger. He hit these shots that just bored through the wind, the wind couldn't affect them.

"He went round that place and didn't bat an eye. It wasn't like a big deal. It was like he was walking around his home course on a Saturday with the boys."

The legend of McIlroy was growing.

He ended a dreamy week with another 72, including a rousing walk-off birdie on eighteen that left him in forty-second place. At the trophy ceremony, McIlroy received the Silver Medal alongside Pádraig Harrington, the second Irishman to win the Open (hat tip to Fred Daly), further expanding McIlroy's notion of what's possible. "Hopefully it's the shape of things to come," McIlroy said of his performance. "I think I'm getting better all the time, progressing as a player. Hopefully I've got a few more Open Championships in me. It's a great performance—first major, first Open Championship—and hopefully I can go on to bigger and better things."

Only one more item remained on the to-do list for his amateur career.

THE 2007 U.S. TEAM has come to be considered the greatest squad in Walker Cup history. It featured a future Hall of Famer (Dustin Johnson), a future U.S. Open champ (Webb Simpson), and four players who would go on to win multiple PGA Tour events (Billy Horschel, Rickie Fowler, Chris Kirk, Kyle Stanley). GB&I did not have the same kind of firepower, but it did have McIlroy, who helped draw huge crowds to Royal County Down, one of the greatest courses on the planet. In the opening session of foursomes, McIlroy and another Northern Irishman, Jonathan Caldwell, earned a hard-fought halve versus Johnson and Colt Knost, the reigning U.S. Amateur champ.

The team score was 2–2 heading into the afternoon singles. McIlroy was sent out first to set the tone. The U.S. team countered with its emotional leader, Horschel, who, with his perfect hair, perfect smile, and upturned collar, looked like the douchey rich kid villain in every teen movie. His on-course demeanor was equally grating. "Listen, I was twenty years old, I've matured a lot since then," Horschel says with a laugh. "At least I hope I have. I said going in, *What Sergio García does at the Ryder Cup, I'm going to be that for the Walker Cup. I'm gonna be the cheerleader, I'm gonna be the fist-pumper.* Rory had ten thousand people pulling for him and his team, we only had a few friends and family. I wanted to make sure that when we did something good it was known across the golf course. I probably went over-the-top. I turned into Sergio on steroids. I know I rubbed Rory the wrong way." Especially when Horschel prevailed in their match, 1-up. At the end of the first of two days of competition, the score was tied 6–6.

In the next morning's foursomes, GB&I captain Colin Dalgleish again sent McIlroy out first with Caldwell as his wingman. U.S. captain Buddy Marucci countered with Horschel and Fowler. McIlroy and his partner were 4-up after five holes, but the Yanks battled back. On the fourteenth hole, Horschel played an exquisite sand shot. "I come out of the bunker like a damn cheetah, running after the ball and yelling at the top of my lungs, 'Go in! Go in!' And it lipped out. I guess [McIlroy] was pissed about that. I guess he was pissed about the day before when we played our singles matches." It didn't help McIlroy's mood that he and Caldwell lost 2 and 1.

The U.S. led 10–6 going into the final session of eight singles matches. GB&I again sent out McIlroy in the first match. Naturally, the U.S. team countered with Horschel. "That outburst of his [in the preceding match] was probably the worst thing he could have done," says McIlroy. "I set out to be as loud as he was. On the first tee I ripped a drive up the middle, hit my 7-iron approach to maybe 15 feet—I was shouting 'Be good! Be good!' all the way—and holed the putt for an eagle. When the ball went in, I gave it the loudest 'Come on!' you've ever heard. I think he got the point."

Indeed he did. Says Horschel, "He was letting me know, *This shit ain't happening anymore. This is my house today.* And I was like, *Damn, I'm fucked.*"

McIlroy spanked Horschel 4 and 2, but the U.S. won the Walker Cup in a thriller, 12.5–11.5. It was a bittersweet ending to a stellar amateur career for McIlroy. It hurt to lose in front of the home folks, but no tears were shed. The kid from Holywood was all grown up, and now the bright lights of the professional game beckoned.

5.

Despite Rory McIlroy's amateur accolades, he still had to earn his place in the meritocratic structure of the European Tour. In September 2007, a week after the Walker Cup, McIlroy matriculated to the first stage of European Tour Q School, at which the low 29 players in a field of 110 would survive and advance. After an opening 70, McIlroy put himself in plum position with a 67 at the Oxfordshire Golf Club. Q School is the most pressure-packed event in golf, filled with beleaguered journeymen fighting for their livelihood, but McIlroy brimmed with hubris, saying of his second round, "It really could have been a 59. I had so many chances but the good thing was I keep my cool even when the putts didn't go in." McIlroy followed with two more solid rounds to finish thirteenth and punch his ticket to the second stage. Then he blew into the British Masters for the launch party of his professional career.

When McIlroy rocked up to the Belfry, he was plastered in so many logos he looked like a NASCAR ride. The selling of McIlroy had presented a unique challenge. He plainly possessed superstar potential but, with his rounded physique and unruly curls, did not present as dashing a figure as, say, 6'4" Dustin Johnson, who also turned pro in the wake of the '07 Walker Cup. McIlroy had a cult following in Europe but minimal name recognition in the United States, the home of the golf equipment industry. Chubby Chandler found a clever solution by looking east. He had spent the preceding year quietly assessing (and stoking) the endorsement market on McIlroy's behalf; now, having officially signed on as the kid's agent, he closed an eyebrow-raising deal with Jumeirah, a luxury hotel chain based in Dubai, which would pay McIlroy $400,000 a year to wear its (big, ugly) logo on his chest and hat.

"Chubby had a global vision, much more so than most agents," says Wally Uihlein, the then-CEO of the parent company of Titleist and FootJoy. "He was the first one to exploit the fact that Dubai was willing to spend big money. He was the first guy to open the floodgates out of the Middle East."

Decades ago, the farsighted leadership of the United Arab Emirates began planning for a post-oil economy, and golf played an unlikely role. (In more recent times, Saudi Arabia has used golf as a blunt instrument to advance its economic and political interests, with far-reaching ramifications for the sport.) The inaugural Dubai Desert Classic was conducted in 1989, marking the first European Tour event on the Arabian Peninsula. Every year, the wide-angle TV shots from behind the eighth tee of the Emirates Golf Club would highlight to a global audience the relentless expansion of the Dubai skyline as the city became a commercial and tourism hub for the Middle East and Europe. By the turn of the century, the Desert Classic had become one of the marquee events on the Euro Tour, its field vastly upgraded by bloated appearance fees (which are verboten on the PGA Tour): in 2001, Tiger Woods began making an annual trek, lured by seven-figure appearance fees. Given the Desert Classic's high profile, it was a pretty big deal that an amateur like McIlroy was granted sponsor exemptions in 2006 and the following year. (Woods won the tournament for the first time in '06.) McIlroy's good play and good cheer at the Desert Classic did not go unnoticed, particularly by the folks at Jumeirah. The brand was owned by Dubai Holding, Sheikh Mohammed bin Rashid Al Maktoum's personal corporate profile, but in the mid-2000s, much of the company leadership came from Europe: Jumeirah's chief marketing officer was Irish, and its CFO hailed from Northern Ireland. They were eager to get in on the gold rush that Woods launched. Chandler admits to being surprised at how much Jumeirah was willing to pay but says, "It was really easy selling Rory because I could say from the heart that this is the best young European player I've ever seen."

McIlroy showed off a spiffy new Titleist staff bag at his introductory press conference at the British Masters, having signed a deal through 2013 to use Titleist balls and clubs and wear FootJoy gloves and shoes. Woods famously landed a five-year, $40 million deal with Nike upon turning pro; McIlroy's contract was far more modest—$150,000 annually—but the time horizon of the deal showed a larger commitment. "Chubby and I were on the same page, and even Gerry: Let's be patient about this," says Uihlein. "Let's not put a ton of pressure on Rory right out of the box, and let's give him the space to grow up intellectually, physically, cognitively." Titleist/FootJoy did offer a sweetener that was unusual in its contracts, paying out a bonus equal to 20 percent of McIlroy's on-course earnings.

McIlroy nabbed a noteworthy deal with Oakley, heretofore known as an edgy apparel company catering to surfers, skateboarders, BMX riders, and other hipsters who no doubt thought of golfers as weenies. In the Woods era, golf was becoming . . . if not quite cool, definitely less nerdy, and brands were eager to latch on to fresh-faced talent. For $80,000 a year, McIlroy would wear the Oakley logo on his shirt and belt buckle. All the contracts had big bonuses built in for winning a major championship or ascending to certain benchmarks in the World Ranking.

McIlroy, a budding automobile enthusiast, was most excited about the pimped-out BMW he got for free as part of an endorsement deal with a chain of Irish car dealerships. He was already looking for a place to park it. "We had a meeting on the patio at Carnoustie [during the 2007 Open Championship]," says Chandler, "and went through all the deals and possibilities. Rory took it all in and said, 'I want to get on the ladder.'" That's a British term for buying one's first house, thus beginning the climb upward into something bigger and grander. "This was months before he turned pro," says Chandler, "but we managed to get him a mortgage even though he didn't have any actual earnings. All because he was

Rory Fucking McIlroy." Within a few months, Rory f'ing McIlroy had bought one of the nicest homes in Holywood, for £600,000. Holly Sweeney moved in with him so the teenagers could play house.

For all the endorsement income pouring in, McIlroy cared most about his on-course earnings: if he could make enough euros over the final three months of the season to finish in the top 115 on the Order of Merit, he would lock up his playing privileges for 2008 without having to endure the crapshoot of the next stage of Q School. The pressure to perform was severe, and, once again, Woods had warped expectations; he faced a similar need for job security after turning pro in August 1996 but turbocharged his career by winning two of his first seven PGA Tour starts.

At the British Masters, McIlroy played like a young man fretting about his future, shooting a second-round 78 and finishing forty-second. That paid out €15,128.50; the Tour's number crunchers projected it would take €212K to finish in the top 115. McIlroy rated his play a B-minus but called the overall experience "absolutely fantastic," adding, "I've enjoyed the attention and signing autographs as a professional. I can give stuff away now, too, now that I'm getting it for free."

It didn't take long for McIlroy—who had topped out at 5'8"—to make a big impression on his colleagues. "He's worked incredibly hard on his physique, but back then he didn't walk into the room and you'd think, *Wow, that's an athlete*, know what I mean?" says Justin Rose. "But he had this effortlessness and pop to his swing. It didn't quite stack up. There was something under the hood that was extra. There was a bit of a superpower there for sure. Everything was in a beautiful sequence, there was such a rhythm to his swing, that you didn't notice the violence. When he first came out, guys on the range would be stealing glances at him. There was something unique about him, and it was obvious from the very beginning."

McIlroy delighted in his reputation as golf's young slugger. Asked about the emotional impact of blasting his drives well beyond his playing partners, he said, "It shouldn't give you an extra boost, because it's not a long driving contest, but, if I'm honest, yes, it does. As a professional golfer, the lowest score is your priority and it shouldn't matter if you're flying it by your playing partners . . . but it's still nice. It's a nice thing to have in your repertoire."

Next up for McIlroy was the most glamorous tournament on the European Tour, the Alfred Dunhill Links Championship, contested on some of the finest courses in the world: Carnoustie, Kingsbarns, and the Old Course. The pro-am format brought out a sparkly mix of professional athletes and corporate titans, creating the kind of big-time atmosphere that McIlroy loved. The €5 million purse had McIlroy running numbers in his head. "When I talked about my chances of making my card this week to Lee [Westwood], he told me I could win the tournament," McIlroy said. "When someone like Lee tells you that, it gives you a lot of confidence." He got off to a decent start with a 71 at windy Carnoustie, but McIlroy began his second round on the Old Course by dumping a wedge shot into the burn on the first hole and taking a brutal double bogey. But he played airtight golf the rest of the way, shooting a 67 that included a walk-off thirty-five-foot birdie putt from the Valley of Sin. A third-round 67 at Kingsbarns propelled McIlroy to fourth place, two shots off Paul Lawrie's lead, and gave him a tantalizing opportunity: if he could finish solo third or better, he would earn enough euros to lock up his Tour card.

McIlroy roared home in the final round on the Old Course, stuffing his approach on the Road Hole and then making a second straight birdie at eighteen. His 68 pushed him to −15, and then he stood behind the eighteenth green to watch his fate unfold. It all came down to Lawrie, the reigning Open champion, who arrived at the home hole one stroke behind McIlroy. Lawrie played an excellent pitch to five feet. If he were to make the birdie putt, Lawrie would snag a share of third place, diluting the payout just enough to keep McIlroy on the outside looking in. But the Scot missed, keeping McIlroy alone in third place. "Well, that's my Tour card," McIlroy said matter-of-factly to Lloyd Saltman, his teammate just a few weeks earlier at the Walker Cup. McIlroy earned €211,321 to rocket 158 spots on the Order of Merit, to 105th. It had taken him all of two events to secure his future on the European Tour. A couple of days later, he took some cash out of an ATM and was thunderstruck to see that the payday from the Dunhill had hit his account. "It's something I'll remember for the rest of my life," McIlroy says. He went out and bought the fanciest watch he could find, giddy at the financial freedom. (Years later, McIlroy made an offhand press conference remark that he now considered the diamond-encrusted, new-money timepiece to be "horrific," but he refused to name the make and model since he's sponsored by a different watchmaker. Raymond Williams, the style editor at large at Skratch Golf, identified the offending watch as a 2007 Breitling Chronomat Evolution.)

The week after the Dunhill, McIlroy finished tied for fourth at the Open de Madrid. *Hola, mundo.*

The McIlroy Christmas hit a little different in 2007 after Rory's audacious European Tour debut. Gerry and Rosie had always spoiled their only child with gifts, but this time, it was the young pro's turn. Waiting in the driveway was a token of Rory's gratitude for his parents: a brand-new Mercedes C-Class sedan. The silver Benz became one of the nicest cars in the parking lot the second Gerry drove it to Holywood Golf Club. Not bad for an abruptly retired barkeep.

6

Rory McIlroy continued to make a name for himself as a rookie on the European Tour. At the Qatar Masters, in January 2008, he earned a third-round tee time alongside Adam Scott, one of the biggest stars in the game. "There was a fair amount of hype around him, and I wanted to see it for myself," says Scott. "We both played nicely, and I remember toward the end of the round thinking, *Okay, I actually need to play well to beat this kid.* It was a bit of a thing, like no eighteen-year-old should come out here and whip my ass. I know every older guy said that about me when I was a kid, too. That's actually a thing with veteran players. I ended up shooting 65 and beat him by a shot. We did a joint interview afterward, and I got to say, 'Here's the next superstar.' It was a no-brainer. This might be taken wrong by all the guys who followed him, but Rory's the last player where I thought, *He can't miss.*"

Game recognize game, but what exactly about McIlroy left such a strong impression?

"Look," says Scott, "it wasn't a million years ago, but it was 2008. We didn't talk about speed like we do today, as an essential item. The game was played a little differently, but Rory had speed to burn. The greatest players, they always hit that one shot where you go, *Wow!* That's why they're great. Rory had a few of those during that round. And he had that bounce in his step and that twinkle in his eye. You could see he had that it factor."

McIlroy had a chance to justify all the hype, heading into the final round in third place, one back of Scott and three off the lead of Andrew Coltart.

Yet McIlroy played the first three holes on Sunday in +3, losing his composure while Scott was tearing up the golf course. The Aussie shot 61 to blow away McIlroy (and everyone else). Rory limped home with a 74 to fade to thirty-third place. "In the amateur game, Rory was always going to be the best player in the field, so he could dictate the result," says Scott. "If he played well, he was going to win. You come out here, and someone else is always going to go low. They don't care who you are. You have to learn to manage the emotions and stay within yourself and not let the other players affect your mindset and your play."

There were plenty of other growing pains. McIlroy missed cuts in Dubai and Malaysia and then went to Korea and missed a third straight cut. "I had never been to a country that felt so alien to me," he says of Korea. "I felt so far away from home and remember sitting at the end of the bed with a box of Pringles from the minibar and crying . . . You're on the road and you're on your own and just feeling so alone. It was tough. I couldn't wait to get on a flight home."

McIlroy took a monthlong vacation that forced him to reassess his priorities. "Those cuts have sort of given me a kick up the backside," he said. "You have to work really hard out here to keep your position. You have to work as hard as all of the other guys in the gym, hitting balls and working on short game and everything else. That's one thing I've learned: you have to work extremely hard out here." Not an insignificant revelation for such a natural talent.

More work equaled better results, including a seventh at the Irish Open that came two weeks after his nineteenth birthday. But a summertime swoon prevented McIlroy from qualifying for the Open Championship and forced the first (but hardly last) difficult business decision of his young career: he sacked his caddie, Gordon Faulkner. They had been together going back to McIlroy's breakthrough at the '07 Open. Enter J. P. Fitzgerald, a known quantity among the International Sports Management stable, as he had previously caddied for Darren Clarke and Paul McGinley. "J.P. was a decent enough caddie, but the key to that was his personality," says the matchmaker, Chubby Chandler. "He's an extrovert and knows everyone. So he could take Rory around and introduce him to people and go with him to any social event. He played a big part in Rory getting settled on tour."

The coupling of McIlroy and Fitzgerald led to much amusement back at East Tennessee State University. Fitzgerald's enrollment there had helped create the pipeline of players from the Irish island to the school, leading to the near miss in landing McIlroy. ETSU coach Fred Warren remained fond of Fitzgerald even though he had driven him crazy during his days as a Buccaneer. "J.P. was a big personality, a big-time character," says Warren. "He's a gambler. He loves the action. If two flies were on the wall, J.P. would want to bet on which one would fly away first." Warren had carefully followed McIlroy's progress and wondered how the kid would alchemize with Fitzgerald. "I figured there could be some fireworks on the golf course," says Warren.

McIlroy missed his first three cuts with Fitzgerald on the bag. J.P. was flummoxed that his man often employed irons off the tee. "That was the Gordon influence," says McGinley. "He was old-school, and a lot of the old-school caddies were conservative by nature. To them, it was about minimizing mistakes. J.P. was different. He caddied like a gambler. I distinctly remember J.P. telling me, after they had been together for only a short while, 'This guy's best club in the bag is his driver, and all he's been doing is hitting 2-irons off the tee. Fuck that! I'm going to get him to hit driver everywhere.' I know this is a big statement, and I don't mean it to be a big statement, but in some ways, J.P. changed golf. Because back then, it wasn't bombs away. And J.P. made Rory play fully aggressively. And by doing that, he unlocked something in Rory's psyche. He unburdened him, he unshackled him, and Rory went to another level very quickly."

In his fourth start with Fitzgerald on the bag, at the European Masters, McIlroy shot 63-71-66 at Crans-sur-Sierre Golf Club in Switzerland to take a four-stroke lead into the final round. But he looked vulnerable again amid the final-round pressure, bogeying the second and third holes to lose the lead. McIlroy hung in there and regained the lead with a twenty-foot birdie putt on the fifteenth hole. He needed a par on the seventy-second hole to become the third-youngest winner in European Tour history. (Naturally, Seve Ballesteros held the record at the time.) But McIlroy flew the green with his approach shot, pitched on, and then faced a five-footer for glory. He missed it and headed to sudden death against journeyman Jean-François Lucquin, who was winless in 175 career starts. Both faced midrange birdie putts on the first extra hole. McIlroy missed his and then committed the biggest blunder of his career, blowing the eighteen-inch comebacker and gift wrapping the victory for Lucquin. McIlroy tried to be philosophical in defeat, saying, "It would be great to get a win this year, but if not, I have the rest of my career. C'est la vie." (Seventeen years later, he would admit to still thinking about the missed gimme.)

The gutting crunch time mistakes could have spooked a less cocksure player, but McIlroy just kept coming. He shot a final-round 65 to join a three-way playoff at the Hong Kong Open, in which he was pipped by Lin Wen-tang's birdie on the second extra hole. McIlroy finished 2008 with a tie for third at the South African Open. The year had been a whirlwind: twenty-seven tournaments across sixteen countries and three continents. He racked up eight top-ten finishes and over €900,000 in prize money (to say nothing of the 20 percent bonus from Titleist). As Adam Scott forecast, McIlroy was looking inevitable. The rookie began 2008 outside of the top two hundred in the World Ranking and ended it thirty-ninth. That came with a nice little perk: an invitation to his first Masters.

THE ROAD TO AUGUSTA began in the Middle East in January 2009. McIlroy loved competing over there because it was like playing golf in a dome: warm temperatures, benign conditions, and flat golf courses that could be easily overwhelmed by a big hitter. After a tie for fifth in Abu Dhabi, he arrived at what was becoming his home away from home, Dubai. (In fact, McIlroy was already in the process of making Dubai his official residence for tax purposes.) The tournament was his to lose from the moment he took the lead with a first-round 64. If it felt like generational change was imminent, that might have been because of McIlroy's playing partner: fifty-two-year-old Mark O'Meara, long known as Tiger Woods's mentor. (O'Meara also won a Masters and an Open Championship.) When McIlroy was a wee lad, he and his mates loved to spectate at the World Match Play at Wentworth. In 1999, during the thirty-six-hole final against Colin Montgomerie, O'Meara jarred a greenside bunker shot on the eighteenth hole of the morning round. He gave the ball to nine-year-old Rory, who was lingering greenside, and even signed the souvenir for him. Ten years later, they were walking the fairways as equals, and McIlroy blew O'Meara's mind by relaying the story and informing him that he still had the ball in a drawer at home. O'Meara created a stir after the round when he said, "Ball-striking-wise, he's probably better than what Tiger was at nineteen. His technique, I think, is better. Certainly, Tiger has developed his game and swing over the years and made modifications to be able to hit the ball pin-high, but Rory is already doing that and he's nineteen, so he's already a step ahead." The European press spooned it up. With typical nuance, a headline in *The Scotsman* declared, "McIlroy Is Better Than a Young Tiger Woods."

McIlroy kept pressing forward in Dubai, forging a two-stroke lead heading into the final round. This was the moment of truth for the can't-miss kid. The Sunday collapse in Switzerland, the playoff loss in Hong Kong... those could be chalked up to the acquisition of data if he pulled through in Dubai. But were McIlroy to blow another lead, it would constitute a troubling trend. The whispers would begin, and the press conference questions were sure to become more barbed. An insidious doubt could creep in. Golf history is littered with awesome physical talents whose careers were torpedoed by emotional fragility, lack of mental toughness, and metaphysical turmoil.

McIlroy began the final round like a man playing for his reputation, birdieing the first three holes, including a deft up-and-down after driving it *over* the green on the 351-yard par-4 second hole. Justin Rose, tied for third at the outset of the round, birdied three of the first ten holes to stay in the fight. McIlroy responded by birdieing the ninth hole. And the tenth. Then the eleventh. And the twelfth. And the thirteenth! He was six shots clear, and the grillroom at Holywood Golf Club was delirious. *Go on, Rors!* He had finally done it. Gerry and Rosie were in the gallery in Dubai, fighting back tears. All those graveyard shifts at the 3M factory, the grungy toilets at the rugby club that had to be cleaned, the putting sessions as the sun set, and then schlepping all over the world just to give their only child a chance . . . it was all worth it now. What a story.

McIlroy's coronation over the closing holes hit a little snag on the fifteenth hole, when he caught a 7-iron heavy and made bogey, but no big deal. On the sixteenth, McIlroy drove it into the trees and had to chip out sideways, leading to another bogey. Still, the lead was a comfortable three shots with two holes to play. Nobody had really noticed when Rose eagled the thirteenth hole amid McIlroy's birdie barrage, but then Rose birdied seventeen, too, while McIlroy made a third straight bogey after driving into a waste area. Just like that, the lead was sliced to a lone stroke. The mood in McIlroy's gallery shifted from jubilation to foreboding, perhaps even dread.

On the watery par-5 eighteenth hole, McIlroy hit a good drive into the wind but left himself 241 yards to cover the hazard in front of the green. Getting there with a 5-wood was iffy, and the 3-wood would likely carry into the back bunker; that was the least desirable leave with the pin cut in the back of a green sloping toward the water. So, after consulting with Fitzgerald, McIlroy did something they both loathe: lay up. That left a wedge shot from ninety yards. Flooded by adrenaline, nerves, and perhaps a touch of fear, he nuked his third shot over the green . . . into the back bunker. A collective groan emanated from the crowd, including the army of Jumeirah executives who had gathered to celebrate their poster boy. As McIlroy settled into the sand, it felt like his entire future was riding on this up-and-down. He executed the shot flawlessly, somehow getting his ball to stop three feet from the hole. He had that par putt for victory, and salvation. Said Rose, "It took a lot of guts just to hole that putt." The celebration married joy and relief, a portent of things to come. "It was probably the best shot I've hit under pressure," the champ said of his play from the bunker. "It's definitely a burden off my shoulders or a monkey off my back. If I had not won today, having a 6-shot lead, it would have been pretty tough to take, and it would have been hard to come back from that, I think. You know, you watch it on TV, and you see guys coming down the stretch with a lead, and you think it's easy, but it's not."

The win was worth €323,514.99, and visions of exotic cars were already dancing in McIlroy's head. Asked about a splurge to celebrate, he said, "I'm thinking about something, but I don't know if I could get insured on it."

The win shot McIlroy, nineteen, into the Ryder Cup conversation and to second on the European Tour money list, which for 2009 had been rechristened the "Race to Dubai." This was the most tangible sign yet of the Middle East's game-changing commitment to golf, which McIlroy had helped stimulate. Only sixteen months after turning pro, he had cemented his status as the boy king of European golf. Now, like so many before him from the Irish island, it was time for McIlroy to make a name for himself in America.

•

A MONTH AFTER HIS victory in Dubai, McIlroy made his PGA Tour debut at the WGC Match Play Championship in Tucson. The big storyline coming in was Tiger Woods's return to action as he recovered from knee surgery following his epic win at the 2008 U.S. Open. Few observers noticed when McIlroy beat Louis Oosthuizen in the first round. That led to a second round match versus U.S. Ryder Cup stalwart Hunter Mahan. "I don't know much about him, but I know he's a great player," Mahan said, speaking for many. McIlroy dispatched Mahan 2 and 1 on the same day that Woods was upset by short-hitting Tim Clark. Needing a new storyline, the golf press quickly glommed on to the fresh-faced McIlroy. A breathless report by Mark Cannizzaro in the *New York Post* began, "Maybe Tiger Woods was just clearing the stage. Woods' early exit from the Match Play Championship left the door open for a 19-year-old kid from Northern Ireland who, at least in Europe, is being hailed as the next great one. Remember the name: Rory McIlroy. Baby-faced, with untamed black hair flaring out of his cap in every direction, he may not look like an eventual challenger to Woods' throne until you watch him hit a golf ball." The story included an eye-popping quote from Ernie Els: "You're probably looking at the next No.1 in the world with him. He's got all the tools."

McIlroy was the toast of the town after he beat Clark to gallop into the quarterfinals. He delighted in the attention. "I don't want to say I always expected to get to this point, but I always hoped that I would," he said. "But I am surprised how quickly I've done it." Unfortunately for McIlroy, he had to play Geoff Ogilvy; the former Match Play champ boasted a 14-2 lifetime record in the tournament. He dispatched McIlroy 2 and 1. Still, it was a helluva debut, and how much McIlroy's star had risen became evident when he flew to Palm Beach Gardens, Florida, for the ensuing week's Honda Classic. Rory and his dad were in a mall parking lot when a retired golfer who lived in the area recognized them. "Hi. I thought that was you," the man said to Rory. "I'm Jack Nicklaus."

"Hello, Mr. Nicklaus," McIlroy said.

"Hi, Jack!" said Gerry.

Rory scolded his father as soon as the Golden Bear ambled away: "You don't call him Jack—he's Mr. Nicklaus."

Rory continued his strong play, finishing thirteenth at the Honda. That was worth $90,000. Gerry spent much of the week holding court at the bar at PGA National. He was having the time of his life traveling with his son and watching him take on the world. At the conclusion of the Honda, reporter Michael Bamberger said to Gerry, "Well, he made more than he spent this week." Gerry loosed a hearty laugh and said, "Not when he gets my bill!"

Rory followed with top-twenty finishes at Doral and Houston and then arrived in Augusta for his first look at a course that has defined so many careers. Those expecting the teen to be awed by the setting failed to realize that he had already become a hardened pro. "I thought I would be nervous hitting my first shot here," McIlroy said following a Monday practice round, "but, you know, I think maybe if I was a little younger and maybe if I played here as an amateur, it would have been a little different and I would have been in awe of the place. But having been on tour now for a year and a half, I'm not saying that it's not different, but I just treat it as if it were another golf tournament. I'm not really one to get overwhelmed by much these days for some reason. Don't know why."

Jordan Spieth has credited his fine play at Augusta National to the sloping terrain, saying the varied stances and improvised swings unlock his creativity. In that regard, the home of the Masters has something in common with a more humble track: Holywood Golf Club. "It is often criticised for its steep slopes," says Robert Cooley, a former secretary at McIlroy's home club. "They often say you have to have one leg longer than the other to be able to play it."

McIlroy shot a solid even-par 72 in his Masters debut and then caught fire during the second round. A towering long iron into the thirteenth green set up an eagle that propelled him to −4 and onto the leaderboard. At the Masters, the pressroom has always been divided into different ghettos: magazine writers over here, newspaper scribes over there, the Asian press in one corner, the Europeans in another. McIlroy's eagle sent a current of electricity through the Fleet Street hyperbole slingers. But he hooked his tee shot into the water on sixteen, taking a double bogey, and then lost another shot on the seventeenth hole due to an errant drive. After fanning his approach on eighteen into the greenside bunker, McIlroy needed to get up and down to get to the house under par. But he fluffed the shot, leaving his ball in the bunker. Looking like a striker for his beloved Manchester United, a frustrated McIlroy made an aggressive, sweeping motion with his right foot, sending sand flying. He blasted out with his fourth shot and then three-putted for a ghastly triple bogey. McIlroy signed for a 74 and then skulked away, having been defeated by Augusta National for the first (but hardly the last) time.

A few hours later, the intrigue began. Fred Ridley, then the immaculately coiffed chairman of the Masters competition committee, began fielding questions as to whether McIlroy had kicked the sand in frustration or merely smoothed it vigorously after his first, ill-fated bunker shot. Why would it matter? Because smoothing the sand is acceptable under the persnickety USGA Rules of Golf, but kicking it would be considered testing the surface of the bunker, which brings a one-stroke penalty. If McIlroy did, in fact, break the rule, he had not accounted for the resulting penalty stroke in recording his 7. Per the rules of the day, he would be disqualified for having signed an incorrect scorecard.

Ridley called McIlroy and asked him to return to tournament headquarters to review footage of the incident with the rules committee. With the hubris of youth, McIlroy declined. *Nah, I'm good.* Ridley called again half an hour later, and now his tone was much sharper. "I said no because I'm confident I didn't do anything wrong," McIlroy said. "And [Ridley] rang me back and said, 'It would be in your best interest to come up and see the tape.'

"It's a natural instinct for me," McIlroy continued. "I didn't kick it; it was more of a sweep. A smoothing of the sand is what I did. I might have done it a little vigorously, but that was my intent. It wasn't my intent to test the sand."

Just to clarify, McIlroy added, "It wasn't a tantrum."

The founder of the Masters, the great Bobby Jones, was once celebrated for calling a penalty on himself, and he sniffed, "You might as well praise a man for not robbing a bank." Given the ambiguity of the kick/sweep, McIlroy could have followed in the Jones tradition and settled the matter by calling a penalty on himself. But Rory steadfastly maintained his innocence. The Masters is an invitational, and in the matter of potential rules infractions, the old boys who run the tournament have always been predisposed to be good hosts and let things slide. McIlroy was exonerated by Ridley. Rory shook off the lingering awkwardness with a 71-70 weekend to finish a very credible twentieth.

McIlroy made another cut the following week, at Hilton Head, and then the curtain fell on his grand American adventure. In one fortnight, he had become a headliner on both sides of the Atlantic.

McIlroy took a month off after Hilton Head, during which he returned home to celebrate his twentieth birthday. He and Holly Sweeney, who had enrolled in university, were still a couple, though McIlroy admitted, "We've had a couple of five or six week breaks, which you are going to have." All the better if they occurred around his birthday: McIlroy had begun an annual tradition of hosting a boys' trip to Ibiza. They would pile into a private jet, where goodie bags awaited: a Gucci belt, Prada sunglasses, little gifts like that from McIlroy to class up the lads' appearance. Much debauchery ensued. Later in life, McIlroy was asked if he missed anything about life before he became famous. He replied wistfully, "Being like eighteen, nineteen, twenty, and just going out and getting hammered with your mates and not worrying about a photo of it getting on social media. The amount of fun times we had at eighteen, nineteen, twenty. You're on tour, just started to make money, you can go do whatever, basically, and not have a worry in the world about being photoed or be in the paper the next day."

The halcyon days of his youth were now over. For McIlroy, life was about to get much more complicated.

7.

Rory McIlroy continued his fine play for the rest of 2009. At the U.S. Open, at venerable Oakmont, he shot 68 on Sunday to tie for tenth. At the PGA Championship, McIlroy tied for the lowest round on Sunday to move up to a tie for third. He had been too far back after fifty-four holes to have a chance to win either major championship, but the strong results confirmed that he had already developed into a contender whenever the best players gathered on the toughest courses in the most important tournaments. He also threatened to emerge as the leading man of the European tour. McIlroy had seven top-five finishes in his final nine starts, climbing to second in the final Race to Dubai standings behind Lee Westwood. (McIlroy earned €2.86 million in prize money, plus a €800K Race to Dubai bonus.) In a testament to his all-around excellence, young Rory led the tour in scoring average (71.1).

The golf world changed irrevocably over Thanksgiving 2009, when Tiger Woods's domestic dispute touched off the tawdriest sex scandal of the internet age. Tiger had long been Rory's role model, and it was disorienting for the young pro to witness the crumbling of his hero's artfully curated facade. Publicly, McIlroy pledged his support with carefully worded sound bites. Privately, "he was shocked like everyone else how it all unraveled," says Chubby Chandler. "I don't recall Rory talking about it very much. He was just taking it in—what it now meant to be in the public eye and the pitfalls that came with that."

When Woods woke up on that fateful Thanksgiving morning, his vanquished colleagues had accepted that his unprecedented dominance would continue indefinitely. Tiger, then only thirty-three, had always been fueled by a sense of entitlement. The money, the fame, the adulation, the women . . . in Woods's worldview, he deserved it all because he worked harder and burned to win more than every other player. The scandal destroyed Woods's sense of self and the idolatry felt by his peers and the public. Fearing eye contact at his return to action at the 2010 Masters, Woods hid behind sunglasses as if they were the tinted windows of a limousine.

Tiger would never be the same player. (Mounting injuries were certainly a factor, too.) Who could possibly fill the void? The answer began to reveal itself three weeks after Woods's awkward return at Augusta, when McIlroy turned Quail Hollow into his personal playground. He had planned to skip the tournament to rest a bone bruise in his lower back that had plagued him for months, but McIlroy got restless sitting on his couch. He struggled across the first two rounds and looked like he would miss the cut, until a gorgeous 4-iron set up a gimme eagle on his thirty-fourth hole. "Most important shot of the year, to be honest," McIlroy said. He made the cut on the number at one over 145, nine strokes back of leader Billy Mayfair.

McIlroy's back finally loosened up in the Charlotte heat, allowing him to overwhelm Quail Hollow on Saturday: he had five eagle putts during a 66 that moved him into a tie for seventh, four strokes off the lead. McIlroy followed with what remains one of the finest rounds of his career. On a firm, fiery course that Anthony Kim described as "Augusta hard," McIlroy birdied five of the first eleven holes . . . and then finished with six consecutive 3s, including a kick-in eagle on the par-5 fifteenth hole. His 62 shattered the course record; his 10.714 total strokes gained remains the best final-round performance of any player in a PGA Tour event since the stat was introduced in 2004.

McIlroy finished off his four-stroke victory in style with a walk-off forty-footer, which moved Jim Nantz to exclaim on the telecast, "Welcome to the big time, Rory McIlroy!" Said Phil Mickelson, who finished second, "He's got the game of a veteran. That 62 is one of the best rounds I've seen in a long, long time. He's an amazing talent. [But] you just never expect something like 62."

McIlroy's first Tour victory was a significant milestone, because the most dominant European player of his adolescence, Colin Montgomerie, famously failed to win in the U.S., and the best Brit of the aughts, Lee Westwood, won only twice in America, twelve years apart. Two days shy of his twenty-first birthday, McIlroy became the youngest Tour victor since—who else?—Tiger Woods, in 1996. With his boyish smile and old-world manners, Rory was suddenly positioned as the anti-Tiger: wholesome, unproblematic, universally liked and admired. A month after Quail Hollow, McIlroy was lounging on a couch in the locker room when Tour veteran Billy Andrade strolled by. McIlroy jumped up to greet him. Here Andrade picks up the tale: "He walked over to me and said, 'Hey, Billy, I'm Rory McIlroy. I just want to say I've been a big fan of yours for a really long time.' When I turned pro in the late eighties, I went up to every star and introduced myself: Ben Crenshaw, Ray Floyd, Tom Watson. They were guys I looked up to, and I had to pay homage. Fast-forward to when I was older, the young guys were on their own program. They wouldn't even give you a nod. They didn't care at all. Rory, that kid, I was blown away by what he did."

McIlroy rode all this momentum and goodwill to the Old Course for the 2010 Open Championship. He had risen to ninth in the World Ranking and was now presented with a course that rewards power like few others. (See *Daly, John.*) McIlroy entered with the second-shortest betting odds at +1,600, and then he went out and torched the Old Course for an opening 63, tying the lowest round in the long history of the major championships. (Branden Grace would lower the record to 62 at the 2017 Open at Royal Birkdale.) On a windless day, McIlroy kick-started his historic round by driving the green of the 352-yard par-4 ninth hole and making the fifteen-foot eagle putt. He followed with five birdies in the next six holes, including one of the two-putt variety after driving another par-4, the twelfth hole. On seventeen, the fearsome Road Hole, McIlroy played a towering 6-iron to four feet. "It sort of went through my mind on seventeen that 62 would have been the lowest round in a major," McIlroy said. "That's probably why I missed the putt." But he atoned with another birdie at eighteen.

Without a breath of wind, the course could not have played easier—"The old lady had no clothes on today," Tom Watson said. Still, McIlroy's round had the Fleet Street headline writers all but hyperventilating. *The Guardian*: "The Open 2010: Masterful Rory McIlroy Makes Hay and History." The *Daily Mail*: "Rory McIlroy Explodes at St Andrews with a Stunning 63."

And then McIlroy self-immolated with a second-round 80.

In fairness, wind gusts touched forty miles per hour and forced play to be suspended for sixty-six minutes because balls were being blown around on the greens. The round played out like a seven-hour nightmare: bogies on holes 4, 6, 7, and 8 and then a double on 11. McIlroy had taken sixty-three strokes by the time he played the fourteenth hole. Doug Ferguson of the Associated Press reported, "Rory McIlroy looked like he was on the verge of a full-scale tantrum." McIlroy closed with three good pars to avoid the ignominy of missing the cut. "I just let it get away from me a little bit," he said. McIlroy's fatal flaw was that, instead of playing for par and accepting the occasional bogey, he kept trying to force birdies, compounding his mistakes. Dan Jenkins, the dean of the golf beat, famously rendered a succinct verdict: "He was too young to realize 75 was a good score."

For the time being, 63-80 would become shorthand for McIlroy's volatility, though the 69-68 weekend was a testament to his resilience; he climbed all the way back in to tie for third (still eight shots behind runaway winner Louis Oosthuizen). Setting aside the freakish winds, McIlroy had played three stellar rounds and established himself as a contender for the next three or four Opens at St. Andrews, Lord willing and the creek don't rise.

McIlroy had a chance for redemption three weeks later at the PGA Championship at Whistling Straits. Though still only twenty-one, he was already bothered that he had three top tens in the major championships but zero victories. He was so hot to trot in a practice round with Darren Clarke that his old mentor snapped at him: "Be patient, you muppet!" On the eve of the PGA, McIlroy said, "Everyone tells me, 'Rory, just be patient.' But sometimes it's hard to do that [when] you're trying to get somewhere so fast." Opening rounds of 71-68-67 presented him with a delicious opportunity, leaving McIlroy tied for second, three strokes behind Nick Watney. Rory looked a little shaky at the outset of the final round, bogeying two of the first eight holes due to what he called "tentative" play. But none of the other would-be contenders were pressing forward. McIlroy birdied the tenth hole and then the fourteenth, and just like that, he was tied for the lead. For the first time, he faced the heart-pounding, nerve-jangling pressure of trying to win a major on the back nine on Sunday. McIlroy did not meet the moment. On fifteen, he jerked his drive into the rough, skied the green with his approach, and then missed a must-make four-footer. Bogey. Then an errant 5-iron doomed him to par on the sixteenth hole, a gettable three-shotter. McIlroy had one last chance at the seventy-second hole with an eighteen-footer to tie the clubhouse lead. He missed it on the low side. After finishing one shot out of a playoff (won by Martin Kaymer), McIlroy chose to look on the bright side. "This is what we all want to do," he said. "It was great fun out there. It was fun when I birdied ten and fourteen to give myself chances to really make a run at it. The putt on fifteen will be the one I will look back on, but it was great to be there, and I'll be part of many more major battles in the future."

McIlroy's high finishes throughout the summer of 2010 came with a sweet consolation: a spot on Team Europe for the Ryder Cup, the most overheated, jingoistic event in golf.

GROWING UP AS CATHOLICS in a Protestant world, Gerry and Rosie McIlroy embraced a pragmatic, apolitical secularism they passed down to their son. Rory attended a Catholic elementary school but rarely went to church. The Golfing Union of Ireland was his portal into top-flight amateur competition; it represented all of the Irish island as if the border between north and south didn't exist. The team was simply Ireland—not Northern, not the Republic. McIlroy represented Ireland at the European Boys' Team Championship, Eisenhower Cup, and European Amateur Team Championship. The announcement that golf would return to the Olympics came at the dawn of McIlroy's professional career, and it filled him with dread; he knew the Games would force him to pick a flag. Great Britain or Ireland? Either one was the wrong answer. The most provocative public statement of McIlroy's life remains his declaration that "I've always felt more British than Irish. Maybe it was the way I was brought up, I don't know, but I have always felt more of a connection with the U.K. than with Ireland." There are those in the Republic who will never forgive McIlroy for speaking his truth. His Northern Irish compatriot David Feherty empathized with the feeling of being caught between two worlds. "To be an Ulsterman is a strange thing," says Feherty. "It's almost as if you're a special needs Irish person. Being from Northern Ireland is not geographical or political—it's emotional. I captained the Irish side when we won the Dunhill in 1990. I hadn't thought about whether I was Irish or British until they raised the [Republic of Ireland's] flag and played the anthem. I felt a lump in my throat and thought, *Fuck me, I'm Irish, too.* I consider myself as British as I am Irish, but it's not something any of us ever wants to discuss publicly, because no matter what you say, it will put someone's nose out of joint."

Having spent his life avoiding the kind of flag-waving nationalism that killed his great-uncle, McIlroy was understandably lukewarm about the Ryder Cup. In May 2009, he said, "The Ryder Cup is a great spectacle but an exhibition at the end of the day, and it should be there to be enjoyed. In the big scheme of things it's not that important to me." This was miles from the prevailing European orthodoxy, in which the Ryder Cup was both a holy war and a financial lifeline; for much of its history, the European Tour stayed afloat only because of profits from the Cup. McIlroy had grown up listening to Tiger Woods's bland nonanswers in press conferences. It took admirable courage for Rory to speak so candidly, despite the inevitable blowback, including from Colin Montgomerie, Team Europe's captain. (GolfChannel.com headline: "Monty: The Ryder Cup Is Not an Exhibition.") McIlroy's teammates did their best to let him know there were no hard feelings, donning huge, curly wigs during a practice round in a showing of solidarity. "We had fun with it," says Paul McGinley, who served as a European vice captain at that Cup. "It was like the little puppy got a little bit excited. The little puppy will grow up and realize what it's all about." It didn't take long. On the eve of the Ryder Cup, the team received a phone call from the patriarch of European golf, Seve Ballesteros. He was gravely ill, but his voice exuded passion, even as it was piped through an old-school conference call box, à la Charlie speaking to his Angels. "I got into that team room at Celtic Manor, and I just saw how much it meant to everyone," says McIlroy. "I was like, *Maybe I got this wrong.* [Seve] is speaking to the team, and we're all in the team room. I look around, and the majority of the team is crying as Seve is talking to us. And I'm like, *That's it. That's the embodiment of what the European Ryder Cup team is.* I think that was the moment—that conference call with Seve in 2010 was the moment for me."

This was the first Ryder Cup to be played in Wales, and predictably, heavy rainfall scrambled the schedule. McIlroy was sent out in the second match of the competition in a four-ball alongside fellow Northern Irishman Graeme McDowell, who had won the U.S. Open at Pebble Beach a few months earlier. The magnitude of the Ryder Cup hit McIlroy as soon as the competition commenced. "I felt the pressure of having to perform for the team, and that made my play a little tentative and go into my shell a little bit," he said. He and McDowell were lucky to eke out a halve versus Stewart Cink and Matt Kuchar. Then they lost a rematch to the same Yanks in foursomes. As the sun set on day two, Europe trailed 6–4.

McIlroy and McDowell helped turn the tide, winning a crucial foursomes match 3 and 1 versus Zach Johnson and Hunter Mahan. That squared the Cup, 6–6, and touched off a European rally that resulted in a three-point lead heading into singles, which were delayed by the weather until Monday. Montgomerie showed immense trust in McIlroy by sending him out second. He again had to play Cink, who had ridden a hot putter all week while going unbeaten. As expected, McIlroy was a crowd favorite. On the first tee, the massive grandstand serenaded him: "*Rory, Rory McIlroy, Rory, Rory McIlroy / You've got Big Mac, we've got wee Mac!*"

It was a tense, tight match that always looked like it would go down to the wire. McIlroy made a ten-footer on sixteen to stay all square, leading to a fist pump and shout of "C'mon!" Still even playing the par-5 eighteenth hole, McIlroy earned the scorn of the old-school broadcasters on the European feed by going for the green from 273 yards out. He smashed a 3-wood, but his ball faded into a cavernous bunker on the short side. Cink laid up and then hit a good wedge shot to ten feet. McIlroy faced a brutally hard bunker shot and he tried to get too cute, leaving his shot in the sand. But Cink missed his birdie putt, handing McIlroy a do-or-die four-footer to salvage a halve. When the putt went in, McIlroy exhaled a long, billowing breath of relief. The half point wound up being crucial as the Cup went down to the last match, with McDowell vanquishing Mahan to give Europe a 14.5–13.5 victory.

By the end of the Ryder Cup, McIlroy couldn't stop gushing about the experience. In the freewheeling victors' press conference, McIlroy said, "This has been the best week of my golfing life, by far. It's been absolutely incredible. To share every moment with these guys up onstage, it's just been fantastic. And, you know, I'm still very, very young, and I don't want to miss a Ryder Cup for the next twenty years."

With typical cheek, Lee Westwood interjected: "It's the best exhibition, isn't it?"

"It's the best exhibition in the world," McIlroy said, drawing a big laugh. He added, "You know, I realize now what the Ryder Cup means and how much it means to everyone, and I'm a big fan."

It was a charming flip-flop and the sign of an open mind; presented with new information, McIlroy changed his opinion rather than double down on his old, obsolete statements. This would hardly be the last time he walked back a controversial take.

Having proven his bona fides in America and on the Ryder Cup stage, McIlroy had a lot to think about heading into the offseason. He made a momentous decision to renounce his PGA Tour membership and focus on the European Tour in the new year. Commuting between tours had prevented him from being dominant on either one. In 2010, McIlroy made sixteen starts on the PGA Tour but finished a mediocre thirty-sixth in the FedEx Cup standings, even with his breakthrough win at Quail Hollow. Not counting the majors and World Golf Championships, McIlroy made ten starts on the European Tour and failed to win any of them, slipping to thirteenth in the Race to Dubai. There was an inescapable pressure to keep up with his mates at International Sports Management: in addition to Louis Oosthuizen's Open win at St. Andrews, Westwood ascended to number one in the World Ranking in October 2010. "It's no disrespect to the PGA Tour," McIlroy said. "It's a great tour. It just doesn't quite fit for a European. You have to really be living over there full-time. I thought it was going to be easy this year: *It's okay, I can just go back and forth.* But it sort of took its toll. By the end of the PGA Tour season, I was a bit jaded and had to sit back and look at it, and came to the conclusion that it just wasn't for me."

McIlroy's decision on where to ply his trade touched off a series of events that would have sweeping ramifications for his career and the business side of the sport. But before all that could play out, he had a date with destiny in Augusta.

8.

Having given up the bright lights of the PGA Tour, Rory McIlroy looked stifled at the outset of the 2011 season. He led after two rounds in Dubai but blew up on the weekend (75-74) to fade to tenth place. He made three cameos in the U.S. leading into the Masters but didn't sniff the leaderboard in any of them. He arrived at the Masters still a tender twenty-one years old but eager to remind the golf world that he still mattered.

That took all of one round, as McIlroy blitzed Augusta National with a bogeyless 65 to become the youngest player in Masters history to hold a share of the first-round lead. McIlroy overwhelmed the course off the tee and relentlessly attacked the rain-softened greens with his approach shots. A shift in attitude helped, too. After missing the cut at the Masters the year before, McIlroy realized that he had let the hype get in his head, so, this time around, he took a studiously low-key approach, not arriving until Tuesday and becoming the last player to register for the tournament. This was the height of *Entourage*'s popularity, and McIlroy channeled Vince Chase by rolling into Augusta with a posse of old friends from Holywood: Harry Diamond, Mitchell Tweedie, and Ricky McCormick. They killed the hours before McIlroy's first-round tee time by tossing an American football in the front yard of their rental house. "I was actually told off by the lady living across the street—we were making a bit too much noise," McIlroy said. "Had to cut it short. I just said, 'Sorry, we'll go inside now.'" McIlroy received plenty of hazing when photos surfaced of his Eurocentric throwing motion: "Yeah, everyone said, 'You look like you're throwing it to the moon.' I was trying to throw it far—maybe it was a little too high, I don't know. I need to work on my technique."

McIlroy may have radiated good cheer, but he knew an almighty test awaited in the coming rounds. For perspective, he only had to think back nine months to his 63-80 at the Old Course. "It was a very valuable lesson in my development as a golfer," McIlroy said. He followed with a second-round 69 to build a two-stroke lead, yet Saturday's 70 was even more impressive. McIlroy labored to play the first twelve holes in 1 over par, but he never lost his cool and was rewarded with three birdies in the final six holes to reach −12 and stretch his lead to four strokes. "I've been talking about it with my little team all year about just playing stress-free golf," he said afterward. "I felt as if last year, I had a chance to win a lot of tournaments and I didn't do it just by making a few little mistakes here and there. Patience was huge for me today."

McIlroy's newfound discipline had him on Tiger's tail, trying to become the second-youngest winner in Masters history, only eight months off Woods's pace. Saturday night in Augusta, there was a giddy feeling in the air, a sense that the game was on the precipice of generational change. Only a year earlier, Tiger had returned to Augusta with his life on fire. He was greeted by a haughty scolding by club chairman Billy Payne, who said, "It is simply not the degree of his conduct that is so egregious here. It is the fact that he disappointed all of us, and more importantly, our kids and our grandkids. Our hero did not live up to the expectations of the role model we saw for our children." Now here was the squeaky-clean McIlroy to ring in a new era. Graeme McDowell spoke for many with a curt text to his Ryder Cup wingman following the third round: "I love you." Said McIlroy, "I don't know what that means. I don't know if that's him or the beer talking."

Every fifty-four-hole leader at the Masters is haunted by the specter of Greg Norman. In 1996, as he sat on a six-shot cushion, Norman was unwinding in the locker room when the English writer and raconteur Peter Dobereiner grabbed him by the lapels and said, "Greg, old boy, there's no way you can fuck this up now!" The next day, Norman burned up his six-shot advantage in the first eleven holes. Then, on twelve, he dumped his Maxfli into the water, losing the lead for good to his archnemesis Nick Faldo, who was McIlroy's favorite player. (That was the first Masters that Rory remembers watching as a kid.) Two other players in Masters history had blown a fifty-four-hole Masters lead of four or more strokes: Ed Sneed in 1979 and Ken Venturi in '56. Augusta National is an eighteen-hole high-wire act, often with the tiniest margin between a great shot and calamity. The pursuers knew what McIlroy faced, and they, too, understood the enormity of the opportunity. "It's an amazing feeling to wake up on Sunday in Augusta with a chance to win the Masters," said Bo Van Pelt, who was in eighth place, six shots back. "You've grown up watching it on TV, you've dreamed about it your whole career . . . you're trying not to be too giddy."

Added Luke Donald, who was in seventh place at −7, "It feels as if it takes forever for your tee time to come. The minutes crawl by. It's brutal. And if you're sitting on a four-shot lead, I can imagine the pressure builds and builds."

McIlroy spent Sunday morning watching the telecast of his favorite rugby team, Ulster. "But even after that, I still had time to kill," he says, and he couldn't resist a little channel surfing. "If I turned on ESPN, I was on TV. If I turned on Golf Channel, all I could hear was people talking about me. I learned after that not to watch television, go on Twitter, or anything like that. Any little outside influence you let into your bubble can be detrimental."

McIlroy had the 2:40 p.m. tee time. In the group ahead, Charl Schwartzel played a pitch-and-run from outside the rope line short and right of the first green. His ball dipsy-doodled across one of Augusta National's most undulating surfaces and, after a long, circuitous journey, clanged off the flagstick and disappeared for a birdie to send him to −9. "As great a shot as I've seen at Augusta," said Gary Player.

McIlroy split the first fairway but then yanked his approach shot long left. "That was the first point in the tournament where I made a very tentative swing," he says. "I came up and out of the shot. That's when I knew I didn't feel the same as the previous three days." He missed a four-footer for par. In one hole, his four-shot lead had been sliced in half.

McIlroy drove it into the bunker of the par-5 second hole and then clipped the lip with an overly ambitious second shot. Now there was a stirring in the gallery, a feeling of unease. McIlroy played two solid shots to leave himself four feet for par. As he surveyed the putt, a roar emanated from the third green: Schwartzel had spun his approach shot into the hole (again!) for an eagle. "I knew that's my lead gone," said McIlroy.

Up ahead, Woods was trying to recapture his pre-scandal magic. Having started his round tied for ninth at −5, he made birdies at two, three, and six and then stuffed his approach shot at seven. "We were in the seventh fairway when he made his putt up on that green," says Geoff Ogilvy, who began Sunday in ninth place. "Two birdies in a row—you could feel it building. I don't think Tiger wants to be considered a setup man, but he made the day what it was with his front nine. No one else can bring that kind of electricity to a golf course. No one."

When Schwartzel three-putted from one hundred feet on the fourth hole, McIlroy was back in the lead by a shot. Playing the par-5 eighth hole, Woods ripped a 3-wood to ten feet and then buried the putt to move within one of the lead. Says Ogilvy, "You know what was really cool? Across the course, you could hear when they posted the eagle on the leaderboards. Down by eleven, over at thirteen, then fifteen. One roar after another. Not for a golf shot but for the changing of the leaderboard."

McIlroy's approach to the fifth green came up miles short, and he failed to get up and down, falling to −10. Tiger Woods was tied for the lead. Pandemonium reigned at Augusta National. "A big mistake

I made was thinking too much about what everybody else was doing instead of concentrating on myself," McIlroy says. "In situations like that, you can't let your mind wander."

Woods made a twenty-five-footer to save par on nine, shooting a front-nine 31. McIlroy dropped a fifteen-footer on the seventh hole for his first (and last) birdie of the day, regaining sole possession of the lead at −11. He hit a good drive on the par-5 eighth hole, but his approach shot, with a 3-wood, took an unlucky bounce off the greenside mounding, away from the flag. McIlroy chunked the ensuing chip and settled for a disappointing par. "That's sort of the turning point of the round," he said. "If I got it up and down, I would have gotten a lot of momentum. When I didn't, it sort of felt as if it might not be my day."

But he was still in the fight! Woods missed a 2.5-footer for par on twelve and then, at the par-5 thirteenth, pulled a short iron left of the green, leading to a disappointing par that killed his momentum. Luke Donald rinsed his tee shot at twelve. The Sunday pressure was exacting a toll; McIlroy arrived at the tenth tee still leading by one at −11. But he smother-hooked his drive dead left, and the ball caromed off a tree even farther left, toward a row of cabins that have never been considered in play. The photos of a forlorn McIlroy peering at the distant fairway, with a black-shuttered cabin looming behind him, would become symbolic of his struggles at Augusta National. "I was literally in a daze," he says. "I'm like, 'What the fuck is going on?'" He punched back into the fairway but then hooked a 3-wood left of the green. McIlroy could still have gotten up and down to salvage a crucial bogey, but he clipped a tree branch with his chip. "Just tried to be a little too cute with the fourth shot," he says. It was funeral quiet as he left the green.

The triple bogey sent McIlroy skidding to seventh place. Still, he was only two back of coleaders Schwartzel, Adam Scott, K. J. Choi, and Ángel Cabrera. "On the back nine everything was happening very fast," says Choi. "It was one roar after another, or people kind of groaning so you knew something bad happened. It was impossible to keep track of who was doing what."

At fifteen, Woods hit a towering approach shot to four feet and strutted down the fairway as if he already had one arm in the green jacket. The eagle would give him sole possession of the lead . . . but he bricked the putt! The ensuing birdie created a five-way tie for the lead. At eleven, McIlroy played a gutsy long iron to the back-left flag. The eighteen-foot birdie putt could've gotten him within one of the lead, but he missed it and then—gasp!—blew the 2.5-foot comebacker. The tee shot on ten was so comically bad it could almost be dismissed as a fluke, but the three-putt revealed something deeper. "I sort of unraveled," McIlroy says. "I lost a lot of confidence in my putting around the turn. I didn't really get anything going and was sort of second-guessing lines and second-guessing my speed. On these greens, you can't do that."

Ken Venturi could relate. Long after his collapse in '56, he said, "I hit fifteen greens that day but three-putted six times. The hardest thing in golf is trying to two-putt when you have to, because your brain isn't wired that way. You're accustomed to trying to make putts, and when you change that mindset, your brain short-circuits, especially under pressure."

At sixteen, Ogilvy made his fifth consecutive birdie to reach −10, becoming the eighth player to hold at least a share of the lead during one of the wildest Sundays in Masters history. McIlroy played a solid tee shot on the dangerous twelfth hole, leaving himself fifteen feet for birdie. He missed, and then missed again . . . and again. "I was just gone, completely gone," says McIlroy. The four-putt left him 7-over on his round and now five strokes off the lead. A sickening feeling was swirling in the dogwoods. "I can't believe it," Ian Baker-Finch intoned gravely on the telecast; his brilliant playing career ended prematurely because of the driver yips, and he was more attuned than most to the mental warfare of championship golf. "It's a brutal game, and we are all a little fragile. And we all feel for him."

On the thirteenth tee, McIlroy snap-hooked his drive into the hazard and then slumped over, his face buried in the crook of his arm. "I felt like crying," he says. Masters Sunday was supposed to be a joyous coronation, but it turned into a wake. In an act of mercy by CBS, McIlroy mostly disappeared from the telecast. "All the rest of us did Rory a huge favor," says Ogilvy. "It could have been a death march for him, where his struggles were the focus of the rest of the day. But there were so many birdies flying around, everyone pretty much forgot about him. He was spared a lot of agony."

McIlroy had dumped Holly Sweeney at the start of the 2011 season but reconsidered within a month and had to do what he called "a lot of begging and grovelling to get her back." Her university studies and job as a cheerleader for the Ulster Rugby club precluded Sweeney from being in Augusta throughout Masters week. But on the down-low, International Sports Management flew her in on Sunday to partake in the expected victory party. McIlroy saw her for the first time after signing for his 80 and couldn't help but apologize, saying, "I'm sorry I wasted your time." He maintained his composure for the cameras. "I didn't handle it particularly well, obviously, but it was a character-building day, put it that way," McIlroy said. "I'll come out stronger for it." The real emotion flowed when Rory called Rosie back home in Holywood. The young master sobbed into his cell phone.

Schwartzel won a topsy-turvy Masters by birdieing the final four holes. That night, McIlroy repaired to the hospitality house that International Sports Management had rented. Deep into the night, David Feherty stopped by. The CBS announcer grew up in Northern Ireland and worked for years as an assistant pro at Holywood Golf Club. Wee Rory was six years old the first time Feherty saw him swing a club, on the downhill par-3 sixth hole nicknamed "Nun's Walk." McIlroy hit his tee shot stone dead. "He just walked back to the bag and put his club away like that was meant to happen," says Feherty. "No emotion, no celebration. I remember thinking, *Jesus, this kid is something special.*" Now, fifteen years later, Feherty sought out McIlroy, expecting to have to talk him off the ledge. "I was so worried about him," Feherty says. "That sort of thing can really change a player's career. It can detonate their self-confidence. I wasn't sure how he was going to handle it until I walked into the house and saw him sitting with Harry [Diamond] and his pals. I said, 'You all right, son?' Rory said, 'I've had worse days.' That was another holy shit moment to me. He had such an incredible attitude about it. And so much fortitude. That's when I knew he'd be a superstar." Feherty stuck around and eventually had McIlroy laughing so hard he was gasping for breath.

But there was no escaping the haunting reality of what might have been. The next day, the International Sports Management players piled into a private jet to fly to New York, where they would catch a flight to the Malaysian Open. McIlroy had to put on a brave face when Schwartzel rocked up to the plane wearing the one thing money can't buy: a green jacket.

How do you recover from one of the worst collapses in golf history? For McIlroy, the road back began with a phone call from the one person on the planet who understood his pain: Greg Norman. The Shark reached him in Malaysia and preached perspective. In a weird way, the '96 Masters was the best thing that ever happened to Norman. He played at Hilton Head the week after, and the most imperious and polarizing player of his day was thunderstruck to discover that, overnight, he had become a lovable loser. *The Sydney Daily Telegraph* published Norman's office fax number, and more than three thousand supportive messages poured in. Norman was paired with Paul Azinger, with whom he had a frosty relationship, but Zinger said, "Everyone who's played this game has been humbled and humiliated, and he had an extremely humbling experience. I would have just said congratulations had he won, and probably not much else, but we talked quite a bit. I told him that he showed more dignity in defeat than he ever could have in victory, and he talked about what it was like to feel that way, the kind of stuff that I probably would never have shared with him. It means a lot to him to know that players do care." Said Norman from Hilton Head, "The best thing is that I'm less cynical now, which is going to make my approach to the game much easier as years go by. It's easier to deal with situations when you know that people really care about you; it picks you up when you're feeling down. It's been an amazing few weeks . . . It's been a lifetime of experiences." The Shark shared all of that with McIlroy, who was similarly being enveloped by good vibes. "I got a lot of text messages and a lot of emails congratulating me on how I handled everything afterward, and I really appreciated that," McIlroy said. "But I mean, what else was I going to do? I can't come off and sulk and say, *Oh, this is the worst day of my life*, because a bad day on the golf course is better than a good day in the office." He joked that, if he appeared composed in his post-round TV interview, it was because he had five holes to think about what he would say.

And then, in one of the more remarkable performances of his young career, McIlroy picked himself off the mat and finished third in Malaysia.

After that, Northern Ireland beckoned for a staycation at the new €2.2 million estate he shared with Holly Sweeney. The thirteen-acre grounds included four par-3s, a driving range, multiple putting greens, and a soccer pitch, all of it tended to by a pair of greenskeepers. In the garage was McIlroy's new Ferrari. "She definitely keeps my feet on the ground, and she knows me better basically than anyone else," Rory said of Holly, adding, "She has been such a great support, and it was great to get back home and see her and spend time with her. She takes my mind off golf and everything else that is going on."

One of Norman's messages was to look on the bright side: McIlroy's game was good enough to lead the Masters for sixty-three holes. But while at home, McIlroy watched video of his swing with his coach, Michael Bannon, searching for clues. McIlroy's putative mentor, Lee Westwood, had offered a blunt road map: "When he gets under a bit of pressure he's got a pull hook in his bag." Bannon detected that on Masters Sunday the club had dropped behind McIlroy on the downswing, leading to the disastrous left misses. McIlroy put in long hours to get his swing more on plane. When he returned to competition, at Quail Hollow, McIlroy sought out Dave Stockton, who in his heyday was one of golf's most celebrated putters, leading to victories at a pair of PGA Championships. In his seventies, Stockton began ministering to a new generation of players with his old-school ways and folksy aphorisms. With McIlroy, he eschewed any mechanical talk and focused on feel and routine. Rory had been taking three practice strokes before every putt; Stockton convinced him to abandon all of them. McIlroy's new routine? "One look at the hole, go. Very instinctive," he said, "instead of almost thinking about it too much. Just trying to let it all flow, let it all go." McIlroy putted beautifully in his last start before the U.S. Open, a fifth-place finish at the Memorial. He felt his game beginning to crest.

But on the way to Congressional Country Club for the U.S. Open, McIlroy took an unexpected side trip: to Haiti, in his new capacity as an ambassador for UNICEF. For two days, he experienced firsthand how UNICEF was improving sanitation and combating cholera in one of the world's poorest countries, which was still reeling from a 2010 earthquake that killed a quarter million people. McIlroy visited maternity clinics and schools, singing songs and playing soccer with the kids. He came to the delightful realization that not a single person on the island cared about the mistakes he made on the back nine of Augusta National. "Yeah, I thought I had perspective before going to Haiti, and then actually seeing it, it just gives you a completely different view on the world and the game that you play," he said.

Perspective. That was the most important thing McIlroy gained during the two long months between the 2011 Masters and the U.S. Open. McIlroy had grown up reading the books of Bob Rotella, the most celebrated sports psychologist in golf, and they worked together throughout 2010. "From the beginning, the message was: *Don't be afraid to be great,*" says Rotella. "But to be great, you have to be willing to get ripped to shreds. If you just kind of hang around and play for a top ten, there's no attention on you, there's no criticism. If you play to win, you're going to get your heart broken sometimes. You have to be willing to go through that because that is the price of greatness." After the Masters disaster, McIlroy consciously avoided reaching out to Rotella or any other trained professional. "I like to figure things out on my own," McIlroy said. "I've always said that, you know, the responsibility should be on me. You learn for yourself and learn from your mistakes, and that's what I've tried to do. I've taken my own views from what happened and moved on, and that's the most important thing."

Perspective kept arriving, even at the expense of his good friend Graeme McDowell, who took a fifty-four-hole lead at the Players Championship but blew up on Sunday with a 79. Said McIlroy, "I sent him a text saying, 'It happens to the best of us.'" The scribes probed for weakness in every press conference, but McIlroy always had a ready answer. He pointed out that other young guns had recently blown leads on major championship Sundays: Dustin Johnson's 82 at the 2010 U.S. Open, and Nick Watney's 81 at the '10 PGA Championship. "I mean, it's tough to finish off tournaments, no matter who you are," McIlroy said. "Tiger made it look so easy for fifteen years or whatever, but it's really tough."

In the endless reflection after the Masters, McIlroy concluded it wasn't one snap hook or four-putt that cost him the green jacket. No, it was a betrayal of his core belief in himself. He had been hunting trophies since he was a boy, always attacking, always betting on himself. But he turned timid on the most critical day of his golfing life and played not to lose, a disastrous shift in approach. He resolved that next time it would be different. Said McIlroy in the run-up to Congressional, "Watching the [Masters Sunday] tape back, I was always looking at the ground. I was very insular. My shoulders were a little bit [hunched over]. Sort of like I didn't want the outside world to get in, instead of embracing the situation and saying, *You* know, I've got a four-shot lead at the Masters—let's enjoy this ... I went out on the last day at Augusta just trying to keep the lead, instead of being, *Right, I'm going to shoot 65, beat everyone by 8, and just show everyone how good I am.* That's really what you should be going out and looking at."

•

THE NOTION THAT MCILROY would face lowered expectations at Congressional was exploded in Ernie Els's pretournament press conference, when the two-time U.S. Open champ raved, "He's got all the talent in the world. He's a future number one without a doubt. He is incredible. And he's still learning. He's twenty-one years old; he's not perfect. Nobody is perfect. But he can really change the—maybe the history of the game. He's got that kind of talent. If he keeps learning and keeps going, keeps his head up, boy, I think he's going to win a lot of majors, but obviously he has to win the first one to win a lot."

Congressional is a big ballpark, with a sense of scale to match its massive, overly formal clubhouse. The undulating terrain and expansive greens instantly reminded McIlroy of Quail Hollow, his favorite course on the PGA Tour. The USGA offered a more imaginative setup with slightly wider fairways and less rough around the greens. Summer storms left Congressional's greens soft and vulnerable. In other words, it was the perfect time and place for McIlroy's brand of long ball. In a blockbuster first-round pairing alongside Phil Mickelson and Dustin Johnson, McIlroy unleashed a lifetime of want and will. With the split start, his round began on the tenth tee. McIlroy birdied the twelfth hole with a sand wedge to six feet. He birdied seventeen with an 8-iron to ten feet and then holed a twenty-footer on eighteen. McIlroy was smashing his drives so far in the swampy air that he reduced a national championship test to a glorified pitch-and-putt. He hit a sand wedge to six feet on hole number one. Three birdies in a row! On four, he hit another wedge tight and the lead was his. Playing the fearsome par-5 sixth hole, McIlroy pounded a drive and then, from 240 yards out, assessed whether he should attack a green guarded by water. His mind wandered back to the week before, when he was in Haiti. "I was thinking about laying up," he said, "and then I thought: 'You've just been in a place where millions of people have no clean water, and millions of kids get no education, and you're nervous about hitting a golf ball into some water!'" He produced a perfect 3-iron to the heart of the green and two-putted for another birdie. For the round, McIlroy hit seventeen greens in regulation, leading to the most stress-free 65 imaginable. Meanwhile, Mickelson needed a series of miraculous saves to salvage a 73. "He's striking it flawlessly," Phil said with a sigh.

After the round, McIlroy was hammered with questions about his fatal 80s at St. Andrews and Augusta National and how this week might be different. It took heroic restraint to betray only mild irritation. Did this round relieve any of the post-Masters angst? "Well, there's definitely no relief in it," McIlroy said. "You know, it's always nice to shoot a good first round at any tournament, let alone a major. But no relief. I know I'm playing well. I know this golf course. I know I'm pretty comfortable on this golf course, so I expected to go out there and—if I hit it the way I hit it in the practice rounds—I was going to always do pretty good."

McIlroy had the lead by two strokes and the gift of the late-early wave; he was back on the course again the next morning. He stood on the first tee box like a seasoned showman commanding the stage. "It felt like he grew a foot that week," says Chubby Chandler. "His presence was immense."

McIlroy birdied the fourth hole. And the sixth. Then on the eighth, from 114 yards out, he played a crafty, sawed-off pitching wedge; his ball flew right over the flag and sucked back into the hole. Eagle. The crowd was in a tizzy. "It felt like a home match," McIlroy said. The United States Motherfuckin' Open had devolved into chaos, and it was not yet lunchtime on Friday.

"He was hitting it so good it was a joke," says Jim "Bones" Mackay, who was caddying for Mickelson. "Like, we were actually laughing about it. I remember on the [par-3] seventh hole on Friday, he started his ball thirty feet left of the hole and it just kind of stayed there. It was the first shot in two days that didn't knock over the flagstick. Rory stood there like he was confused. He couldn't believe he hadn't hit it closer."

On the par-5 sixteenth, McIlroy smoked a 4-iron from 223 yards that settled eight feet from the hole. "I told him, 'I don't think you'll see a better golf shot,'" said caddie J. P. Fitzgerald. McIlroy made the putt to reach −12, a magic number at the national championship. Gil Morgan touched it during the third round at the 1992 U.S. Open but ultimately flew too high on borrowed wings. Woods finished the 2000 U.S. Open at −12 on a firm, fiery Pebble Beach—what is widely regarded as the most masterful performance in golf history. McIlroy kept pushing. On seventeen, he made a twelve-footer for another birdie. He was −13, deeper than any man had ever gone before at a U.S. Open. It was like walking on the bottom of the Mariana Trench.

Bones has seen a lot of stellar golf across thirty-five years around the Tour; for sustained excellence, where do McIlroy's first two rounds rate?

"Right near the very top," he says.

But it was never going to be entirely stress-free with McIlroy. On the eighteenth hole, he misplayed his approach shot into the water and took a double bogey. Still, two rounds running he had produced the low score of the day, and his 131 total was a U.S. Open record. "You know, it's funny to me, it feels quite simple," he said. "I'm hitting fairways. I'm hitting greens. I'm holing my fair share of putts . . . I don't really know what to say. It's been two very, very good days of golf."

But that was all foreplay. The stressfest of the weekend awaited, with the torturous wait until a midafternoon tee time; swollen, overserved galleries; crusty, spiked-up greens; and God and Johnny Miller waiting to pass judgment. Would McIlroy's closing double bogey shake his confidence and stir the ghosts of Augusta National? Shoulders back, head held high, with even more bounce than usual in his stride, McIlroy brought a commanding presence to the third round. He hit an errant drive on the third hole, punched out sideways, and then, from ninety yards, stuck a wedge to three feet to save par and send a message. He poured in a twenty-five-footer on five for his first birdie and then made another one on the par-5 ninth. McIlroy hit his tee shot on the par-3 tenth hole a little too good, flying the green and making bogey, but on eleven, facing one of the scariest shots on the course, from deep rough, he hit a 7-iron that flew right over the flag and settled eighteen feet away. McIlroy pumped his fist when he drained the birdie putt. It felt like a knockout punch; the only thing missing was Roger Maltbie exclaiming, "It's just not a fair fight!"

"I think they go hand in hand, having a little bit of attitude and a killer instinct," McIlroy said. "I think that's what you need on the golf course, especially in the position that I find myself in. You can't get complacent. No lead is big enough, so you need to just keep going."

McIlroy's 68 gave him a three-day total of 199, yet another U.S. Open record. His lead was eight strokes. But, says Rotella, "the most impressive thing he did that day was his press conference performance. In the years since, I've reread Rory his own quotes many times." Said McIlroy on that fateful Saturday evening, "What I did today, I tried to set myself a little target, little goals, just because it kept me from focusing on the leaderboard and focusing on how far ahead I was or anything like that. That really kept me in the present and kept me focused on my game. I'm really focusing on the process of making a good decision and making a good swing. That's all I've been trying to do, especially today, really lose yourself in that shot that you're playing at that moment in time and not think about anything else." As for the fraught, impending Sunday, McIlroy said, "At Augusta, it was all a little bit new to me, going into the final round with the lead. I didn't know whether to be defensive, aggressive, go for it, not go for it. But now I know what I need to do, which is a great thing to have. I have a clear mind going out there tomorrow, and I just need to stick to my game plan."

Everyone else in the field had already conceded defeat. "Bones said [Rory's] played out there the last few rounds like it's the Bob Hope Chrysler Classic," said Graeme McDowell. "He's free swinging it and aiming at every pin like he's supposed to shoot 65 . . . I hope he goes on and does it, because I've been waiting for this to happen. He's going to be a great ambassador for the sport. Will he achieve what Tiger has, [14] major championships to date or whatever he's got? Can he be that good? Yeah, potentially. He's got that potential."

Pádraig Harrington went one step further, saying that it was McIlroy, not Woods, who was now the biggest threat to break Jack Nicklaus's record of eighteen career major championship victories, even though at the moment Rory trailed Tiger 14–0. When Harrington's words were relayed to McIlroy, he shook his head and said in his lovely lilt, "Oooh, Paddy, Paddy, Paddy."

The curiosity of how McIlroy would handle the Sunday pressure lasted all of one hole, as he began his round by splitting the fairway, knocking a wedge to ten feet, and then making the putt for a resounding birdie. Then he birdied the fourth. The rout was on. Whereas McIlroy had been too inward on Sunday at Augusta, this time he cruised the fairways yapping in J. P. Fitzgerald's ear about rugby, cars, and other miscellanea. McIlroy came home with a showman's panache. At the par-3 tenth hole, surrounded by a huge amphitheater in front of the clubhouse, playing partner Y. E. Yang hit a tee shot to two feet. Then McIlroy did him one better, his ball stopping inches from the hole. (For the week, he would hit sixty-two greens in regulation, another U.S. Open record.) McIlroy's closing 69 brought two more tournament records: a four-round total of 268 and a winning score of –16. The eight-shot win had never been in doubt, so, in the end, the overriding emotion was joy, not catharsis. As he stepped off the eighteenth green the kid got a big, burly hug from Gerry. "Happy Father's Day!" Rory shouted in his ear.

Ankle and Achilles injuries had forced Woods to miss the U.S. Open for the first time since 1994. McIlroy made the cover of *Sports Illustrated* and the headline said it all: "Golf's New Era."

The hyperbole went to another level. "He's the best player I've ever seen," said McDowell, who was, in fact, alive during Woods's prime. Added Luke Donald, then the number one player in the world, "As I've said before, I think he has probably the most talent I've ever seen from a golfer."

Holly Sweeney captured the giddy mood in one tweet: "My fabulous boyfriend has played flawlessly all week! Drink up Northern Ireland, he's done us proud! Champagne flowing . . . Sooo happy for the curly one! 1st major down, millions to go!"

•

THE WORLD WAS AT McIlroy's feet following the U.S. Open. Quite literally. Two weeks after Congressional, he took in the Wladimir Klitschko–David Haye fight in Hamburg, Germany. He was delighted to discover Caroline Wozniacki, 20, seated in the row in front of him. McIlroy loves tennis and had long admired the fine form of the world number one.

"I always suspected he had a thing for her," says Sweeney. "When he was watching the women's games he always said he fancied her but I didn't take it that seriously—little did I know."

McIlroy made enough of an impression on Wozniacki for her to tweet, "Fantastic fight! Also met Rory McIlroy, who was sitting just behind me. Really down to earth great guy."

Says Sweeney, "I saw a tweet from Caroline saying she met Rory and that he was a great guy or something along those lines and my heart sank. I thought something was up because I didn't really hear from him during the trip to that boxing match in Germany that she was at."

In the days after the prizefight, McIlroy summoned Chubby Chandler to a hotel in London to share a secret: he was infatuated with Wozniacki and wanted to pursue a relationship. With visions of Tiger's sex scandal dancing in his head, Chandler told McIlroy, "Bloody hell, this could ruin your career if it's not handled properly." He beseeched McIlroy to keep the budding romance under wraps for the time being.

McIlroy's impulsivity is a family trait: his father proposed to Rosie after only a three-month courtship. Says Rory, "Yeah, that's what everyone says: 'You're definitely Gerry's son.'"

After his consultation with Chandler, McIlroy found Sweeney at the house they shared outside of Holywood. "[Rory] went straight to see the dogs instead of me," says Sweeney, "dodged me when he came through the door, and then sat me down and told me that he met with [Wozniacki] in Germany and that he wanted to see how it would go with her."

McIlroy's first start after the U.S. Open breakthrough came at the Open Championship at Royal St. George's. He played like a man with a lot on his mind, finishing a distant twenty-fifth. International Sports Management put out a one-sentence press release the morning after the Open concluded: "Rory McIlroy's long-time relationship with Holly Sweeney came to an amicable end before the Open Championship." "Amicable" might've been a stretch. Says Sweeney, "It killed me—that's why I went away to Dubai as soon as we split up, so I didn't have to look or think about it." McIlroy and Wozniacki went public the day after the statement dropped, canoodling on the streets of London. The photographs of the lovebirds instantly went around the world.

"A U.S. Open and a celebrity girlfriend all in the same fortnight," says Chandler. "It was like, *Okay, here we go. Things are about to get very interesting.*"

9.

The winner's check for the 2011 U.S. Open was $1.5 million. Rory McIlroy made nearly as much from all the win bonuses built into his endorsement contracts. Overnight, his appearance fee to play around the world tripled. (The PGA Tour is the only circuit that forbids appearance fees, though clever tournament sponsors have long paid six-figure thank-yous to top pros who pressed the flesh at off-course functions.) Four days of spectacular golf, preceded by a lifetime of preparation, put McIlroy on the fast track to generational wealth. His agent, Chubby Chandler, was delighted, of course, but also uneasy. International Sports Management took a 20 percent commission on McIlroy's appearance fees, 15 percent on his endorsement income, and 5 percent on his on-course winnings; these were on the high side of industry standards. "It was coming too fast," says Chandler. "The amounts were getting too big, and obviously Rory knew that. I had in mind that at the end of the season we would sit down and adjust the percentages so they were more favorable to Rory." But he hadn't told McIlroy that.

There were other sources of tension. Chandler remained very close to his clients Darren Clarke and Lee Westwood, and he fussed over them like a helicopter parent ... but he had outsourced day-to-day oversight of McIlroy to his young associate Stuart Cage. Older, wiser, and long celebrated as the future of European golf in the post-Faldo era, Westwood treated McIlroy like a pesky little brother. "Lee is very sharp, he has a very quick wit, and he would make little comments that were funny but a bit harsh," says Cage. "I'd feel uncomfortable listening to it. Rors may well have felt the same, but he never responded. I always had the feeling that Rory knew in his heart he'd be the better player. It was like, *I'll show you*. Which he has, even though Lee had a phenomenal career." Indeed, it took only four days at Congressional Country Club for McIlroy to eclipse Westwood, upending an already complex dynamic.

It is a truism of professional sports (and showbiz) that the talent must always take top billing. Tiger Woods broke with Butch Harmon in part because he resented his swing coach's increasingly high profile in the media. (Golf Channel analyst Brandel Chamblee contends that Tiger leaving Butch and remaking his swing is "the craziest thing in the history of sports" and that Woods would have won at least twenty-five major championships if he had stayed with Harmon.) The gregarious Chandler had long been a darling of the typing class. A month after McIlroy's victory at the U.S. Open, Clarke, then forty-two, finally fulfilled his promise and won the Open Championship. Chandler had guided Clarke for two decades—the victory was the high point of both of their careers. Chandler became ubiquitous in the media; given that ISM clients had won the first three majors of 2011, the run-up to that year's PGA Championship featured much talk about "the Chubby Slam." This was not McIlroy's favorite press conference topic. The Chubby Slam didn't happen—Keegan Bradley won the PGA—but, at the Irish Open, a spectator asked for Chandler's autograph. He claims to hate that type of attention, but Chubby obliged the fan just as McIlroy happened to walk by. "Oh, look," Rory said, "there's my celebrity agent signing autographs." Says Chandler, "It was a biting comment, meant to hurt."

In September 2011, two months after McIlroy began his romance with Caroline Wozniacki, he had another furtive rendezvous, summoning Conor Ridge to his home. Ridge was a native of Galway who had worked in public relations before founding Horizon Sports at the tender age of twenty-five. (His father was the firm's primary financier.) Ridge was a smooth talker who enthusiastically embraced the agent aesthetic: slicked-back hair, bespoke suits, and shiny, pointed shoes. Horizon was decidedly boutique until 2008, when Ridge stole Graeme McDowell from ISM. Part of the lure was the 10 percent stake in Horizon that McDowell received, creating a murky arrangement in which there was, at the very least, the appearance that G-Mac could profit from the play of his competitors. It has long been thought that Chandler had a similar equity arrangement with Clarke and Westwood, but Chubby adamantly denies this, saying, "I gave them bonuses because they undoubtedly helped me build the business, but never equity. I think it is unethical for a player to make money off of another player." Ridge landed another boldfaced name in 2009 when he signed McIlroy's friend Shane Lowry, who had recently won the Irish Open while still an amateur.

Now, sitting on the couch in the McIlroy living room as both sipped coffee, Ridge had a once-in-a-career opportunity to woo a disgruntled megastar. McIlroy explained that he wanted a younger, cooler image. He wanted to transcend golf. A point he made more than once was that he desired a cleaner, uncluttered look. (On his hat and chest were still the big, ornate logos for Jumeirah, the Dubai-based hotel chain that had little name recognition in most of the places where McIlroy teed it up.) He also expressed regret at giving up his PGA Tour membership in 2011; McIlroy had stewed at home watching on TV while one of the season's biggest events, the Players Championship, went on without him. When it was Ridge's turn to talk, he offered a detailed twenty-year plan for McIlroy's career. The meeting stretched for four hours. They quickly realized that they saw McIlroy's future in a remarkably similar way. It was like falling in love on a first date.

Hovering over the clandestine meetup was one word: Nike. The post-scandal Tiger Woods was approaching rock bottom in the summer of 2011, having been absent at the U.S. and British Opens due to injury and missing the cut at the PGA Championship. He dropped out of the top fifty in the World Ranking for the first time since October 1996, his second month as a professional. Nike is fueled by star power; the swoosh needed a new leading man in golf. Company executives had already begun cozying up to McIlroy, subtly signaling their interest without running afoul of the unwritten rule not to poach a player under contract (his clothing contract with Oakley ran through 2012 and equipment deal with Titleist through 2013). "I knew Nike was interested, but I hadn't engaged with them yet," says Chandler. "Maybe I'm old-fashioned, but I felt Rory should fulfill his contracts first, especially because they were with companies that supported him before he had won anything. That's the problem with Rory—he'll sign a deal and a year later want something better." Back then, when I asked the president of Nike Golf about the courtship of McIlroy, Cindy Davis chose her words carefully: "Our team is always developing relationships, at all levels of golf. Put it this way: we've been a fan of Rory's for a long time."

McIlroy's post-Congressional play had been sluggish, in part because he was chasing Wozniacki around the globe. The meeting of the minds with Ridge seemed to energize McIlroy: he followed with three straight top-three finishes. Then he took a trip to Bermuda for the Grand Slam of Golf, a made-for-TV exhibition reserved for winners of each year's major championships. On the way home, McIlroy pulled Chandler into a private lounge at JFK Airport in New York. "He told me he was going in a different direction, and that was that," says Chandler. "It was very clinical, very mature. We shook hands and let the lawyers handle the rest." They tabulated the remaining commissions on McIlroy's endorsement deals and upcoming appearance fees, and the barristers negotiated a payout to ISM in the high six figures.

In McIlroy's first public comments, he said, "For four years, Chubby was the best guy and ISM were fantastic for me, but sometimes to progress you need to have a fresh view on things. It's about me trying to play my best golf and that's all there is to it . . . To be honest, I feel as if I just needed a fresh view, and I'm excited about the future now." The PGA Tour membership issue loomed large, as did the opinionated presence of Westwood, who had skipped the 2011 Players Championship when he sat atop the World Ranking. "That's another example of being involved with Chubby and ISM and maybe being led down the wrong path, or a path that I didn't want to go down," McIlroy said. "It was something I sort of felt like I had to do. I think just spending a little bit of time around Chubby and Lee and hearing their view of the PGA Tour—obviously they're very pro–European Tour—while I've always been one who wanted to play on the PGA Tour."

Shortly after McIlroy signed with Horizon, he teamed with Graeme McDowell to represent Ireland at the World Cup of Golf. G-Mac was sensitive about insinuations that he had helped Ridge steal his friend from ISM. "I purposely took a back seat in it all," McDowell said. "Rory makes his own decisions. I certainly wasn't going to sway him."

McIlroy had begun 2011 as a boy wonder but ended it as a man newly empowered by calling the shots in his career. Hubris can be expensive: when it came time to officially sign his contract with Horizon, at a company Christmas party that may or may not have been a little boozy, McIlroy did not have it vetted by a personal attorney. Chandler was gobsmacked when he inevitably learned of McIlroy's terms with Ridge and Horizon Sports. "I had thought his leaving was about money," Chandler says, "but come to find out Rory was paying them the exact same fees he was paying us! It was too much." Neither McIlroy nor Ridge knew it, but the clock was already ticking on their relationship.

●

THE IMPACT OF MCILROY'S growing fame could be felt acutely around his hometown of Holywood. In the weeks after his U.S. Open victory, seemingly every member of the Golf Writers Association of America came to town to report McIlroy's origin story. (Scribes are forever searching for assignments that yield boondoggles to the linksland; Royal County Down is less than an hour's drive from Holywood.) With notebook in hand, *ESPN The Magazine*'s Gene Wojciechowski approached a teenager at Holywood Golf Club, and the kid sighed wearily. "I've already done five of these interviews," he said.

When celebrities date each other, their fame isn't added together—it's multiplied. Rory and Caroline had already acquired a doozy of a nickname: "Wozzilroy." Good-looking, über-talented, and prone to public displays of affection, the young couple became fixtures in the European tabloids. As the Scottish newspaper *The National* put it, "The young sweethearts . . . are so cute that we risk insulin shock by looking too closely." But no one could look away. It was barely contained chaos when Wozniacki attended a McIlroy tournament for the first time, the WGC-HSBC Champions in China in November 2011. (The week before, McIlroy had won the Shanghai Masters, an upstart tournament unaffiliated with any established tour, claiming the $2 million winner's check, at the time the largest in golf.)

Pre-Caroline, McIlroy had conspicuously avoided going to the gym. He began reshaping his body in the latter half of 2011, motivated by the most powerful force in the universe: male pride. "I'd never really [jogged] before," says McIlroy, "but I thought I was pretty fit. So we went for a forty-five-minute run. After thirty, I was completely dead. I did the extra fifteen but was in pain. I've slowly built up my cardiovascular fitness, not because I need it for golf but because I want to keep up with her when we go running." Wozniacki won five WTA titles in 2011 and finished as world number one for the second consecutive season; McIlroy loved that he could share pillow talk with an elite athlete who understood the pressures and sacrifices that come with life at the top. "It's working so well because we have so much in common," he said. "Obviously different sports, but we're pretty much in the same position at a young age and we can talk about things that probably a lot of 21, 22-year olds can't talk about. It's nice to have someone that understands what you're going through."

McIlroy had a final highlight in 2011 when he won the Hong Kong Open with a closing 65. After dunking a bunker shot on the seventy-second hole to seal the deal, he uncorked a series of lusty fist pumps, a mini-catharsis after months of off-course drama. "Yeah, I've never been that excited or animated on a golf course before," McIlroy said. "I think it just shows you how much it meant to me." The victory shot him to number three in the World Ranking. It had been a helluva year. What could he possibly do for an encore?

•

AFTER A SEASON OF discontent, which included parting ways with his longtime caddie, Steve Williams, and hiring yet another swing coach (Sean Foley), Tiger Woods ended 2011 with a bang by finishing third at the blue-chip Australian Open and then winning his own Hero World Challenge against a small but strong field. During Woods's previous, imperious reign, no one would have gotten too excited about him winning an unofficial tournament that many of the competitors treat like a working vacation in the Bahamas. Still, it was his first victory of any kind in two long, hard years and rekindled hope that there might still be some magic left.

McIlroy was keeping tabs on Woods, as always, and he couldn't help but pine for a showdown with his resurgent boyhood hero. "You want to test yourself against the best in the game, and if I were to come up against Tiger on a Sunday, it would probably be the biggest challenge of my career, obviously," McIlroy said. "It's something I would look forward to. It would be a huge experience and a huge learning curve for me just to see how I would handle it. It's not something that a lot of players in my sort of generation have experienced yet." Indeed, Woods had won his most recent major championships by dusting old dudes with minimal star power: Rocco Mediate, Chris DiMarco, Woody Austin. Would Tiger ever tangle with the young studs who had filled the vacuum following Thanksgiving 2009?

The golf world finally got its wish at the 2012 Honda Classic. McIlroy came in hot after making the finals of the WGC Match Play Championship, in which he was upset by Hunter Mahan. McIlroy was unbothered by the loss because, in the semifinals, he had deliciously dispatched his old antagonist, Lee Westwood. "This is no disrespect to the guys in the other semifinals, but [the Westwood showdown] was like my final in a way. That was the one I wanted all week, and I got it. And that's what I got myself up for." That kind of personal vendetta was right out of Tiger's playbook; the pupil was becoming the master.

Woods would add another name to his extensive enemies list during the Honda Classic, when excerpts dropped from *The Big Miss*, his former swing coach Hank Haney's scathing tell-all book about their days together. Tiger looked edgy throughout the first two rounds and had to birdie seventeen and eighteen on Friday to make the cut. McIlroy was one off the lead with rounds of 66-67, and then he shot another 66 on Saturday to summit the leaderboard. Woods, with a third-round 69, was nine shots adrift. And then, on Sunday, all heaven broke loose. Woods played the front nine in 4-under in a strong wind, flying up the leaderboard but still five shots off McIlroy's lead. Then Woods birdied the eleventh hole and poured in a thirty-footer on the seventeenth, followed by a vintage fist pump. McIlroy tenaciously held on to the lead and was still up three strokes as Woods played the par-5 eighteenth hole. Tiger mashed a 5-iron to six feet, buried the eagle putt for a 62, and then uncorked two more fist pumps. It was the lowest final-round score of Woods's career and sliced the lead to a lone stroke. The wall of noise could be heard throughout South Florida, most especially on the thirteenth green, where McIlroy was idling. "Definitely wasn't a birdie roar," he said. Then he coolly rolled in a slick, downhill five-footer for his own bird to double the lead. "You know, I always had putts on the putting green when I was ten years old to beat Tiger Woods," McIlroy said after the round. "Thought it would be great to turn that into reality at some point."

McIlroy played airtight golf down the stretch to close out the two-stroke victory. He drove straight from the champion's press conference to jump on a jet to New York City for a rendezvous with Wozniacki.

The next morning, the World Ranking finally made official what everyone already knew: Rory Daniel McIlroy, of Holywood, Northern Ireland, at the age of twenty-two years, ten months, and one day, was the number one golfer on the planet.

There are only a few titles more impressive than best golfer alive. Perhaps leader of the free world? Both men met a couple weeks after McIlroy's triumph at the Honda Classic, when the kid pressed flesh with President Barack Obama at a state dinner at the White House honoring British Prime Minister David Cameron. Among the other guests were George Clooney and Sir Richard Branson, with music provided by Mumford & Sons. McIlroy looked grown-up in black tie, but his boyish charm came through in an ensuing tweet: "Unbelievable experience at the White House last night! Big thanks to @BarackObama for the invite! We'll get that golf swing sorted soon!"

•

THE RUN-UP TO THE Masters is always overheated, but it reached a fever pitch in 2012 thanks to a resurgent Woods and a streaking Phil Mickelson, who earlier in the season had enjoyed one of the highlights of his career by dusting Tiger 64–75 on Sunday at Pebble Beach to win his fifth Crosby Clambake. Then there was the new boy king, McIlroy. The oddsmakers made Tiger the favorite, but just: +325, with McIlroy at +400 and Mickelson +900.

McIlroy's return to Augusta, a year after his stunning unraveling, was always going to be fraught. On the first hole of his first round, he uncorked a wild drive and made double bogey. But McIlroy refused to capitulate, birdieing the next hole. Despite a misbehaving driver, he grinded out a 71 that kept him in the tournament. Then he shot a second-round 69 to put himself in a tie for third place, only one stroke off the lead shared by Fred Couples and Jason Dufner. Afterward, there were endless questions about McIlroy's redemption tour, but he downplayed the narrative and stressed that the third round would be just another eighteen holes: "I grew up watching this tournament on TV, and it's like sacred ground. The first time you get here, you're scared of taking a divot out of the fairway. But now it's just one of the places we come to play, and it's a great honor to come back here and play, but I think definitely every year you get a little more comfortable."

For Masters Saturday, McIlroy was paired with his friend Sergio García in the sparkly second-to-last tee time. With Woods not in contention, they would be the keynote group. But it took only a couple of hours for their two-ball to devolve into slapstick. McIlroy looked overwhelmed while touring the front nine in 42 . . . and García was only two strokes better. Then they both bogeyed the eleventh hole. At twelve, each made his first birdie of the day, and they went in for a long hug, clinging to each other like survivors in a life raft. "We started with a chance to win but were both struggling so bad," says García. "It was just a little consolation for each other. Like, we were both feeling bad about ourselves, and we just needed a hug."

McIlroy sounded utterly defeated in the wake of his 77. The emotional hangover lasted into the summer, as he missed the cut at the U.S. Open and was a nonfactor at the Open Championship. A year that began with so much promise was starting to feel like a dud. He would try to salvage his season at the PGA Championship at Kiawah Island's Ocean Course, a house of horrors replete with ball-gobbling dunes, tangly native grasses, woolly bunkers, diabolical greens, ever-present zephyrs, and other booby traps.

McIlroy came in a tad defensive about his lackluster play in the preceding major championships, saying, "I'm not going to be able to play golf like I played at Congressional every week." He stressed that he had become a more complete player since Congressional, citing a more varied short game and upgraded putting. (He had continued to work with Dave Stockton on refining an instinctive, freed-up routine on the greens.) McIlroy, whose towering draw was the most drooled-over shot shape in the game, had also been laboring to add a fade to his arsenal. Though he hadn't won since the Honda Classic in March, the competition had noticed McIlroy's efforts. "There was criticism about his attitude and his work ethic, and he really stepped it up," said Luke Donald. "Rory has realized he has such an amazing talent, and he doesn't want to waste it. The big difference I've seen this year is his short game. He's obviously worked very hard. He has the whole package now, which is kind of scary."

McIlroy opened the PGA Championship with a bogeyless first-round 67, during which he hit fifteen greens in regulation and was three-for-three on sand saves. But in a weird way, his second round was more impressive, despite his score soaring in wind gusts that touched thirty miles per hour. It was reminiscent of the second round of the 2010 Open, when McIlroy followed his 63 with an 80 at the Old Course. This time, he didn't panic while playing the first thirteen holes in 4 over par. When McIlroy stepped to the tee of Ocean Course's par-3 fourteenth, the wind was howling off the right. Instead of his usual high draw, he held up a hard cut against the gale, what his caddie, J. P. Fitzgerald, later called "maybe the best shot of the week." That led to a crucial birdie, and McIlroy added another one coming in, holding it together for a 75 on a day when the field averaged 78.1. "I definitely feel as if I'm getting better at handling conditions like that and being able to know when a 74, 75, is a decent score and move on and know that the next day should be better," he said. McIlroy was tied for fifth, two shots off the lead held by Tiger Woods, Vijay Singh, and Carl Pettersson.

Lightning delayed the start of the third round, and McIlroy got in only nine holes before darkness fell; he made the most of it with five birdies during a front-nine 32 that gave him a piece of the lead alongside Singh.

(Woods shot 40 to blow himself out of the tournament.) It was a tour de force with his driver as McIlroy missed only one fairway in the persistent crosswinds and led the field at 319 yards a pop. Looking on approvingly was McIlroy's lifelong swing coach, Michael Bannon. He noted one visible change in his pupil: poking out of McIlroy's shirtsleeves were actual biceps on what used to be spindly, freckled arms. Woods pushed his body to the breaking point out of vanity and an attempt to prove his manhood to his Green Beret father. McIlroy started hitting the gym so he wouldn't look like a weenie in front of his tennis star girlfriend, but his continued commitment to fitness had more practical benefits. "He needed to strengthen parts of his body," said Bannon. "He creates so much power on the downswing, he has so many levers, his lower body and core muscles have to be stronger to stabilize him. And now they are."

McIlroy was plenty pumped for the twenty-seven-hole Sunday. By the time he completed his third-round 67, he led by three strokes. McIlroy felt so relaxed he went back to his rental house and took a nap. "My dad had to come wake me up because I overslept," he says. "He said to me, 'Rory, you realize you have to play some golf this afternoon?' I didn't know where I was." He arrived at Ocean Course a mere half an hour before his 1:45 tee time. Ian Poulter had already birdied five holes in a row on his front nine to slice the margin to one stroke. Unbothered, McIlroy blunted that charge with birdies of his own on the second and third holes. As Poulter regressed to the mean with four back-nine bogeys, McIlroy just kept charging ahead, overpowering the par-5 seventh hole for a two-putt birdie that restored the lead to four strokes. His ball-striking wasn't perfect, but he simply refused to make a bogey, repeatedly getting up and down. One by one, the would-be contenders fell away, but McIlroy never let up, even after the outcome was no longer in doubt, reminiscent of the way Woods grinded so hard during the final round of the 2000 U.S. Open despite a double-digit lead, simply because he had vowed not to make a bogey. "That was a statement," said Keegan Bradley, who finished third. "That was a message from Rory to the rest of us."

McIlroy holed a twenty-footer for birdie on the eighteenth hole for a final flourish, loosing a joyous fist pump; it was only his twenty-third putt of the round. Then something broke loose inside of him. "It was the first time I've ever cried after I won a golf tournament," he says. "I see my dad and give him a hug and there's a few tears. 'What are you doing?' he said. I said, 'I don't know.' For some reason it was quite emotional."

McIlroy's bogeyless closing 66 pushed his margin of victory to eight strokes to break Jack Nicklaus's tournament record. Not for nothing, McIlroy was only a few weeks older than Big Jack had been when he bagged his second big one, the 1963 Masters. With a second blowout major championship victory in the span of fourteen months, it had become abundantly clear that McIlroy was no longer competing against his peers. No, the only relevant comparisons now were with the game's all-time greats.

10.

Rory McIlroy rode the momentum from his PGA Championship win into the 2012 FedEx Cup "playoffs," and there was no stopping him now: at the Deutsche Bank Championship, he roared to victory with a final-round 67, and the following week, at the BMW Championship, he outdueled Phil Mickelson and poor Lee Westwood to win again. McIlroy went a combined 40 under par across the two tournaments, becoming the first European player to win four PGA Tour events in a season. His would-be competition could feel that something had shifted. "He has always been driven and motivated," said McIlroy's friend and mentor Graeme McDowell. "Now he's obsessed with being the best he can be."

McIlroy took his newfound alpha status into his second Ryder Cup, at Medinah Country Club outside of Chicago. To the surprise of no one, he was sent out in the very first match, alongside McDowell, and they put a point on the board for Europe with a hard-fought foursomes win against Jim Furyk and Brandt Snedeker. "A lot had happened with Rory between those Ryder Cups," said European stalwart Luke Donald. "In a way, he had grown up before our eyes. Whether he wanted it or not, he was now one of the team leaders. We all fed off his confidence." Still, anything can happen at the Ryder Cup, and McIlroy and McDowell lost in the second session to Mickelson and Keegan Bradley. Then the boys from Northern Ireland lost again on Saturday morning in a rematch versus Furyk and Snedeker. Team USA kept rolling in the Saturday afternoon four-balls, getting an early blowout to push the score to 9–4.

McIlroy was playing in the third match alongside Ian Poulter. They were 2-down through seven holes to Jason Dufner and Zach Johnson and then halved the next five holes. In the match in front of them, Paul Lawrie and Nicolas Colsaerts were on their way to losing to Dustin Johnson and Matt Kuchar, which would push the U.S. lead to 10–4. For Europe, the Ryder Cup was quickly slipping away, and delirium reigned among the sodden American fans. But McIlroy was never going to give in. On Medinah's thirteenth hole, he rifled an approach shot to the heart of the green and then rolled in a big-breaking eighteen-footer for birdie, allowing him and Poulter to win a hole for the first time since number four. McIlroy turned to his pard and screamed in his face: "Come on!" Poulter obliged, birdieing fourteen for a halve and fifteen to square the match. "We were just struggling to get anything going," McIlroy said. "We just needed a spark, anything, a chip-in or a holed putt just to get something going. Thankfully, I was able to make a birdie on thirteen, and that definitely got this man going, anyway. He just took over from there." Poulter, eyeballs bulging, birdied sixteen, and Europe led for the first time in the match. Then he matched Johnson's birdie at seventeen! It felt like all of Chicago had encircled Medinah's eighteenth hole as the final two matches reached their climaxes. Europe needed two full points to have any hope of a comeback in Sunday singles. McIlroy and Poulter watched from the fairway as Woods and Steve Stricker missed birdie putts on the final green to lose 1-down to Donald and Sergio García, making the score 10–5 and giving Europe a glimmer. McIlroy hit a so-so approach to the front of the green, but Poulter played a gorgeous shot to ten feet and then buried the putt to win the match. It was his fifth straight birdie.

Europe was down 10–6 but suddenly had all the momentum. When the singles draw came out that night, McIlroy was in the third slot to help lead the charge. He would face Bradley, who had been the U.S.'s best player across partner play, with a 3-0 record. They would tee off at 11:25 . . . Central time.

A SUBPLOT THROUGHOUT RYDER Cup week was the distracting presence of Erica Stoll, a willowy, elegant PGA of America staffer working with the transportation committee at Medinah. "There was a lot of talk about 'the PGA girl,'" says one Team USA caddie, who demanded anonymity so as not to get yelled at by his wife. "She stood out because she was so incredibly beautiful. You see a lot of babes at golf tournaments, but they usually have a drink in their hand. It was unusual for a girl like that to actually be working for the PGA."

Stoll grew up near Rochester, New York, as part of a sporty family—she played tennis in high school before matriculating at the Rochester Institute of Technology. She was close to completing her degree when the Senior PGA Championship came to town in 2008. Stoll snagged a job working on-site as an office manager and couldn't help but be a little starstruck. The highlight of the week? "Tom Watson walked into the office and said 'Hi,'" Stoll told her local newspaper, the *Democrat and Chronicle*. Yes, that's the whole story. Being a small part of a big tournament revealed an unexpected career path. "The way PGA employees present themselves is so admirable and professional," Stoll said. "That's the kind of job I want, and it's doing something I love."

The PGA of America hired Stoll full-time after she graduated. Like everyone else, McIlroy took note of her at Medinah. "Erica that week was always the one that was checking us in and out," he says. "She was there at transportation, so she was always in the car park over there (by the clubhouse)."

McIlroy was quite obviously smitten with Stoll, according to three PGA Championship staffers who worked that Ryder Cup. "He was throwing every ounce of game he had at Erica," says one. "It was not subtle. It became a running joke among a few of us: Has Rory closed the deal yet?"

The Ryder Cup can be logistically challenging for players as they try to stick to their individual routines within the team framework. Each player has an idiosyncratic warm-up regimen, so for the staggered start of singles play, they arrive at the course at varied times. But forty-five minutes before McIlroy's tee time, panic swept through the European side when they collectively realized that no one had laid eyes on McIlroy. Team Europe and PGA of America officials began frantically making phone calls, including to Stoll, who coordinated player shuttles from the hotel, the Westin in Lombard, to Medinah Country Club, 12.2 miles away.

"As soon as it went out over the internal radios that Rory was missing," says the tournament official, "I texted [a colleague who worked alongside Stoll] and asked what the heck was going on. And all [they] replied with was a winking emoji."

Pat Rollins, then Lombard's chief of police, dispatched one of his men to fetch McIlroy from his room. "Obviously, I panicked, and I got ready as soon as I could," Rory says. "The thing that I was worried about was letting the team down. We were already in a bad position . . . But I was panicking, I really was."

His tee time was now less than forty minutes away, with nothing but Ryder Cup–related gridlock between the hotel and the golf course; it was at least a twenty-minute drive on a normal day. What would happen if McIlroy showed up late? "Turns out if you miss the tee time—if you're five minutes late—you lose the hole," says Michael Belot, then Ryder Cup director for the PGA of America. "Ten minutes late, you lose the match."

Keegan Bradley wasn't having it: "I had already told [Ryder Cup officials], 'I don't care what your rules are, I'm not taking a forfeit. Whether it's now, an hour from now, two hours.' I don't care what they would have said, we still would have played our match. I wouldn't have wanted to finish [with a forfeit]."

Rollins volunteered to drive McIlroy to the course. "Rory climbs in the front passenger side," says Rollins. "It's just us two. I turned on the lights and sirens . . . As we were driving, there was one point where I ended up slamming on the brakes pretty hard. I looked at him, and he was a little frazzled. I asked him if he got carsick. Then I said, 'Don't worry, I'll get you there in time.'"

Rollins called ahead so local law enforcement could clear the roads into Medinah. NBC reported on McIlroy's mad dash in real time. His agent, Conor Ridge, told network staffers that McIlroy had been watching Golf Channel the night before when his tee time was displayed as 12:25. But that was Eastern time. After nearly a week in Chicago, with an army of support staff fussing over him, could McIlroy really have mixed up his time zones? That became the official story broadcast by NBC and amplified by McIlroy. "We went out for dinner that night," says the tournament official, "and [colleagues who worked alongside Stoll] were openly mocking the narrative that was being peddled by the media. They were like, *Can you believe all the reporters fell for that shit?*" (McIlroy has always maintained that he got the time zones confused; when I spoke to his manager, Sean O'Flaherty, he declined to discuss any aspect of his boss's personal life.)

Rollins made the drive to Medinah in sixteen minutes, delivering McIlroy eleven minutes before his tee time. He did a few half-hearted stretches, gobbled an energy bar, stroked five putts, and sauntered to the first tee for his showdown with the twitchy Bradley, who had begun his obsessive pre-round routine two hours earlier. The crowd on the first tee was in a frenzy, aroused by the news of McIlroy's mad dash to the course. The fans offered a cheeky chant: "Central time zone! Central time zone!" McIlroy was going to either be the feckless screwup who cost Europe the Ryder Cup or pull off a legendary act of carefree heroism—there was no in-between. McIlroy made small talk with his opponent while waiting for the first fairway to clear. "He was great, he apologized—not that I was mad at him," says Bradley. "His vibe was a little like, *I can't believe this is happening.* But he's such an awesome player, he settled into the match pretty quickly. If I had to play a Ryder Cup match after arriving like that, I would have been a basket case."

McIlroy's swing looked out of sequence on his opening drive, which missed badly to the right, but he saved a gritty par for a halve. A chant broke out from U.S. fans, who had their own theories about McIlroy's tardiness: "Was she worth it?" *Clap, clap, clap-clap-clap.* McIlroy got up and down on the next two holes to keep the match even and then went 1-up when Bradley made a hash of the fourth hole. On six, McIlroy chipped in to win another hole, and he punctuated the moment with a guttural scream. Bradley fought back to square the match through twelve holes but McIlroy took the fourteenth hole with a beautiful bunker shot to go 1-up. At that moment, the U.S. led 10–7 and was ahead in three matches and all square in six others. For Europe to have any prayer, McIlroy would have to put a full point on the board, and he knew it. On the fifteenth hole, he flagged a wedge shot for yet another birdie, taking a commanding 2-up lead with three holes to play. McIlroy clinically closed out the match on the seventeenth hole. "The best golf I played the whole week," he says. Four hours earlier, he had been in a squad car. *Let the legend grow.*

McIlroy's win closed the gap to 10–9. The scoreboard kept bleeding blue. When Luke Donald, Ian Poulter, Justin Rose, and Paul Lawrie all secured full points, it meant that Europe had taken the first five matches. The Miracle at Medinah was underway. Europe went on to win 8.5 points out of 12 to steal another Ryder Cup. Having gone 3-2, McIlroy was one of only three Europeans with a winning individual record.

At the boozy victory party, European captain José María Olazábal presented McIlroy with an alarm clock.

THE SCALE OF MCILROY'S worldwide popularity could be felt during his trip to China in the wake of the Ryder Cup. A year earlier, McIlroy had headlined a thirty-man exhibition called the Shanghai Masters.

His victory was not recognized by any sanctioned tour. Now, BMW had come in and turned the tournament into a big deal, with a $7 million purse that was one of the fattest on the European Tour. No one denied the cause and effect. "Rory is a very important part of growing the game in Asia," said tournament director Marco Kaussler.

McIlroy, candid and chatty by nature, was still getting used to the white-hot spotlight that comes with being the world number one. At a pretournament press conference, a Chinese reporter asked a question that was translated as, "You have a lot of fans in China. Do you enjoy having local juniors go crazy about the way you play golf and the way you dress and your hairstyle?" McIlroy chuckled and then paused for a couple of beats, Fleet Street headlines dancing in his head: "I don't want to say anything wrong here, but I haven't seen many Chinese people with hair as curly as mine. I think it would be pretty tough to copy my hairstyle." Later, lounging on a couch in the clubhouse, he analyzed the exchange. "I was trying to be funny," he said. "Was that funny? I wanted so badly to make a joke, but if it goes wrong, I don't want there to be headlines like, you know, 'Racist Rory.'"

His agent, Conor Ridge, knew he had to let Rory be Rory, but that came with inevitable tension. "The fans, the media, corporate sponsors, the tours—they all want their piece," said Ridge. "Tiger dealt with it by slamming down the shutters. That's not Rory's way. We're still struggling to find the proper balance."

Market forces were conspiring to further complicate McIlroy's world. During the week in Shanghai, McIlroy's money manager, Donal Casey, flew all the way from Ireland for a 3.5-hour dinner, propelled by the $100 million that was about to land in McIlroy's lap by way of a five-year deal with Nike that Ridge had been stealthily negotiating for months. (Since Ridge hadn't overseen McIlroy's current crop of endorsement contracts, he felt no qualms in extricating his client from them.) The Nike deal remained a secret for the time being, but McIlroy was happy to publicly gloat about the fifty-dollar bet he took from his buddy Graeme McDowell by eating a mound of broccoli covered in blueberry yogurt in player dining in Shanghai. "I didn't realize he's that hard up for cash," said McDowell.

McIlroy was in second place heading into the final round in Shanghai. That morning, he received a wake-up call from his girlfriend, Caroline Wozniacki. "She's in Europe right now, and she'll set her alarm for four a.m. so she can call and wish me good luck before my rounds. It's . . .'"—he stammered a bit, his cheeks reddening—"it's really nice of her."

McIlroy got beaten down the stretch by a scrappy veteran, Peter Hanson, and afterward pulled a black hoodie over his head while sulking in an airport waiting room. Watching him, Ridge whispered, "He won the PGA Championship and three other tournaments on the PGA Tour this year—whether he wins the BMW Masters isn't consequential to anyone except Rory. But he's already thinking about his career victory total." Two days later, McIlroy rendezvoused with Wozniacki in—where else?—Bulgaria. They would meet up in a half dozen countries on three continents over the ensuing two and a half months. Earlier in the year, McIlroy had bought his first beachhead in the U.S.—a $11.75 million spread on the Intracoastal Waterway in Palm Beach Gardens—but he said, "Sometimes I forget what it's like to sleep in my own bed."

•

ON A CRISP MORNING in January 2013, a few minutes before the first round of the Abu Dhabi Golf Championship, Ridge was loitering near the first tee box when approached by Wayne "Radar" Riley, a salty European Tour commentator. "Where's your wheelbarrow?" Radar asked. "I thought you'd be out here carting around a pile of gold."

McIlroy's blockbuster deal with Nike had been announced a couple of nights earlier in a ceremony Liberace would have considered ostentatious: thumping music, blinding lights, tribute videos, and a Tupac-style hologram of McIlroy. The spectacle was made slightly more palatable by Rory's obvious embarrassment. Changing equipment just as he emerged as golf's dominant player was the biggest gamble of his young career. McIlroy took pains to explain that he made the choice with his heart, not his wallet. "I don't play for money—I feel I'm well past that," he said at a press conference during which one scribe addressed McIlroy as "Moneybags." "I play for titles, not money." In a quieter moment, he added, "People may not want to believe this, but money was not my motivation. I wanted to be part of something special. I wanted to be associated with a company that has nurtured so many of the world's greatest sportsmen. I've always been a fan of the company, going back to when I was a kid. I like the image they projected. They've been associated with so many great sportsmen, and even now I can remember a lot of the adverts from ten or fifteen years ago. It always seemed like a good fit to me. Golf needs a younger and more athletic image, and Nike has always had that. I'm young enough. I'm not sure I'm athletic enough . . . but I'll try!"

McIlroy's contracts with Titleist/FootJoy and Jumeirah were supposed to run through the end of 2013, but each company was willing to terminate the deal a year early; Titleist has never liked to pay top dollar because all those golf balls fly off the shelves no matter who is endorsing them, while Jumeirah had already enjoyed more exposure than its execs could have ever imagined when they signed McIlroy five years earlier. His deal with Oakley expired at the end of 2012, but the company had already filed a lawsuit claiming it had been denied the contractually mandated "right of refusal" to match Nike's offer; the case would eventually be settled.

McIlroy had taken eight weeks off before Abu Dhabi to dial in his equipment, working with a variety of Nike craftsmen and the company ball guru, Hideyuki "Rock" Ishii. "Sometimes with a new athlete, you can see there is nervousness, there is apprehension," said Ishii. "They are worried change will hurt them. Not Rory. He had a powerful confidence. Tiger is very cautious and conservative with new products. Test, test, test. Talk, test, talk more, test more. Rory is a different personality. He is more like, *Let's try it and see what happens.*"

McIlroy used his old Mitsubishi Diamana prototype 70x shaft for his driver in Abu Dhabi, but after missing the cut, he sighed: "I just need to find a driver I'm comfortable with." Watching McIlroy hit a mountain of balls on the driving range, fellow pro Greg Chalmers sounded the alarm, saying, "When you change everything, you lose your baseline for what's wrong if something is wrong. Is it the shaft? The ball? The head? How do you know what's wrong? Like, if I change my driver right now, I know it's not the ball because it's the same ball. I can put my finger on what's wrong. But if you change everything—and even if it tests great—it's different in competition. You're excited, so the shaft flicks differently. There are a lot of parameters going into how the ball flies, and when you lose that baseline with at least one thing being constant, how do you know what's wrong when it's wrong?"

Woods, who played the first two rounds in Abu Dhabi alongside McIlroy, seemed to enjoy pointing out that he had never changed his entire bag of clubs at the same time. It was startling to see Tiger reduced to a supporting role: of the twenty questions he fielded in his pretournament press conference, fourteen were about McIlroy. "It's great—he's doing all the media," Tiger said. "I love it. He can have it all. I can do my own thing with a lot fewer distractions."

One of the unspoken motivations for signing McIlroy was that it gave Nike someone appealing to cast alongside Woods; since his sex scandal three years earlier, Tiger had been radioactive in the marketplace. Now, McIlroy's arrival allowed for Woods's graceful transition into the elder statesman role. It was no accident that McIlroy's first TV commercial for Nike featured him and Woods playing a version of H-O-R-S-E on the driving range. Cindy Davis, president of Nike Golf, called McIlroy's signing "one of the most important moments in the history of the company." No pressure, kid.

How McIlroy was keeping his feet on the ground became evident one night in the hotel bar in Abu Dhabi, when, nearing midnight, he held court with his small, fiercely loyal tribe, including his parents and Ridge. Rory was wearing jeans, an untucked oxford shirt, and a sweet pair of vintage white-black-red Nike trainers. He recounted in excruciating detail a match he had played against his dad a few weeks earlier. Gerry remained a serious player and back then carried a 3 handicap; for their medal-match play tussles, Rory would give his old man eight or ten shots, depending on how generous he was feeling. In their holiday game at the Bear's Club, Gerry was three strokes ahead going into the eighteenth hole, a watery par-5. He proceeded to take an 11, and as Rory recounted every ghastly stroke, he was laughing so hard tears streaked his cheeks.

Gerry is a man of immense pride. He barked a shorthand reference at his son, alluding to a long-ago blowup that had cost Rory dearly in one of their matches. Rory instantly turned into a petulant teen: "Shut up, Dad!" With a twinkle, Gerry looked around the small gathering that was hanging on his every word. "I've still got him in me pocket," he said.

Before he left Abu Dhabi, McIlroy offered a verdict on all the hullabaloo. With a tight smile, he said, "I just need to keep winning tournaments and everything will be fine."

Alas, it's not that easy. McIlroy's poor form continued, including a loss to Shane Lowry in the first round of the WGC Match Play Championship. The stress, the pressure, the scrutiny, the wild drives, and McIlroy's corresponding crappy attitude conspired to create quite a headache at the 2013 Honda Classic. He started the second round on the tenth tee and went par, double bogey, par, bogey, par, par, triple bogey, bogey . . . 7-over for eight holes. Then he pumped his second shot into a pond on PGA National's eighteenth hole. McIlroy was overwhelmed by one thought: *I don't want to be here.* He shook hands with his playing partners, walked to the parking lot, and then zoomed away.

The tournament's defending champion and the number one player in the world had flat-out quit. Much eye-rolling ensued when Horizon Sports quickly put out a statement in which the hasty withdrawal was blamed on pain from a shifting wisdom tooth. Doug Ferguson of the Associated Press caustically reported that McIlroy had been munching on a sandwich in the eighteenth fairway moments before his WD.

McIlroy took a couple of days to cool down and then called a reporter with whom he had forged a close relationship, Michael Bamberger of *Sports Illustrated*. "It was a reactive decision," McIlroy said. "What I should have done is take my drop, chip it on, try to make a five and play my hardest on the back nine, even if I shot 85. What I did was not good for the tournament, not good for the kids and the fans who were out there watching me—it was not the right thing to do."

It was an admirable bit of ownership from a twenty-three-year-old, and the withering self-critique did not end there. McIlroy would forever measure himself against his boyhood hero, and in one critical department, he realized he was falling short. "He might be the best athlete ever, in terms of his ability to grind it out," McIlroy said of Woods. "I could have a bit more of that, if I'm honest."

A month later at Augusta, McIlroy was five strokes off the lead after two rounds but suffered another demoralizing blowup with a 79 on Saturday. On the eleventh hole, he had to punch out of the trees after an errant drive. His third shot, with a wedge, came up short and died in the hazard, leading to a triple bogey. McIlroy blamed a switch in the wind for the miscue. "I never recovered from that," he said. The metamorphosis into a gritty grinder would have to wait.

Things would only get messier. The spring of 2013 brought splashy announcements of McIlroy's new megadeals with Bose, Omega watches, and Santander Bank. His blue-chip endorsement portfolio would propel McIlroy to number twenty-one on *Forbes*'s 2013 list of the one hundred highest-paid athletes in the world, at $29.6 million, placing him between

Maria Sharapova and Peyton Manning. Ridge had fulfilled his pledge to turn his prized client into a global brand that transcended golf.

And then McIlroy fired him.

Word of the split leaked in June 2013, meaning their business relationship lasted only a year and a half. The divorce was entirely about money: Horizon Sports's commissions for 2013 would weigh in at a hefty $6.8 million. McIlroy was disinclined to have that much of his earnings siphoned in perpetuity. He resolved to set up his own shop and keep the money in-house. But McIlroy would still need a wingman to handle the details, and he found one in Sean O'Flaherty, a young, low-level staffer at Horizon. O'Flaherty had the apple-cheeked good looks of a boy-band singer. Ridge had always enjoyed hazing him; on one occasion, I witnessed Ridge grab O'Flaherty by the scruff of his neck and say, "Have you ever seen a more punchable face?" Little wonder that O'Flaherty chose McIlroy over Ridge, creating a farcical scene at the Irish Open. As *The New York Times* reported, "McIlroy was shadowed at his news conferences and on the course by the Horizon co-founders, Conor Ridge and Colin Morrissey, but was tended to by a former Horizon employee, Sean O'Flaherty, in his nebulous new role as McIlroy's personal assistant. It was like watching warring spouses hunker down in an unhappy house so they cannot be charged with abandonment."

Horizon would eventually give up custody of the boy wonder. McIlroy took his grievances to court, filing suit against Horizon in October 2013 for the "unconscionable" contract he claimed to have been coerced into signing. All this created ever more strife for McIlroy, who later in the year lamented that he'd "seen enough lawyers to last a lifetime." With all this melodrama swirling, it's little wonder that McIlroy was a nonfactor in the summertime major championships—at the Open at Muirfield, he admitted to feeling "brain dead" and said more generally of his struggles, "It's a very alien feeling. It's something I've never had to deal with before." He ceded the top spot in the World Ranking to

Tiger, who had climbed the mountain yet again. McIlroy went winless on the PGA and European Tours. It was a lost year.

Well, not entirely: on New Year's Eve, while watching fireworks in the harbor in Sydney, Australia, McIlroy asked Wozniacki for her hand in marriage. The next morning, he tweeted a picture of a well-manicured finger adorned with a gigantic diamond ring, along with the caption: "Happy New Year everyone! I have a feeling it's going to be a great year!! My first victory of 2014 #shesaidyes!!"

11.

Rory McIlroy's on-course malaise continued into 2014. He opened with a 63 in Dubai but faded to a tie for ninth with a closing 74. "Just one of those days," he said with a sigh. "Anything that could go wrong did." At the Honda Classic he led by two strokes heading into the final round but, on the sixteenth hole, duffed a fairway bunker shot into the pond, leading to a double bogey. Then McIlroy flew the green at seventeen and made bogey to fall out of the lead. At the par-5 eighteenth hole he ripped his best shot of the day, a 5-wood from 236 yards to 12 feet, setting up an eagle putt for the win. He missed it and was then dispatched by Russell Henley on the first playoff hole. At the Masters, a solid opening round 71 left McIlroy in twelfth place... until he blew up with a 77 during which he hit it into a bush on four, the trees on ten, and a patch of azaleas on thirteen. "I've seen a lot of this golf course in the last few years," McIlroy said; it marked the fourth straight Masters he had posted a 77 or worse. McIlroy had the ignominious first tee time on Saturday, paired with noncompeting marker Jeff Knox, an Augusta National member with a cult following from his previous Masters cameos. Knox beat McIlroy by a shot, 70–71. *Fer fook's sake!*

The struggles between the ropes—McIlroy's World Ranking dipped to eleventh in April—weren't helped by the distractions of planning a glitzy wedding to Caroline Wozniacki. The ceremony was to be held at a small chapel in New York City, followed by a reception at the Top of the Rock high above Manhattan. Among the boldfaced names expected to attend were former President Bill Clinton and tennis superstar Serena Williams, who was busy planning the bachelorette party. The invitations were mailed on May 17, a couple of days after Rory and Caroline were photographed holding hands as they strolled through London. By May 18, they had settled in Wozniacki's flat in Monte Carlo. They dined at Nobu that evening, with a view of the sea. McIlroy tweeted a picture of the sunset and tagged @CaroWozniacki. The next day, he headed to London for the BMW PGA Championship at Wentworth Club.

From London, McIlroy called Wozniacki and ended their relationship in a conversation so abrupt Caroline later said she thought it was a joke.

McIlroy's new manager, Sean O'Flaherty, swiftly issued a press release in the voice of his boss: "There is no right way to end a relationship that has been important to two people. The problem is mine. The wedding invitations issued at the weekend made me realise that I wasn't ready for all that marriage entails. I wish Caroline all the happiness she deserves and thank her for the great times we've had. I will not be saying anything more about our relationship in any setting."

The *Belfast Telegraph* panned the statement as the kind of "impersonal, civil-servicey thing a football club says after sacking its manager." An hour after the statement dropped, McIlroy ventured into the press tent at Wentworth and opened a vein for the assembled reporters. "Look, I think I'm no different than anyone else," he said. "Everyone has been through breakups, and it's obviously very, very difficult. But look, I'm here to try and concentrate on this week and answer questions about golf, and that's what I'm going to do." Asked if he ever considered withdrawing from the tournament, McIlroy said, without irony, "I made a commitment to be here. You know, once I gave my word that I would, I wasn't going to go back on it."

This marked the beginning of McIlroy becoming golf's most human superstar. With his rawness and emotional availability, McIlroy let fans into his world in an unprecedented way for one of the game's leading men. McIlroy's boyhood hero, Nick Faldo, reminisces about meeting then twelve-year-old Rory at a junior clinic he hosted: "At that time, my daughter Emma had just been born, and some of the kids had come over to see her and hold her. Fast-forward seven years, and I see Rory for the first time again at a tournament. The first thing he says to me is, 'How's Emma?' I found that extraordinary for someone who was clearly going to be a champion. He's able to do what so many of us couldn't or didn't during our playing days: take the blinkers off and be a whole person."

However, McIlroy did tell one whopper in his Wentworth press conference, saying of the breakup, "It was mutual and amicable, and we both thought it was the best for both of us." That was certainly news to Wozniacki, who had been blindsided.

What went wrong? McIlroy had initially enjoyed the jet-set life with Wozniacki and all the attendant attention, but he became fatigued with the hoopla that surrounded his love life. In an interview with Paul Kimmage of the *Irish Independent*, McIlroy was asked how a global superstar can find true love. "I thought at the time that being with someone that was in a similar position to you was the obvious answer," he said. "But it isn't, because you can never get away from it. You can never detach yourself and try to come back to the real world." In another interview with Kimmage, he offered further perspective, looking back on the 2013 Open Championship when, outwardly, he had seemed blissfully in love. "It was the most homesick I have ever felt, which didn't make sense, because I'd spent the whole week before with my friends and family at home. I don't know, I was just a bit . . . lost I suppose. My game wasn't great, my personal life was very up and down . . . I remember speaking to a sports psychologist the next week, saying: 'I miss home. I miss having a home. I miss my friends, my family. I miss having something that . . . centres you.' That's the word, something that centres you, something that you can go back to and know that everything will be OK. Because I felt at that point I was never able to do that. I'd go from a golf tournament, to a tennis tournament, to an 'event' or sponsorship appearance, and back to a golf tournament. And it was just this . . . cycle. There was nothing familiar from my childhood, or something I could go back to."

As long as Wozniacki was an itinerant tennis star, it would be impossible for McIlroy to feel centered. Golf is an inherently selfish sport, and plenty of players have sacrificed their families at the altar of greatness. After a tabloid divorce from his childhood sweetheart, Colin Montgomerie (McIlroy's first Ryder Cup captain) wrote in his autobiography *The Real Monty*, "What was happening was, little by little, golf was taking over. I was bringing my golf home, and even when I was there, I wasn't giving as much attention to Eimear and the children as I should have done. I was constantly thinking of something else. I wasn't a proper husband or a proper father. It almost broke my life."

Faldo had his own share of high-profile bust-ups in his love life, leading David Leadbetter, the coach who helped Faldo blow up and remake his swing, to muse, "I can see parallels between what he has done with his golf game and what he has done with his personal life." Faldo took his wife, Gill, to the 1994 Ryder Cup even as he was romancing a member of the University of Arizona women's golf team; UA coach Rick LaRose, surveying prospects for the season, said, "We had one player drop out, one transfer, and one run off with Nick Faldo."

After a year and a half of middling play, McIlroy came to the ruthless determination that golf had to come first. It became hard to argue the point when, five days after the Wozniacki breakup became public, McIlroy made up seven strokes on leader Thomas Bjørn in the final round and surged to victory at the BMW PGA Championship, his first win on European soil. After birdieing the final two holes, McIlroy was muted in celebration. He looked almost sheepish. "I can't explain it," he said. "It's obviously been a week of very mixed emotions, but I'm sitting here looking at this trophy going, *How the hell did it happen this week?*" Actually, he answered his own question: "I guess when I got inside the ropes this week, it was a little bit of a release. I was on my own and doing what I do best, which is playing golf, and that sort of gave me four or five hours of serenity or sanctuary or whatever you want to call it." He had lost a fiancée but found himself.

Before leaving Wentworth, McIlroy offered what sounded like a warning to the competition. Tiger Woods had reclaimed the number one spot in the World Ranking in 2013 but missed most of the first half of the '14 season recovering from a microdiscectomy on his back. With McIlroy distracted, there had been a vacuum at the top of the sport. "I think the game is waiting for one guy to kick on," McIlroy said. "I stand by that comment that I'd like to be that guy. I'd like to think that this is a springboard to doing something like that. You know, there are still three majors to play this year, a lot of golf left, a lot of big tournaments to try to win. So even though we're nearly halfway through the season, I feel like mine's just beginning."

•

THE ROYAL LIVERPOOL GOLF Club, colloquially known as Hoylake, is not the most artful course in the Open rota, but the Hall of Fame champions it has produced are testament to the quality of the test: J. H. Taylor (1913), Walter Hagen ('24), Bobby Jones (the Grand Slam year of '30), Peter Thomson ('56), Roberto de Vicenzo ('67). After Arnold Palmer reinvented the Open in the 1960s, Hoylake's infrastructure was deemed insufficient, and it dropped out of the rota until 2006, when Woods produced one of his most masterful performances. The victory was his first since his father, Earl, had died. For all the artful long irons Tiger struck that week, the indelible images from his win are his bittersweet sobs after the final putt dropped. McIlroy, a student of golf history and a Woods completist, felt a special pull toward Hoylake.

In the two months since his reinvention at Wentworth, McIlroy had been, he said, "burying my head in golf." Well, not just golf: he found time to take six friends to Ibiza for a five-day bacchanal, using a rented yacht as their homebase.

McIlroy released even more tension with a surprise announcement at the Irish Open just ahead of Hoylake: he would play for Team Ireland in the 2016 Olympics. This ended years of hand-wringing and uncertainty for McIlroy and the people of both Great Britain and Ireland. Applause erupted in the press tent and throughout the republic when McIlroy made his declaration. Trying to tiptoe through hundreds of years of tortured history, he couched the freighted decision as merely an extension of his amateur days, when McIlroy played for the Golfing Union of Ireland under the Four Provinces flag that makes no distinction between north and south. "I was always very proud to put on the Irish uniform and play as an amateur and as a boy, and I would be very proud to do it again," he said. "Just weighing up everything, and thinking back about the times that I played for Ireland and won the European Team championship with Ireland, won a lot of great amateur titles representing Ireland, I just thought, *Why change that?* Basically, it's just a continuation of what I've always done."

McIlroy rolled into Hoylake having switched up his preparation: he'd played the Scottish Open the week before after having skipped it in previous years. McIlroy was paired with Phil Mickelson at the 2013 Open Championship; Lefty had won the Scottish the week before and would go on to take the Open at Muirfield. McIlroy noted how razor-sharp Phil's game was with an extra week of links golf as preparation, so he decided to replicate the formula. It clearly worked: during the first round at Hoylake, McIlroy shot a bogeyless 66 to seize the lead. It felt like Congressional and Kiawah all over again. But the real intrigue would come the next day. McIlroy had been vexed by inexplicably bad second rounds throughout 2014. The British press had begun referring to them as Freaky Fridays, and Rory admitted it had gotten in his head. At the U.S. Open, he quoted his own stats: 1st in Thursday scoring average, 181st on Friday. Even Jack Nicklaus had taken note. "It's like so strange," McIlroy said from Liverpool. "I don't know if it's because I've got off to such good starts in tournaments where I may be thinking too much about my score, and I'm up near the leaderboard, and I might be trying to push too much and keep it going. I spent two hours with Jack Nicklaus last week in his office in Palm Beach and had a great sort of conversation about everything—business, golf, brand, the whole lot. And he said to me, 'How the hell can you shoot 63 and then 78?' [McIlroy had done exactly that earlier in the year at Nicklaus's Memorial Tournament.] I said, 'I wasn't meaning to, Jack.' He said to me he was never afraid to change things up in the middle of a round if it wasn't going well, if he felt like he wasn't swinging well. He'd make a swing change right then and there. The mental strength to be able to do that and trust what you're doing." Incidentally, how does one get an audience with the great man? Said McIlroy, "Yeah, I mean, I don't ring him up, I ring his secretary up and say, 'I'd like to schedule a meeting, please.'"

McIlroy buried the storyline on British Open Friday, playing the first five holes even par and then rolling in a bending birdie putt on the sixth hole to reach 7-under. The putt was so pure he felt himself dropping into the Zone, the rare, fabled state of being every athlete chases, during which time slows down and the game becomes easy. "I don't know if I can describe it," McIlroy said. "It's just I feel like I have an inner peace."

McIlroy knew this was the moment to take control of the tournament. "Once I got to 7 [under par], I felt like, *Okay, this time I feel good*," he said. "I can get to 8. I can get to 9, 10, 11, 12." And so he did. Another 66 staked him to a commanding four-stroke lead.

But McIlroy had burned through the advantage by the time he played the first twelve holes of the third round, as a red-hot Rickie Fowler grabbed a share of the lead. On the par-3 thirteenth hole, McIlroy flared his tee shot into an awkward spot right of the green and did well to chop out within twelve feet of the hole. This was his first do-or-die moment of the championship. All week long, McIlroy had been repeating two words to himself like a Zen koan: "process" and "spot." The vexing gales and unpredictable bounces of links golf meant sometimes good shots wound up in bad places; McIlroy resolved to focus on the *process* of picking good targets, making committed swings, and leaving the result in the lap of the gods. On the greens, rather than focus on the hole and thus the outcome of each putt, he picked a *spot* a couple of inches in front of his ball and worried only about rolling his ball over the target; he could live with whatever happened after that. Reflecting on the events of the thirteenth green, McIlroy said, "It was a big putt to save par. I felt quite nervous. I tried to take the end result out of my mind. I focused on a spot two or three inches in front of the ball. I said, *Right, all you need to do is roll it over your spot. That's all I kept telling myself. Roll it over your spot. Roll it over your spot.*" He buried the putt and then birdied fourteen to snatch back the lead.

The sixteenth and eighteenth holes at Royal Liverpool are exploitable par-5s. McIlroy had been looking forward to them all day, but he recommitted to his process on the closing holes, merely focusing on the shot at hand. On sixteen, he pounded a drive and then, from 252 yards out, played a gorgeous 4-iron to the heart of the green. Eagle. At eighteen, another perfect drive was followed by a laser-like 5-iron from 239 yards. Another eagle! In an hour and a half, McIlroy went from almost losing the lead to a six-stroke cushion. It was a bravura performance of smash-mouth golf, to say nothing of ruthless competitiveness. (For the week, he would lead the field in driving distance at 328 yards a pop.) Asked if he was trying to send a message to the competition with a walk-off eagle, McIlroy said, "Yeah, definitely. I wanted to finish it off that way."

The first hole at Hoylake is a tight, twisty, heavily bunkered par-4. Many players laid up off the tee, but to begin his final round, McIlroy pulled driver and unleashed a 310-yard piss missile into the wind. That was another statement. After a good approach shot, McIlroy hooped a twenty-five-foot birdie putt to stretch the lead to seven strokes. Fowler and Sergio García tried to make it interesting with their spirited play, but McIlroy always had an answer. As soon as he tapped in for his 71, he motioned for his mum to come give him a hug; this was the first major championship victory Rosie had witnessed in person. She was dabbing at her eyes even before the embrace. At the trophy ceremony, McIlroy made all of England swoon when he said, "Mom, this one's for you."

At twenty-five, McIlroy was now three-quarters of the way to a career Grand Slam, and the would-be competition had begun to run out of superlatives. "I think his A-game right now is almost unbeatable, which is pretty scary how good he is," said Shane Lowry.

Two months earlier, McIlroy was betrothed and playing some of the worst golf of his career. Now unencumbered, he had taken the tournament that he called "the one we all want." McIlroy added, "I've really found my passion again for golf. Not that it ever dwindled, but it's what I think about when I get up in the morning. It's what I think about when I go to bed. I just want to be the best golfer that I can be. And I know if I can do that, then trophies like this are within my capability."

The victory was worth $1.2 million, but that was not the entirety of the family haul. Ten years earlier, Gerry had famously placed a wager that his son would win an Open by the time he was twenty-five. He put down £200 at 500–1 odds. Rory's victory earned his old man a cool $171,000. Two of Gerry's buddies made similar bets and cashed a combined $137K. Said Jessica Bridge, a spokesperson for the betting firm Ladbrokes, "Rory's father and his friends are having champagne on us tonight." As luck would have it, they could borrow a nice little Claret Jug out of which to drink it.

McIlroy took a week off after the Open and then turned up at the World Golf Championship at Firestone Country Club in Akron, Ohio. Rounds of 69-64-66 left him in solo second, three strokes behind García. With his new fervor in the gym, McIlroy had put on seven pounds of muscle in the preceding eight weeks and he was driving the ball ungodly distances in the muggy air; for the week, he would lead the field at 333 yards a pop. On Sunday, he overwhelmed Firestone with a birdie-birdie-birdie start to snag the lead, and then he birdied the fifth hole to go up by two. García never recovered as McIlroy cruised to another win. Poor Sergio. He was serially abused by Tiger Woods and had now become McIlroy's punching bag. "We know how good he can be," García said as he sighed in defeat. "But at the end of the day, the only thing I can do is keep trying."

The scariest part? Winning was becoming routine for McIlroy. "It's the most comfortable I've ever felt trying to close out a golf tournament out there today," he said. "I felt normal. I felt like it was the first round or the second round. It didn't feel like a fourth round. When I say mentally it's the best I've ever been, I didn't get ahead of myself, I didn't start to think about my score, I didn't think about where I was in the tournament. I just kept playing my shot after shot after shot."

From Akron, McIlroy rolled into the PGA Championship at Valhalla Golf Club, outside of Louisville, Kentucky. He was the prohibitive favorite at +500, among the shortest betting odds that pro golf had seen since peak Tiger. McIlroy was trying not to buy into the hype. "If you read everything that's being written, I'd turn up at the first tee on Thursday thinking I'd already won the tournament," he said. But when McIlroy shot 66 in the first round, one off the lead, there was a sense of inevitability. When he shot 67 in the second round to *take* the lead, resignation reigned among his peers. Then on Saturday, he roared home with three birdies in the final four holes to maintain his spot atop the leaderboard, a closing kick highlighted by a 9-iron to within inches of the hole on the 508-yard, par-4 sixteenth. "Christ, I can't reach with a driver and 3-wood," snorted Colin Montgomerie. "He's playing a completely different course, not just from me but a lot of others, too." It was the sixth time in the last seven major championship rounds that McIlroy held the lead.

A funny thing happened on the way to another Sunday coronation: McIlroy sputtered badly on Valhalla's front nine, bogeying the second and sixth holes. "I started the round very tentatively," he said. "I just didn't really have it. Sort of just trying to get through the first few holes, making pars while everyone else was attacking, so that wasn't good."

The second-to-last pairing was straight box office: Phil Mickelson, only one year removed from the career high point of winning the Open Championship, and Rickie Fowler, the perennial fan favorite who had finished top five in the previous three major championships while desperately trying to win his first big one. Each made four birdies on the front nine to zoom past McIlroy. Henrik Stenson played the front nine in 30 to also push past McIlroy, who at the turn found himself three strokes off Fowler's lead. Even worse, Phil and Rickie were yukking it up as if this were a backslapping member-guest, not one of the most important tournaments in golf. "I saw them fist-pump [at each other] coming off one of the greens and remember thinking: 'What the fuck are they doing?'" says McIlroy. "'This is a major championship! You're trying to beat each other!' And it did, it annoyed me. I thought: 'I'm going to beat these two.' And that's sort of what turned it for me."

McIlroy pounded a drive on Valhalla's par-5 tenth hole and then, from 284 yards out, flat-out mishit his 3-wood. On the telecast, Nick Faldo correctly diagnosed that McIlroy "necked it." The ball started fifteen yards left and ten yards lower than expected, knuckleballing through the stale air like a Phil Niekro pitch. McIlroy's wayward ball landed miles short of the green but bounced, skipped, trundled, and trickled to within eight feet of the hole. Then he buried the eagle putt to pull within one of the lead. "You need a little bit of luck in major championships to win, and that was my lucky break," McIlroy said.

A cold-blooded wedge to six feet on the thirteenth hole led to a birdie that tied him for the lead. Fowler blinked first with a bogey at the par-3 fourteenth after an errant tee shot. Then Mickelson bogeyed sixteen after missing the fairway and the green and then blasting his chip way by the hole. McIlroy had brawled his way back into the solo lead. He pushed the margin to two strokes with a spectacular fairway bunker shot on seventeen, radiating a seething intensity when the birdie putt dropped. McIlroy would later be asked how a formerly carefree competitor had acquired such an intimidating game face. "When I realised it was OK to win; when I realised that people liked winners," he said. "I used to feel guilty [about winning]. I felt it was selfish and almost a bad trait to have . . . Early in my career, I was very conscious of trying to be the nice guy. But I realised there are certain times to be that person, and also times to be competitive, and not exchange pleasantries [during] the final round of a major . . . It's OK to make someone feel bad if you've beaten them on the last green. It's OK to be a winner, it doesn't make you a dick."

The action culminated on Valhalla's watery par-5 eighteenth, the easiest hole on the course. (Mickelson eagled it on Friday.) Thunderstorms had delayed the start of the final round, and it was getting dark by the time McIlroy arrived on the tee. He had to idle while Fowler and Mickelson struck their drives. As they walked off the tee box, McIlroy suggested they play the final hole as a foursome to beat the darkness. After a brief discussion, Phil and Rickie decided to play on as a twosome but allow McIlroy (and playing partner Bernd Wiesberger) to hit up. In an act of obliviousness or gamesmanship, Mickelson then ambled toward the fairway directly in line with the tee box, forcing McIlroy to wait. He swished his driver back and forth with visible irritation. McIlroy could have selected any club but driver to play short of the bunker on the left side of the fairway and water down the right; Mickelson, two strokes back and needing an eagle to have a chance, hit a 3-wood off the tee despite his penchant for recklessness. But McIlroy unsheathed the big stick. "For a long time, I thought that was the worst course management I've ever seen in professional golf," says Pádraig Harrington. "He could have thrown away the whole tournament. If he hits iron off the tee, he can still reach the green with an iron! But over time I've come to understand Rory's and [caddie J. P. Fitzgerald's] thinking. The driver is Rory's superpower. If J.P.

hands him anything else, it's damaging. It's saying, *I don't think you're good enough to hit driver here.* Whereas by handing him the driver, he makes a pressure-packed shot feel normal. This is where data scientists don't understand that players have to play to their personality. J.P. knew that if he gave Rory anything but driver, it was breaking that superpower."

McIlroy sliced his drive toward the water and started leaning immediately, willing it to terra firma. He couldn't see his ball land in the gloaming, but it stopped one step above the red line of hazard, atop a mound that sloped straight toward the water; the heavy rain the night before had softened the ground just enough to keep the ball from bouncing hard right into the abyss. A TV cameraman conveyed the news to Fitzgerald, who, with his life flashing before his eyes, gave his boss a wary thumbs-up.

As McIlroy surveyed his second shot, thunder rumbled in the distance. A moment later, a bolt of lightning lit up the sky. "It's gotten kind of gothic," David Feherty said on the broadcast. Mickelson and Fowler knocked their second shots near the green and marched up the hill. They didn't know it, but McIlroy and Wiesberger were about to play their second shots without further delay; on a reachable par-5, players in the fairway would normally wait until the group ahead had completed the hole. It was a hurried and chaotic scene. Facing an awkward hanging lie and his ball in tangly rough, McIlroy tried to lay up short and left of the green but flew his shot too far, into a bunker. With caddie Jim Mackay tending the flag, Mickelson nearly holed his long eagle pitch and then tapped in the birdie putt, slicing McIlroy's lead to one stroke. Now Rory faced the dreaded forty-yard bunker shot, with a steep ridge bisecting the green. Would he dare fly the ball all the way to the hole? If it went long, he'd be looking at a likely bogey and a playoff. McIlroy played a cautious shot, his ball dying below the swale, fifty feet from the hole. "He's going to have to two-putt from there to win, in the pitch-dark," Jim Nantz intoned. It was McIlroy's prerogative to decide if he wanted to play on or return the next day, when there would be actual daylight. On the telecast, Faldo implored McIlroy to walk off the course and come back in the morning. But McIlroy was pumped full of adrenaline by the huge crowds and had a feel for the speed of the greens. The next day, the putting surface would be different and the atmosphere stale. As a showman, he was not immune to the drama of the moment. He stepped up and knocked his putt stone dead. Ballgame.

Noting that McIlroy did not have his best stuff on the weekend, Fitzgerald said of the victory, "It was all heart."

McIlroy joined Jack Nicklaus and Tiger Woods as the only players to win four major championships before their twenty-sixth birthdays. Nicklaus, who designed Valhalla, predicted McIlroy might win fifteen or twenty majors. The career haul of four already tied Rory with an alltime badass, Ray Floyd, and a megatalent in Ernie Els. Following the third round, I had asked McIlroy if, given the big final-round cushions in his previous major championship wins, he was spoiling for a Sunday dogfight. He demurred, but in the champion's press conference, he said, "To answer Alan's question from yesterday, when he said, 'Would today be the most satisfying if I was able to gut it out and win ugly?' Yeah, it is. It is the most satisfying. To win it in this fashion and this style, it means a lot. I know [now] that I can come from behind. I know that I can mix it up with the best players in the world down the stretch in a major and come out on top." Transcendent talent and now an ornery toughness? That's an all-time combination.

•

IN BETWEEN HIS TRIUMPHS at the Open and PGA Championships, McIlroy had been photographed on a lunch date in Belfast with an aspiring model named Sasha Gale. Apparently, this came as news to an aspiring model named Nadia Forde, whom he had also been romancing. The tabloids in Ireland and Britain had a jolly time chronicling the love triangle, and McIlroy had to get used to press conference questions about his love life. He resolved to keep doing his thing, despite the 24/7 scrutiny. "I mean, I don't see any other way to live your life than just to be yourself," McIlroy said. "That's not really advice about living in the public eye or in the spotlight. That's just advice about living your life in general. Be yourself and do the things that make you happy and that's really it . . . Look, I just live my life, and people can say or write whatever they want. I'm very single and very happy at the minute, that's all I can say." He was even briefly linked with the future Duchess of Sussex. In the summer of 2014, McIlroy nominated Meghan Markle—then a mere TV actress and not Prince Harry's wife—for the ALS Ice Bucket Challenge. She accepted on the condition that McIlroy do the dousing, which he obliged with a devilish grin. After they enjoyed a cozy dinner in Manhattan together, Markle wrote a gushing blog post about McIlroy (which has since been scrubbed off the internet): "He is a force who has the propensity to actually work hard and play hard—relishing intense practices to substantiate his title, embracing nights of sipping Opus One (his bold and impressive choice of wine) and indulging in group dinners at Cipriani . . . And yet, beyond his work/play ethic, the most endearing quality of this man is his character—as real and honest as they come, appreciating a simple smile, never shunning a fan photo, enjoying a plate of pasta with veal ragu, and expressing a love for his parents that is rarely seen in men his age. Or at any age, to be honest. He is not just the real deal . . . he is real. And perhaps that is what makes him even more cherished." Little wonder that at the end of the season, *Golf Magazine* would name McIlroy "Playa of the Year."

Even as he was tomcatting around, McIlroy found himself thinking about the fetching PGA of America employee who played a role in his mad dash to the first tee at the Ryder Cup two years earlier. McIlroy began spending time with Erica Stoll in the months after the PGA Championship. "The thing I love about it," he said, "is that we were friends before anything romantic happened. We met when she was renting a condo in

Palm Beach, and I found it refreshing being with someone who was living a normal life rather than, 'Oh! My jet is 30 minutes late!'"

In October 2014, after leading Europe to a third consecutive Ryder Cup victory, McIlroy played in the four-player, thirty-six-hole PGA Grand Slam of Golf exhibition in Bermuda. He rendezvoused there with Stoll for what he has called their first official date. The PGA of America ran the Grand Slam, so Stoll's colleagues were bemused to see her in Bermuda even though she wasn't working the tournament. "It was common knowledge that Rory and Erica were dating," says Ted Bishop, then the president of the PGA of America. "She's a nice person who was very popular with everyone in the office. I had gotten to know Rory through his success at the PGA Championship, and I thought it was a great match."

McIlroy struggled between the ropes at the Grand Slam: beginning on the tenth hole of the second round, he made three bogies and a double bogey in the span of five holes, laboring to a 75 to finish eight strokes behind winner Martin Kaymer. When it was over, McIlroy said, "It's been an enjoyable few days here in Bermuda." It seems unlikely he was referring to the golf.

12.

In the heady aftermath of Rory McIlroy's victory at the 2014 PGA Championship, his father buttonholed TV commentator Shane O'Donoghue and confided, "The big one is in April." That was the Masters, of course, where Rory could become only the sixth player to complete the career Grand Slam and, not for nothing, get three-quarters of the way to the Tiger Slam (winning four consecutive major championships across two seasons, which Woods did in 2000–2001, his greatest achievement). But the road to Augusta took an unusual detour: the Irish High Court. McIlroy had abruptly fired his agent, Conor Ridge of Horizon Sports, in May 2013. Now, a year and a half later, their ugly lawsuits and countersuits had reached endgame.

The brinksmanship spilled into the press as settlement talks broke down in late 2014; the *Daily Mail* reported that Ridge rejected McIlroy's offer of €10 million to make the case go away. A juicy December 2014 court filing accused McIlroy of having "wiped clean" eight cell phones belonging to himself; his father, Gerry; his manager, Sean O'Flaherty; and financial adviser Donal Casey. McIlroy's lawyers said he changed numbers often to avoid unsolicited calls from journalists (insert eye roll here) and that he factory-reset the devices to preserve his privacy.

The legal nastiness seeped into McIlroy's friendships with Shane Lowry and Graeme McDowell, both longtime Horizon clients. Only through the lawsuits did it become widely known that McDowell had been granted an equity stake in Horizon Sports prior to McIlroy joining the firm, which gave the appearance that G-Mac was stealthily making money off his pal. A spokesperson for Horizon was forced to issue a statement saying McDowell "never received any benefits, dividends, profit share or payment of any kind from Horizon [and] did not benefit, nor could have ever benefited, from Rory McIlroy's commercial affairs."

Says Lowry, "It was a shitshow, because Conor has always been good to me and it was almost as if I had to pick a side, so I was in a tough place with Rory. We went from friends to being acquaintances and it was just... awkward. I mean, I'm 'L' and he's 'M' and our lockers were beside each other at every tournament!"

"It was messy," says McIlroy.

"I hate talking about it," says Lowry.

The 2014 Ryder Cup was directly affected by the awkwardness. McIlroy and McDowell had been a formidable duo for Team Europe in 2010 and '12, playing six matches as partners (and going 3-3). Given McDowell's ownership stake in Horizon, McIlroy was essentially suing—and being sued by—his onetime mentor and best friend on Tour. Paul McGinley served as Europe's Ryder Cup captain in 2014 and felt the antipathy firsthand. "G-Mac was very loyal to the management company, and Rory saw him as part of the enemy," says McGinley. "He's kind of tribal, Rory is. He has a little Tiger in him in that regard. [McIlroy and McDowell] weren't talking to each other. I didn't try to bring them back together, I kept them separate. And I made sure that I didn't side with one over the other. It wasn't for me to be the peacemaker or play God, because I didn't know the full story of it, and I didn't want to know it. But it was clear we couldn't play Rory and G-Mac together. We couldn't even put them together for a practice round. However, we weren't going to make a big deal about it in the media—I wasn't going to ignite things by saying, *Yeah, we've got a big issue here.* I told them, 'Let me handle the media.'"

The rift in the team room never became a story, and Europe led 10–6 heading into singles. There was zero doubt that U.S. captain Tom Watson would front-load his lineup to try to win early matches and generate momentum. It seemed like a no-brainer for the Europeans to lead off with McIlroy, the world number one, but McGinley says, "I believe a street fighter is the best choice to go out first, and G-Mac was the best street fighter we had on the team. I wanted Rory to go out number three." McGinley felt compelled to get McIlroy's blessing before locking in his lineup. "I told him the Americans would send out first either their best player or the guy who had been playing the best that week," says McGinley. "Rory had played seventy-two holes in two days, Graeme had played only thirty-six—he was fresher and ready to go. Let him tangle with the top American, and Rory could come in after and get his point. I kept emphasizing to Rory that every point is equally valuable. And he was great about it. You see, Rory is logical. You explain something logical to Rory and he's good."

When the blind draw came out, McIlroy was paired against Rickie Fowler, who had finished in the top five in all four of 2014's major championships. "I had a chat with Rory about the importance of this game," says McGinley, "not just in terms of winning his points for the team, but the fact that Rickie was coming strong and was the heir apparent—the American version of McIlroy. I told him that he was ready to 'knock you off your perch,' and the American media was very eager to write that story. I told Rory he simply couldn't let that happen, not just for the Ryder Cup but for his career going forward. He went out the next day with the pointy elbows and that poised look of a terminator, and he started birdie-eagle-birdie. He went on to beat Rickie 5 and 4. And afterward on TV, Rory said, 'I was up for this match as much as any round of golf I've ever played.' And he had won two majors that year! In some ways, Rory is very complicated, and in some ways he's very simple."

Four months after the Ryder Cup, McIlroy won the 2015 Dubai Desert Classic with a record score of 22-under to reinforce his status as a massive favorite for the Masters. But then it became clear how much the Horizon lawsuits would compromise his preparation for Augusta National: after Dubai, McIlroy withdrew from the upcoming BMW Masters in Shanghai and WGC-HSBC Champions to prepare for up to two weeks of testimony at the Irish High Court, what he called "tedious and nasty business."

McIlroy's refusal to settle the case was further evidence of his deep stubborn streak. In their court filings, McIlroy's lawyers tried to paint their client as naive and almost childlike when he signed his contract with Horizon . . . but Rory had already accrued the life experience of five seasons as a pro, including the business breakup with Chubby Chandler. Just because McIlroy suddenly decided he didn't like the terms of his deal with Horizon didn't mean he could simply void the whole thing. He was already sitting on an empire; only a very specific personality would torpedo his Masters prep just to be proven right in court (and maybe save a few million bucks that he didn't really need).

Dozens of reporters turned up at the Irish High Court to report on the spectacle. The Four Courts is one of the most impressive and beautiful buildings in Dublin, on the banks of River Liffey. McIlroy arrived for the first day of the proceedings looking studious in a suit and dark-rimmed spectacles. Each side had an army of lawyers. *The Irish Times* reported the legal costs at £100,000 a day; as they bickered back and forth you could practically hear the cash registers ringing. Amid this spectacle, McIlroy finally heeded Dermot Desmond's advice. Desmond, an Irish billionaire with deep ties to professional golf, was best friends with another of Ireland's richest men, J. P. McManus, a longtime McIlroy booster. That the son of a bartender counted both business legends as friends and confidants was a sign of how far McIlroy had traveled in life. Desmond, with his decades of experience and acumen, had reviewed McIlroy's contract with Horizon and rendered a succinct verdict: *You're fucked. Settle the case and move on with your life.*

And so McIlroy finally did, before the second day of testimony began. The price of freedom was steep: a reported £18 million. Ridge got his money and kept the support of his client Shane Lowry, who tweeted, "Conor Ridge is definitely one of the good guys." Writing the check was weirdly cathartic for McIlroy. Says his uncle Brian, "Rory told me, 'I want it to sting. It will remind [me] never to make that same mistake again.'"

McIlroy squeezed in three tournaments between the disposition of the lawsuits and Augusta. He didn't contend in any of them. He went all in preparing for the Masters, buzzing into town a couple of weeks ahead of the tournament and playing ninety-nine holes in a quest to solve a few more of the Augusta National's riddles. Gerry tagged along to make it a father-son trip, which deepened Rory's love for the place. "Thirty-six holes each day, and I remember the sun was going down on the first evening and we were walking up to the eighteenth green," McIlroy says. "My dad and I both were exhausted but probably would have gone for another eighteen if we could have. It's such a special place, especially when it's not Masters week. So serene and peaceful. Sharing a moment and setting like that with my dad is something I'll remember for the rest of my life."

In his last casual game at home before Masters week, McIlroy had a putt for 59 at the Bear's Club. (He left it short.) But McIlroy stopped to tie his shoelaces when the starting gun went off at the Masters, playing the first twenty-seven holes in +3. He salvaged his second round with a strong back nine to reach −2 for the tournament, but one problem: that left him twelve shots off Jordan Spieth's record pace. Facing zero pressure on the weekend, McIlroy freewheeled to closing rounds of 68-66 to finish fourth, by far his best Masters performance, but still six shots worse than Spieth. Only ten times in Masters history had the winner bettered McIlroy's four-round total of 276 (−12), a very bitter footnote. I didn't write it, but the headline to my *Sports Illustrated* cover story rankled McIlroy: "Jordan Rules: The Spieth Era Begins Now." "They love an 'era' in the States, because after I won at Congressional *Sports Illustrated* called it 'The Rory Era,'" McIlroy sniffed. "Eras last about six months these days instead of 20 years."

McIlroy reset the narrative in the weeks after the Masters with a victory at the WGC Match Play Championship—in the semifinals, he was 1-down to Jim Furyk with three holes to play but took the match by finishing birdie, birdie, walk-off eagle putt from forty-four feet—and then a rousing victory at Quail Hollow, winning by seven strokes thanks to a third-round 61. McIlroy had clearly been stimulated by finally having an age-appropriate rival in Spieth. During the final round of the 2015 U.S. Open, at Chambers Bay, McIlroy made a twisting seventy-two-foot putt on the thirteenth hole for his sixth birdie of the day. It looked like he was on his way to a Johnny Miller–esque sixty-nothing to steal the Open, but McIlroy limped home with bogies on two of his final four holes and Spieth one-upped him again, conquering Chambers Bay to get halfway to the Grand Slam. McIlroy finished five shots back. For the first time in his life, he had lost the crowd to a younger and equally charismatic player. Jordan had none of Rory's firepower off the tee, but his strengths—putting, wedge play, fighting ferociously for every stroke—threw into sharp relief McIlroy's relative weaknesses. This yin-yang duo was building toward an epic showdown at St. Andrews, but then McIlroy decided to have a kickabout with his pals.

McIlroy has always enjoyed playing a little *fútbol*—his former manor outside of Holywood had a well-manicured pitch. Asked for a scouting report on McIlroy, his onetime minder at International Sports Management, Stuart Cage, says, "He wasn't horrendous. He could control the ball. But he wasn't in the same league as Sergio García or Martin Kaymer." McIlroy had seen firsthand the collateral damage that can come with even a casual game of soccer: circa 2010, Cage pulled his hamstring so violently that the entire back of his upper leg turned black. In December '13, McIlroy sprained his ankle playing soccer and missed one tournament while recovering. Asked whether he would hang up his cleats, he said, "Yeah, sort of . . . probably not a good idea to play anymore." Yet two weeks before the

2015 Open Championship, to be conducted at the Home of Golf, where he held a share of the course record, at the most cherished venue of the game's oldest championship, where he had previously finished tied for third on an artistic canvas that has long confirmed golf genius, McIlroy felt compelled to play soccer with his homies. It went terribly wrong: a few days later, he posted on Instagram a photo of himself leaning on crutches and wearing a walking boot and a dour expression. McIlroy had ruptured the anterior talofibular ligament in his left ankle when his foot caught in the turf. "It's hugely disappointing, especially with him and Jordan and everything that's going on," said Graeme McDowell, speaking for many. He added, "No one would love to stop Jordan in his tracks next week more than Rory. With the fun rivalry going on and everything, he's going to be gutted."

McIlroy was typically defiant, saying he would continue playing soccer because he wanted to lead a normal life. Sure, whatever, pal, pretend you're Wayne Rooney if you must . . . but not two weeks before the f'ing Open! You get only a few cracks at the Old Course in your prime, and McIlroy had cost himself a priceless opportunity. Meanwhile, Spieth chased the Grand Slam all the way to the seventy-second hole, ultimately falling one shot short. The tie for fourth earned Spieth enough points to steal the top spot in the World Ranking from McIlroy.

Rory returned to action a month after St. Andrews, looking rusty en route to finishing seventeenth at the PGA Championship. It was a huge letdown for McIlroy to be a nonfactor in all four of 2015's major championships after his dominance the season before. Meanwhile, Spieth put the finishing touches on one of the greatest seasons in golf history with a run at winning the PGA Championship. He ultimately finished second as another challenger to McIlroy's throne emerged: Jason Day, twenty-seven, took the PGA with a record score and then later that month won back-to-back FedEx Cup playoff events, sending *him* to number one in the World Ranking.

Of course, with McIlroy, the off-course developments are always as interesting as anything happening between the ropes. His devotion to philanthropy went to a different level at the 2015 Irish Open, as his eponymous foundation took over the tournament and McIlroy presided as a genial host. His advocacy attracted enough corporate support to save this proud old tournament from insolvency. It was a great story of a local boy making good, but it was completely overshadowed when McIlroy showed up at Royal County Down with Erica Stoll on his arm, the public unveiling of their romance. During a tumultuous season, she would emerge as a steadying influence. "I don't feel Erica wants to change me in any way," McIlroy said. "I can be myself around her; there's no bullshit, no acting, no show." He would later add, "She has made me realise the person I want to be away from the golf course, which in turn I feel has made me better on it. The only way I can describe it is if golf were to disappear tomorrow, I don't think I'd miss it as much as I would have a few years ago. I felt I needed golf to be complete as a person, as it's been a part of my life since I was born. I don't feel like that anymore." In December they took a trip to Paris and McIlroy proposed. She said yes.

AFTER HIS CAREER-BEST FOURTH-PLACE finish the year before, McIlroy rolled into the 2016 Masters with a little more swagger. Ever since he galloped up the leaderboard in his second-ever round at Augusta National in 2010, there had been the notion that Augusta National was the perfect golf course for McIlroy. That was true off the tee, as his towering draw matched up with many of the most demanding driving holes. But the real test at Augusta National is precision in the iron game. In a very subtle way, McIlroy's swing path was ill-suited for the course's sloping terrain. "I argued forever that it's the worst possible course for him," says Golf Channel analyst Brandel Chamblee. "The reason it became his nemesis is because there are so many hook lies from the fairway—I'm thinking about [hole number] 1, 2, 3, 7, 8, 9, 10, 11, 13, 15, 18. It's very hard to drop the club inside in transition, as Rory always had done, and play great at Augusta National. He's swinging into the slope, and the slope shuts his clubface. He would hit that little pull, and his ball would fly long and left, leaving him exactly the kind of downhill putts that are a killer on that course. The players who have had the most success at the Masters swing across the slope and pick the ball: that's Jack Nicklaus, Tiger Woods, Ben Hogan, Jordan Spieth. The idea that Rory had an advantage at Augusta was a total fallacy."

McIlroy saw some merit in the critiques of his short-iron play. "At Augusta, there is a lot of touch, a lot of finesse," he said. "That is the one thing I am trying to learn and get better at, that style of golf where you manage your way around golf courses. Maybe you just need a little more imagination. I think that's the thing I need if I want to call myself a complete golfer."

Then there was the ongoing psychological torture that followed McIlroy's infamous final-round 80 to blow his four-shot lead in 2011: he posted a 77 or worse in each of the three Masters that followed. Across his first six Masters, McIlroy made an astounding eleven double bogies and three triple bogies. Plenty of curses have swirled among the dogwoods through the ages. There is a subset of Hall of Famers for whom Augusta National was supposed to be the ideal venue, and yet they could never deliver: Lee Trevino, Greg Norman, Ernie Els, Johnny Miller, Tom Weiskopf... the list goes on. "Well, the Masters does funny things to people," says Miller, three times a runner-up there. "Some guys get Augusta fever. I know I did. It's such a sweet tournament, the course is so thrilling, the setting just reeks of golf history—once you get a taste of being in contention it can drive you nuts. It doesn't allow you to play your normal, comfortable game, because you want it too much."

"I wanted it badly," says Norman. "Did I want it too much? Probably."

Adds Els, "I did put quite a lot of pressure on myself there. I always felt I was made for that course. It was to my detriment, unfortunately. It didn't quite work out for me. Sometimes I wish I could've approached it a little differently, but it is what it is."

Unlike the previous year, when he overprepared, McIlroy didn't make his usual pretournament scouting trip to Augusta in 2016, this time trying to unclutter his mind. When tournament week arrived, he aced the sixteenth hole during a Monday practice round, which seemed to portend a change in his luck. A solid opening 70 landed McIlroy in a tie for ninth, and then on Friday, brutal winds buffeted Augusta National; McIlroy's 71 tied for the low round of the day. He was alone in second place at –3, only one stroke behind the leader . . . Spieth—naturally. It was the sixth consecutive Masters round where he had topped the leaderboard. It was happening, the showdown the golf world had been craving.

Alas, McIlroy was not up to the challenge. He bogeyed three of the first ten holes thanks to a hooked drive on number three, a three-putt on seven, and a dead pull off the tenth tee that stirred memories of 2011. At that point, he was five shots back of Spieth and, in the words of *The Guardian*, "falling apart like wet cake." On eleven, McIlroy pulled another drive, his ball stopping hard against a tree trunk. He then played a mystifyingly aggressive shot, running his ball all the way down the hill into the pond guarding the green, leading to a shambolic double bogey. This kind of course management blunder was exactly what Jack Nicklaus was thinking of when he later said, "I only have one criticism of Rory. You have to concentrate 100 percent of the time. For some reason, Rory always has a little bit of a lapse somewhere around the tournament. He'll find a double bogey or triple bogey that sneaks in there. I don't know how he does it or why, but it happens."

McIlroy gathered himself long enough to hit a stellar tee shot on twelve to six feet. But then Spieth rolled in another long birdie putt from the back of the green and everyone knew what would happen next: McIlroy whiffed the putt. The rest of the round was a death march, with McIlroy failing to make a birdie for the first time in eighty-one major championship rounds. Following another 77, he admitted to being thrown off by Spieth's uncanny ability to squeeze the most out of his rounds. "I turned around after fifteen, I said, 'How the hell is he 2 under par today?' But it's his most impressive asset, and as much as it could be annoying to his competitors, it's very, very impressive."

The next day, McIlroy shot an uninspired 71 to tie for tenth. Spieth wound up giving away the tournament with a trainwreck on the twelfth hole, but the outcome didn't exactly hearten McIlroy: Englishman Danny Willett stole the green jacket, his first (and still only) PGA Tour victory. McIlroy and Willett are only a year apart in age and had played alongside each other since their early teens. Rory had always been the vastly superior player, but now the short-hitting Willett had the one thing his antagonist desperately wanted.

McIlroy's funk carried into the U.S. Open at Oakmont, where he missed the cut. That national championship was won by another usurper, Dustin Johnson, who possessed an oily, feline grace and as much firepower off the tee as McIlroy. Johnson's breakthrough helped him win the 2016 money title, the Vardon Trophy for lowest scoring average, and all the player of the year awards, even though McIlroy had nabbed his first FedEx Cup (and won the Irish Open with a kick-in eagle on the seventy-second hole!). When McIlroy arrived at the '15 Masters, he was the best player in the world by a mile and seemed to have a stranglehold on the game's future. A little more than a year later, the competition at the top of the sport had grown far fiercer, and McIlroy looked like he would be forever woebegone at Augusta National, putting the career Grand Slam in doubt.

"Yeah, I'd be lying if I said those guys having success doesn't motivate me," he said of Spieth, Day, Johnson, et al. "Of course it does. I don't want to be left behind. I want to be a part of that conversation. I'm clinging on at the minute, but a few wins will change that."

13.

In the summer of 2016, a strange phenomenon swept the golf world: the best male players were suddenly misplacing their backbones. Related symptoms included myopia and apathy. The cause was a mosquito bite. Or, rather, the hysterical fear of one. Golf was returning to the Olympic Games for the first time in 104 years, and among all the best athletes from around the globe, male golfers were somehow alone in their debilitating fear of the Zika virus. Rory McIlroy was the sixth high-profile golfer to announce he would skip the Rio de Janeiro Games, saying, "I've come to realise that my health and my family's health comes before anything else. Even though the risk of infection from the Zika virus is considered low, it is a risk nonetheless and a risk I am unwilling to take." For a short period of time after an infection, Zika can be transmitted to female sex partners and lead to birth defects; it was recommended that, post-Rio, players who were planning to procreate should wear a condom for a little while. Upon hearing this, Dustin Johnson's exact words were, "Fuck that shit, I'm out."

McIlroy would later admit what everyone already knew: Zika was merely an excuse to skip an event that had always stirred complex feelings within him. When McIlroy made the freighted announcement two years earlier that he would compete for Ireland and not Great Britain, it was suggested that he had a third option: boycott the Olympics altogether. He dismissed that out of hand, saying, "It would have been a very selfish decision. It wouldn't have been good for the game of golf at all. If we, as a golf community, want golf to succeed in the Olympics, we need to have our best players playing. I realized that pretty quickly. Obviously it was an option but it was never going to be an option that I would decide to choose because, ultimately, what we want is to grow the game and make the game better and expose the game more to more people around the world, and not having your best players play at the Olympic Games in its first year back in over a hundred years isn't something that is good for golf."

The backtracking of McIlroy et al. stirred condemnation throughout the sports world. Golf's original global citizen, Gary Player, said, "I would have taken a rowing boat and rowed over to play in the Olympics. And this excuse about Zika is feeble. You have Zika in America in some states right now. You've got more of a chance of being killed by a gun or a motorcar in America than getting Zika. . . . I think it's pathetic and I'm sad to see it."

After Justin Rose won the gold medal in a stirring showdown with another major champion, Henrik Stenson, McIlroy sent him a congratulatory text message. Rose replied by asking if Rory had felt left out of the festivities. McIlory replied, "'Justin, if I had been on the podium [listening] to the Irish national anthem as that flag went up, or the British national anthem as that flag went up, I would have felt uncomfortable either way.' I don't know the words to either anthem; I don't feel a connection to either flag. Not everyone is [driven by] nationalism and patriotism. I grew up in a place where I wasn't allowed to be. And I never wanted it to get political or about where I'm from, but that's what it turned into. And it just got to the point where it wasn't worth the hassle."

A month after the Olympics, McIlroy wrapped himself in the flag of the one jingoistic event at which he feels comfortable: the Ryder Cup, where he wears the blue and yellow of a united Europe. He blew into Hazeltine National Golf Club straight from a playoff win at the 2016 Tour Championship that allowed McIlroy to claim his first FedEx Cup title, one of the few missing items on his CV. The win was worth

$10 million to McIlroy, and a good bit of that flowed to his caddie, J. P. Fitzgerald, who said, "It's like a tsunami hit my bank account."

Europe had won the three preceding Ryder Cups, with McIlroy a key contributor at each. Following the lopsided U.S. loss in 2014, Phil Mickelson, true to his Machiavellian nature, had savaged U.S. captain Tom Watson in the most awkward press conference in Ryder Cup history. Mickelson's criticism had plenty to do with ego—he had been benched by Watson for both of Saturday's sessions—but it was also a calculated move to serve as an agent of change. The U.S. entered its Task Force era in the wake of that debacle, during which top players from the past and present were empowered to reshape every aspect of the American team's efforts. Mickelson competed at Hazeltine as if his reputation depended on a U.S. win, which it kind of did. The boys in Stars and Stripes had the extra emotional punch of playing in the King's memory, as Arnold Palmer died five days before the Ryder Cup began.

The U.S. team had been strengthened by the rise of twentysomethings Spieth, Johnson, Brooks Koepka, Rickie Fowler, and, especially, Patrick Reed. Europe was missing its leader, Ian Poulter, who had been left off the team due to a prolonged slump, making McIlroy the squad's undisputed alpha. But paired with Andy Sullivan—remember him?!—Rory lost on the eighteenth hole to Mickelson and Fowler in the opening session of foursomes. The match featured a tense exchange when Phil tried to get a look at Rory's lie in the rough and was told, in no uncertain terms, to take a hike. Europe got swept 4–0 in the session, and it was all uphill from there. The strain showed in McIlroy's edgy interactions with the lippy American gallery, which at one point sang "Sweet Caroline" in a cold-blooded ode to his breakup with Wozniacki. McIlroy repeatedly, diffidently gesticulated to the crowd while winning his next three matches, keeping the Europeans in the fight. "It's a hostile environment out here," he said, "and I want them to know how much it means to us and sort of silence them and say, *You're welcome.*

It's nice to do that sometimes." In the Saturday afternoon four-balls, McIlroy shepherded rookie Thomas Pieters to a 3 and 1 win over the titanium-denting U.S. duo of Dustin Johnson and Brooks Koepka. "I swear, the first five holes of that match were like a long drive contest," says McIlroy. "We weren't caring where it was going, we were just trying to hit it as hard as we could. I said [to Pieters] if we can keep hitting it hard and straight, those boys will try to keep hitting it harder and harder, and it will start to go left on them. That's sort of what started to happen." Despite McIlroy's macho play, Europe trailed 9.5–6.5 heading into singles. There was little doubt who would lead off for either team.

In the preceding few seasons, Reed had emerged as one of the most polarizing figures in golf. No one doubted his bona fides as a player, as Reed had won three times in the thirteen months leading up to the Ryder Cup on the strength of a wizardly short game. He was one of the few Americans to show any fight at the 2014 Cup, scuffling his way to a 3-0-1 record and inflaming tensions with his signature move, a bratty finger to the lips to shush the partisan crowd in Scotland. Along the way, Reed acquired an over-the-top nickname: "Captain America." But away from the enforced camaraderie of the Ryder Cup team room, Reed was a loner on Tour. He had been dismissed from the University of Georgia golf team after being arrested for underage drinking. Another player might have survived this youthful indiscretion, but Reed had strained relations with his teammates, a handful of whom reached the Tour and were happy to savage him to peers and reporters. "They all hate him—any guys that were on the team with him [at Georgia] hate him and that's the same way at Augusta [State, where Reed finished his undergraduate career]," Tour winner Kevin Kisner, a Georgia alum, told *Golf Digest*. "I don't know that they'd piss on him if he was on fire, to tell you the truth." The public perception of Reed curdled when his estrangement from his parents and sister spilled into public view, thanks to a poisonous social media post by his wife, Justine. All this juju imbued Reed with a me-against-the-word ethos that made him perfect for the Ryder Cup. He went 2-1-1 over the first two days at Hazeltine, carrying Spieth in all four matches. The golf world was atwitter when it was announced that fans on both sides of the Atlantic would get what they were craving: Reed versus McIlroy in the first singles match, both putting their undefeated singles records on the line.

The mood on the first tee had the crackling atmosphere of a prizefight, not a golf exhibition. It was a melee inside the ropes, as every reporter and dignitary on the property wanted to witness the juiciest singles match in ages. Reed looked like he was going to lose the first hole but buried a twenty-footer to salvage a halve, celebrating the made putt with a series of lusty fist pumps. McIlroy drew first blood with a birdie on the third hole. Reed squared the match by driving it to ten feet on the short par-4 fifth hole and canning the eagle putt. The haymakers kept coming. At number six, McIlroy buried a twelve-foot birdie putt. He wheeled around to scream in the direction of the grandstand and then, walking toward Reed, threw a fist pump in his direction. That made it personal. Unbothered, Reed rolled in his birdie putt, bowed theatrically, and then wagged his finger at McIlroy, like Dikembe Mutombo taunting an opponent after swatting away their layup. The atmosphere was reaching a fever pitch.

They traded birdies again on the seventh hole, and this time McIlroy stole his opponent's signature move, putting his finger to his lips and hissing, "Shhhhhhhhhhh." The crowd instead offered a chorus of boos. The Ryder Cup had inspired plenty of histrionics through the years, but never had they been this in-your-face. And the crescendo was still coming.

McIlroy played an indifferent tee shot on the par-3 eighth hole, his ball expiring forty-five feet below the hole. Reed's was a little better, as he left himself twenty-five feet. Surely the pyrotechnics would pause for at least one hole? Eh, not so fast. McIlroy rammed in his putt. As soon as the ball disappeared, his whole body convulsed as seemingly every one of his muscles popped, à la the Incredible Hulk. McIlroy loosed a long, guttural roar, then cupped one hand behind his ear and shouted at the stunned gallery, "I can't hear you!" It instantly became one of the most indelible images in the long history of the Ryder Cup. Reed stepped up and, inexorably, willed his putt into the hole. He turned toward McIlroy and offered a raised index finger and a smirk. *Oh no, you don't!* McIlroy had birdied four straight holes . . . and was 1-down in that stretch. Tiger Woods, sitting greenside in a cart in his role as a U.S. vice captain, just shook his head and laughed at the spectacular absurdity of it all. "Holes 5 through 8 were the best four-hole stretch I've ever experienced on the air in golf," says Dan Hicks, the NBC announcer who has covered the Ryder Cup since 1993. "There have been some great moments, but four-hole stretches—nothing comes close to what we saw from 5 through 8."

Alas, the intensity was unsustainable. McIlroy didn't make a birdie on the back nine, saying, "I ran out of steam." But he grinded hard enough to send the match to the eighteenth hole. One-down, McIlroy flagged his approach shot to give himself a glimmer, but Reed hit it even closer and then brushed in the birdie putt like a practice-round gimme to win the match. He had slain the dragon, and Europe's hope of a comeback effectively ended at that moment. "We mocked each other a little bit and whatever; at the same time it was all in good fun," McIlroy said after his first Ryder Cup loss. "No problems with Patrick Reed at all. He's been immense this week." The fans were strangely subdued once the U.S. had finally clinched the Cup, as if, like McIlroy on the back nine, they had already burned up all their emotion. In a showing of class and sportsmanship, Rory led them in a chant of "U-S-A! U-S-A!"

•

THE RYDER CUP BEATDOWN and birdieless Masters round alongside Spieth did much to damage McIlroy's aura of invincibility. At the 2016 PGA Championship, he rated his season as a B-minus . . . and that was before he took thirty-five putts while failing to make a birdie during his first-round 74. After missing the cut, McIlroy laid all the blame on his putter, and the stats backed him up: at that moment, he ranked 130th on Tour in strokes gained putting, losing .135 strokes to the field per round, his worst numbers since 2011.

Enter Phil Kenyon. McIlroy hired the English putting guru immediately after the PGA. Kenyon had enjoyed tremendous success working with Henrik Stenson, Justin Rose, Martin Kaymer, Louis Oosthuizen, and Lee Westwood, among others. Before turning to teaching, Kenyon played for Liverpool John Moores University, where he also received a master's degree in sports science and psychology. He had been mentored by Harold Swash, Britain's "Putting Doctor," an engineer by trade who invented the Yes! C-Groove putter, the L.A.B. of its day. Kenyon was known for his technical bent and employing all the latest whiz-bang gadgetry, a marked departure from the simple, old-school, feel-based approach of McIlroy's previous putting coach, septuagenarian Dave Stockton.

More change came to McIlroy's game when, in August 2016, Nike announced it was exiting the golf equipment business. McIlroy became the most coveted free agent since LeBron James took his talents to South Beach. He hit an ungodly number of balls across the holidays in 2016, testing out a seemingly endless combination of balls, irons, driver heads, and shafts. McIlroy would ultimately sign a $100 million deal with TaylorMade, even as Nike continued to pay him to wear its apparel. His newly empowered manager, Sean O'Flaherty, received a salary, not a commission, which meant McIlroy saved $15 million on commissions just from the TaylorMade contract—that more or less covered what he had spent to make his previous agent, Conor Ridge, go away. But the bonanza of a new equipment deal came at a steep price: having pushed his body too hard, McIlroy suffered a fractured rib in January 2017 during his season opener on the European Tour. McIlroy's practice time and tournament schedule had to be curtailed, but he did sneak in a casual game in February 2017 with the newly elected president of the United States, Donald Trump, a fellow South Florida resident with deep ties to professional golf. Reflexively apolitical after his complex upbringing in Northern Ireland, McIlroy says he agreed to tee it up with Trump out of respect for the office of the president. He did not anticipate the blowback he would receive for playing golf with such a polarizing politician, and McIlroy displayed some backbone by later saying, "So I will sit here and say that day I had with him, I enjoyed. But that doesn't mean I agree with everything—or, in fact, anything—that he says."

The rib injury compromised McIlroy's preparations for the Masters, where another slow start (72-73) doomed his chances. Afterward, McIlroy was more philosophical than usual, as his mind was on other things: his storybook wedding to Erica Stoll would take place two weeks after Augusta. "It would have been nice to walk down the aisle in a green jacket," he mused.

The wedding took place at Ashford Castle in Ireland's County Mayo, a majestic pile of stones that dates to the thirteenth century. Rory and Erica had spent their first New Year's Eve together at the castle years earlier. Security was stringent, as McIlroy hired Bono's body man to lock down the castle; an army of drones was employed to monitor the surroundings. Guests included Chris Martin, the front man of Coldplay; Niall Horan, a member of One Direction; Northern Irish actor Jamie Dornan; and golfers Pádraig Harrington, Sergio García, and Paul McGinley. Rory's boyhood friend Harry Diamond presided as best man. Music was performed by Stevie Wonder and Ed Sheeran, who had to be imported by helicopter, as he was in the middle of a world tour.

"It was a lovely wedding," says McGinley. "It was small by Irish standards. Very classy, very elegant, very understated. It wasn't ostentatious in any way." McGinley was struck by the bride's reserve. "I've had dinner with her a number of times and she's quiet by nature," he says. "They're a little different in that way. Rory is a big personality; he's gregarious. He's a lot like [his father] Gerry."

The McIlroys honeymooned at the posh Sandy Lane resort on Barbados, co-owned by McIlroy's pals J. P. McManus and Dermot Desmond. (Tiger Woods married Swedish bikini model Elin Nordegren at Sandy Lane in 2004.)

Rory's postnuptial bliss didn't last long: the rib injury flared up a few weeks after the wedding at the Players Championship, forcing him to spend a month resting and doing rehab. He returned for the U.S. Open at Shinnecock Hills and opened with an 80. Adding insult to injury, McIlroy's missed cut was accompanied by electronic heckling from Steve Elkington, the dyspeptic former pro and Twitter muckraker. He tweeted, "Rory is so bored playing golf... without Tiger the threshold is prolly 4 majors with 100mill in bank."

McIlroy was on his flight home when he read Elkington's tweet. He had already enjoyed, in his estimation, three or four glasses of red wine. He wrote a reply, deleted it, wrote a reply, deleted it, wrote a reply, deleted it, wrote a reply, deleted it, wrote a reply, and hit send: "More like 200mil... not bad for a 'bored' 28 year old... plenty more where that came from." He included a screenshot of his Wikipedia page listing his many glittering accomplishments. It was a solid dunk, but Elkington's retort skillfully painted McIlroy as a mercenary: "New you were a money guy. Jack won 18 [majors] and never mentioned his total cash." McIlroy turned into a pedantic English professor in response: "It's knew... mustn't have taught grammar in the 50's." McIlroy almost immediately regretted getting sucked into the spat. "Twitter and alcohol never go well together," he says. He handed his phone to Erica and asked her to log him out and change the password without telling him the new one, forcing McIlroy to give up Twitter. It didn't last, of course. McIlroy has always been extremely online and attuned to what is being said about him by golf fans, reporters, and fellow players. During his injury hiatuses throughout 2017, *he* was reaching out to podcasters asking if *they* might want to have him on, propelled by a mix of boredom and enthusiasm for a younger generation that had energized the golf media. In these long, chatty sessions, McIlroy further endeared himself to golf fans with his open, honest reflections on life and golf.

He also filled the time by moving into a new dream house with Erica, paying $11 million for Ernie Els's pad at the Bear's Club. (This was the beginning of McIlroy becoming a full-time resident of the U.S.; for tax purposes, Monaco had been his official homebase for the preceding four years.) The seven-bedroom, ten-bathroom mansion, weighing in at 12,800 square feet, had long been McIlroy's vision of the American dream. He first visited the property during the 2009 Honda Classic, when Els and his wife, Liezl, hosted Rory and his parents in their sprawling digs. At one point, Rosie looked out the window at a faraway facade and asked, "Who lives over there in that house?"

"No, that's our house," Liezl said. "It's all the same house."

Says Rory, "And my mum is like, 'Oh, okay.'"

Forbes estimated McIlroy's income for 2017 at $50 million, but that didn't include any winner's checks; it was his first season without a victory since his rookie year in '08. Meanwhile, other young studs continued to assert themselves, as Brooks Koepka, then twenty-seven, won the U.S. Open and Justin Thomas, twenty-four, took the PGA Championship. McIlroy's mounting frustration could be seen in his barbed exchanges with caddie J. P. Fitzgerald. (On a few occasions he was also overheard giving his manager, Sean O'Flaherty, a profane tongue-lashing.) During the first round of the Open Championship at Royal Troon, McIlroy played the opening six holes in +5. It was reminiscent of his brain-dead stretches at the Masters, where in five of the preceding six years he had zombie-walked to a nine-hole score of 40 or more. McIlroy admitted to going to a dark place: "I was thinking, *Geez, here we go.* Those thoughts ran through my mind." Walking to the seventh tee, Fitzgerald let his boss have it: "You're Rory McIlroy—what the fuck are you doing?" That woke him up, and McIlroy salvaged a 71. Three more good rounds followed for a backdoor tie for fourth, but he still finished seven shots behind Jordan Spieth, who won his third major championship to begin threatening McIlroy's status as the best player of the post-Tiger epoch. Something had to give, and it turned out to be Fitzgerald's job; McIlroy fired him a month after the Open, saying, "I wasn't myself on the golf course, and I was getting really hard on him. The only time I would talk to him was to text to say I'll meet you at this time on the green or golf course. That was it. The friendship side of our relationship had become so stale and nonexistent. I was like, *This isn't really right.*" He added, "Sometimes to preserve a personal relationship you have to sacrifice a professional one." He went on to say that he looked forward to dining and playing golf again with Fitzgerald. Beneath his genteel veneer, McIlroy had developed a well-disguised ruthlessness; once you're out of his orbit you might as well be dead. In an interview with the *Daily Mail* in 2019, Fitzgerald would say he hadn't spoken to his former boss once since they parted ways.

McIlroy put the best man from his wedding, Harry Diamond, on the bag. It was a full-circle moment for both of them, as a thirteen-year-old Rory had caddied for Harry at the 2002 Ulster Boys. It was supposed to be only until the end of the season, allowing McIlroy time to find a permanent replacement. But in the offseason, Rory and Erica took a second honeymoon, driving across Italy and the South of France. With a little time and space to think, McIlroy realized what an advantage it was to have his best friend on the bag. It made Rory a better version of himself—more patient and less caustic—because he couldn't imagine being mean to Harry. There was plenty of hand-wringing among the cognoscenti when Diamond got the job full-time. The thinking went that McIlroy needed an old-school, hard-ass caddie to rein in his impetuousness. Those who know McIlroy well scoff at that notion. "At the end of the day, people have no understanding of what a caddie is," says Pádraig Harrington. "It's not about getting the yardage. You can train anybody to get the yardage.

What matters in a caddie is that they have your back. It's saying the right thing at the right time and knowing when to say nothing. A caddie is so important, but not for why people think they are. No one is going to tell Rory McIlroy how to play golf. I find that idea bizarre. Rory knows more about playing golf than any caddie ever could. But Harry knows more about Rory than any other caddie could, because they grew up together." In other words, Rory is an expert at golf, and Harry is an expert at Rory.

McIlroy's swing coach Michael Bannon offers the most succinct take: "You can't tell Rory what to do."

McIlroy ended 2017 a pedestrian (for him!) eleventh in the World Ranking, and he continued to grope for answers into the new year. A month before the Masters, he abruptly fired his putting coach, Kenyon. (In 2017, McIlroy ranked 159th on Tour in strokes gained putting.) He hired Brad Faxon, and they worked together for the first time on Monday of Bay Hill week. How much McIlroy had lost his way was evident in that initial session. Says Faxon, "One of the first things he said to me was: 'Is it okay to go back to a thirty-four-inch putter?' I asked why he was using one that was thirty-three, and he said, 'Because that's what Phil wants me to use.' I asked if he had felt comfortable with a thirty-four-inch putter before, and he said, 'Yeah, I won two or three majors with one.' Yeah, Rory, it would be fine to go back. So he hit a few putts, and he asked, 'Is it okay if I get a little open with my body standing over a putt?' I told him a lot of great putters were open at address, including Jack Nicklaus and Ben Crenshaw. I putted that way because it helped me to see down the line better. So we made that adjustment." Faxon thought McIlroy had become too stiff and static over the ball, so they instituted a pre-putt routine with what Faxon calls "continuous motion and flow." To get McIlroy to think differently about his putting, Faxon told him to grab his sand wedge and his 5-wood. He had McIlroy hit three eight-footers with his putter. He made one. Putting with the sand wedge from the same spot, he holed two. With the 5-wood, McIlroy made all three. Turns out it's not that hard to get the ball in the hole when you strip away the mechanics and focus on *getting the ball in the hole*. "You gotta let the athlete come out, let the genius come out," says Faxon. "Rory is as gifted as any player ever, but sometimes the game drives you so crazy. As soon as he got less technical, you could see him relax and let his beautiful natural putting stroke come out."

McIlroy couldn't miss once the tournament began. On Sunday, he raced home with five birdies in the final six holes for a 64 to blow away a group of big-name contenders. For the week he gained 10.07 strokes on the field on the greens, the best putting performance of his career. It was McIlroy's first PGA Tour win in eighteen long months. He was defiant in victory, saying, "Look, I've always believed in myself, and I know that me being 100 percent healthy is good enough to not just win on the PGA Tour but win a lot. So I never lost belief. I know that I've got a gift for this game, and I know that if I put the time in, I can make a lot out of it." Having just won Arnold Palmer's tournament, McIlroy couldn't help but think back to his first dinner with the King, three years earlier. "He liked A.1. Sauce on his fish, which was quite strange," McIlroy said with a laugh.

Palmer went to his grave ruing all the PGA Championships that got away, preventing him from completing the career Grand Slam. Riding the momentum from Bay Hill, McIlroy blew into Augusta for his fourth crack at consummating the Slam. He admitted that the pre-Masters hype had bothered him in the past but, after the challenges of the preceding eighteen months, this time felt different. "You have to embrace and relish the opportunity that is put in front of you and go out and grab it," McIlroy said. "So I'm an avid fan of the history of the game, and I know what a win here would mean and where that would put me in history alongside some of the greatest that have ever played this game, and that would mean an awful lot to me. But I have to try and clear my head of that come Thursday morning, and go out and play good golf." Which he finally did, after having gotten in his own way on previous Masters Thursdays; McIlroy's 69 on a firm setup put him in a tie for fourth, three shots behind . . . Spieth, who held the first-round lead for the third time in the last four Masters.

McIlroy held his ground during a windy second round with a 71 that kept him in fourth place, but now he was five shots behind leader Patrick Reed, his Ryder Cup antagonist, who made nine birdies while taking only twenty-two putts during a 66. On Saturday, McIlroy played the front nine of his dreams: two-putt birdie on the second hole, back-to-back twenty-footers on the third and fourth, a stone-dead tee shot on the sixth. At the par-5 eighth, he was twenty-five yards short of the green and played a pitch that came in too hot . . . but it clanged off the flagstick and disappeared for an eagle, pulling him into a tie for the lead. Across Golf Twitter and the grounds at Augusta National there was a collective giddiness: *Rory's comin'!* But Reed wouldn't go away—he birdied eight, nine, and ten to retake a three-stroke lead. The skies opened up as McIlroy played the thirteenth hole. Trying to dodge the raindrops, he rushed his second shot. The ball sailed into an azalea bush beyond the green, and McIlroy had trouble even locating it in what he called "a sea of pink." He did well to salvage a par, but in the group behind him, Reed stuffed his second shot and made eagle. McIlroy conjured a birdie on fifteen after a wild drive, but Reed chipped in from a tricky greenside lie for his second eagle in half an hour. Still, the golf gods appeared to side with McIlroy: on eighteen he hit another crooked drive, but his ball clanged off a tree and back into the fairway. He converted that into a birdie, punctuated with a restrained fist pump. McIlroy's bogeyless 65 pushed him to solo second. He had withstood Reed's best shot by countering with his lowest round at Augusta National since 2011. Afterward, both players tried to position themselves as the underdog. "Patrick has a three-stroke lead; I feel like all the pressure is on him," said McIlroy. "He has got to protect that, and he has some pretty big-time players behind him. He has to sleep on that tonight. I feel like I have nothing to lose. My game is right there. I don't feel like there is any shot on the golf course that I can't execute, and

I think I've shown that in the last three days. This isn't my first time in this position. I have a lot of experience and experience that I have learned from, good and bad. I'm going to freewheel it and play like I have nothing to lose, everything to gain. Which is true."

"But at the same time, he's trying to go for the career Grand Slam," parried Reed.

Masters Sunday is a kind of religious holiday in Augusta. Church services are moved earlier in the morning to allow locals time to get to the National or prepare all the fixings for a house party. In 2018, one such gathering took place on the northern edge of Augusta at a tidy two-story house with black shutters identical to those on the National's clubhouse. A daughter who was away at college drove home from Athens, Georgia, just to share the Masters with her parents. A dozen friends dropped by, everyone settling in the seating area in the backyard by the pool, where there was a big TV. The family mutts, Murphy and Cooper, scampered underfoot. It was a Masters party just like every other, with one wrenching difference: a few miles away, the hosts' son was trying to win the green jacket. Bill and Jeannette Reed and their daughter, Hannah, were not welcome at Augusta National. Patrick had made that much clear, the final twist of the knife in an estrangement that dated to 2012. So the Reeds gathered at the house their son lived in while leading Augusta State to two national championships. Memorabilia from his playing career was still scattered about: crystal trophies, photographs on the walls, a couple of commemorative golf bags. The bedroom he hadn't set foot in for so long was still referred to as "Patrick's room." As the final round got underway, the soundtrack was buzzing and beeping phones; Bill alone had awakened to 152 text messages.

Augusta is a company town, and sympathy for Reed's parents may explain why the applause was so tepid for their son on the first tee. Meanwhile, the crowd roared for McIlroy. But he had been fighting a hook on the driving range, and then he blocked his opening tee shot forty yards right, deep into the trees, spooking McIlroy to his core. Still, he executed a deft greenside up-and-down to save par and close within two strokes of Reed, who made bogey after an errant drive. On the par-5 second hole, McIlroy expertly drew a 371-yard drive around the corner of the dogleg. Short and chubby with T. rex arms, Reed could only dream of such a majestic poke. Then McIlroy cut a mid-iron to within three feet of the hole. Augusta National shook. Reed was doomed to make par out of the greenside bunker, meaning McIlroy's eagle would draw him even. Going back to Bay Hill, he had not missed a putt of consequence in a month. But this time McIlroy made a jittery, rushed stroke and pushed his ball wide right. You could practically see him shrink from the crushing cosmic weight of his previous Masters failures. On the next hole, McIlroy laid up and then, from the middle of the fairway, spun a wedge off the green—"That was really an unforced error," CBS's Peter Kostis said with a touch of disdain in his voice. McIlroy made bogey while Reed holed a tricky putt from off the green for birdie. Fifteen minutes earlier, it looked like McIlroy would be tied for the lead. Now he was three strokes back and it might as well have been a million. McIlroy made four more bogies and bled out to a 74, falling to fifth place. Reed's victorious walk up the eighteenth fairway was met with a smattering of awkward applause. The people had wanted to see McIlroy make history. Instead, he was left to lament, "I was very, very tentative with my swing. I was guarding against the left [miss] I had on the range and started missing it right." There would be no respite from the ongoing malaise.

14.

In May 2018, the Reuters wire service carried a curious item: a British-based concern, the World Golf Group, was attempting to launch something called the "World Golf Series," which would consist of fifteen to twenty annual tournaments worldwide, each offering a whopping $20 million purse. The series was designed to offer a jazzier, more consumable product, with fifty-four-hole tournaments and shotgun starts that put every player on the course at the same time. The Reuters story, written by Andrew Both, reported, "The series sounds eerily similar to the world tour proposed by then–number one Greg Norman more than two decades ago—a plan that went nowhere after the PGA Tour played hardball. It divided and conquered by issuing an 'us or them' ultimatum, threatening to scrap the membership of any player who signed up for the doomed venture." It was a one- or two-day story in the golf world, and then this upstart golf league receded from view. But behind the scenes, powerful forces had been unleashed that would culminate years later in the game-changing launch of LIV Golf.

The Reuters article didn't mention by name the propulsive force behind the series, which would later be rebranded as the Premier Golf League: Andy Gardiner, a corporate finance lawyer and obsessive golf fan. Like many folks who consumed a lot of professional golf, he had become disenchanted with the product. The well-connected Gardiner sought out friends and clients in the golf world, and for four years before the Reuters story broke, he had been engaging them in discussions about ways to improve, if not entirely rethink, the professional game. "Funny enough, one of the first conversations I ever had was with Rory," Gardiner says. "I was explaining the concept, and at the time, he was of the view that actually this is what golf needs. That was some time ago. He's entitled to change his opinion, but had Rory said to me, *Andy, that's rubbish*, I would've probably stopped. But on we went."

•

RORY MCILROY FINALLY CAUGHT a spark at the 2018 Open Championship at Carnoustie. Rounds of 69-69-70 left him in sixth place, tied with a resurgent Tiger Woods, who had lost most of the preceding three seasons while undergoing four back surgeries. Woods and McIlroy were four shots behind coleaders Kevin Kisner, Xander Schauffele, and Jordan Spieth (once again!). McIlroy became an afterthought when he bogeyed the second and fifth holes of the final round. By then, the whole golf course had tilted in the direction of one man: Tiger.

The living legend was trying to return from the ashes yet again. To cheer for Woods at Carnoustie was to believe in the power of redemption. Over the preceding decade, he had been to hell and back: tabloid infamy, sex addiction therapy, divorce, the police blotter, rehab for an addiction to painkillers, leaked dick pics, and a slew of back problems that literally brought him to his knees on the golf course. He was playing this Open Championship with a newly fused spine; it felt like every violent lash from the heather could be his last. In his heyday, Woods was revered but never beloved. Now he had reinvented himself as a vulnerable forty-two-year-old single dad, an underdog who hadn't won a tournament in five years or a major championship in a full decade. Woods had talked about reconnecting with his Buddhist roots in the wake of his scandals. The underpinning of that religion is gratitude, and you could feel that in the air at Carnoustie—Woods grateful to be back where he belonged, the rest of us mesmerized to bear witness. On the fourth hole, Tiger played two gorgeous shots through the wind and gutted the birdie putt. Carnoustie exploded and the internet melted, but Woods offered only a perfunctory nod; he had a familiar, ravenous look in his eye. On the par-5 sixth hole, Tiger made a textbook two-putt birdie. Suddenly, incredibly, he held the lead. With every step he was serenaded by shouts of *"TI-gaaaa!"* but he sailed through the cacophony, having retreated into himself.

As Woods made gritty pars on the next four holes, McIlroy began to stir. At number nine, he rolled in a fifteen-footer for his first birdie of the day. On the par-4 eleventh, he nearly drove the green and then pitched it close, offering a wee fist pump when the birdie putt drew him within two of Woods's lead. No one was afraid of Tiger anymore. On Sunday evening, Spieth relayed an exchange he had with caddie Michael Greller: "I looked up and I saw Tiger was leading solo, and . . . Michael was like, 'He hasn't been in this position in ten years, and you've been here how many times in the last three years?'" Point taken. On cue, Woods made a mess of the eleventh hole, missing the fairway and green and then fluffing a chip, leading to a gutting double bogey. Then he bogeyed the twelfth hole after an errant approach shot. The unraveling was stunning in its swiftness. McIlroy also bogeyed twelve, three-putting from fifty feet, but on the par-5 fourteenth, he unleashed two mighty blows and then buried the eagle putt. From out of nowhere, he was now tied for the lead.

"Carnoustie is a course where I struggle to comprehend exactly how to take it on, strategically," says Matt Kuchar, McIlroy's playing partner that day. "There are a lot of bunkers that start at, let's call it, 280 [yards] off the tee and go to 330. You could pick something that stayed short of the bunkers but then leave yourself a long approach shot, or you could challenge the bunkers with some sort of wood and try to fit your ball between them and have a much more reasonable approach. But if you hit it into the bunkers, they are basically a one-shot penalty. Rory, he hit driver everywhere and he took most of the bunkers completely out of play. It was golf like

I had not seen it played before. He played it in a different manner than I could or even envisioned it could be played. It was pretty incredible."

Strong winds and tucked pins on a bone-dry golf course made birdies scarce on the closing holes. McIlroy hit every green coming home but didn't give himself a good look at birdie until the eighteenth hole. By then, it was too late: Francesco Molinari won by two strokes thanks to two birds on the final five holes. McIlroy was peaceful afterward, saying, "I have no regrets. I played the way I wanted to play this week. It was great just to be a part of it and hear the roars. For a while I thought Tiger was going to win. My mindset was to go and spoil the party."

Behind the scoring trailer, Woods's children awaited in matching tomato-red attire. All week long, Tiger had spoken movingly about wanting to win for his kids, to show them who he used to be. When he finally made his way to Sam, eleven, she squeezed her dad hard. "Almost," Tiger said softly. Next, he wrapped Charlie, nine, in a great big hug. "I tried my hardest," Tiger said. Like McIlroy, he was discovering how challenging it can be to recapture former glory. Charlie wore a T-shirt emblazoned with a message that applied to both Woods and McIlroy: LOVE THE HATERS.

Two months after the Open, Tiger and Rory tangled again at the Tour Championship as they played alongside each other in the final group. It had been six years since McIlroy dusted Woods at the Honda Classic to ascend to number one in the World Ranking for the first time. But they had been in different groups that day; the final round of the Tour Championship was, incredibly, the first time they would be able to look each other in the eye with a tournament on the line. Entering Sunday with a three-stroke lead, Woods made a tone-setting birdie on the first hole and then followed with the kind of plodding, efficient golf that had carried him to seventy-nine(!) previous Tour victories. Meanwhile, McIlroy was all over the place as he fought a two-way miss with his driver: bogies at 4 and 5, a birdie on 6, double bogey on 7, bogey on 8. By the turn, he was eight shots back and reduced to spectating as Woods finished off one of the most meaningful victories of his career. Delirious fans swarmed the fairway as Tiger and Rory marched up eighteen. McIlroy said to Woods, a fellow golf historian, that the wild scene evoked Jack Nicklaus almost being swallowed by the crowd on the final hole of the 1980 U.S. Open at Baltusrol. "I said, yeah, I just didn't have the tight pants and the hair, but it was all good," said Woods. Despite the levity, Tiger felt the magnitude of his accomplishment: "I mean, I'm having a hard time not crying on the last hole."

McIlroy could relate—he would later call his 74 in front of his boyhood idol one of the most dispiriting rounds of his career. He added, "Everyone was like, 'Wasn't that a great moment?' And I'm like, 'No, it was fucking shit!' It was terrible. I birdied the last to shoot four over! I got the bigger picture that it was wonderful for golf, and I'm sure I'll look back and think 'That was pretty cool,' but it hurt. It really hurt."

Amid the array of on-course disappointments, McIlroy continued to stand out as a mensch among superstars. In the 1990s, Brad Faxon and Billy Andrade founded a pro-am to raise money for charities in their native Rhode Island. They had no trouble recruiting big names to donate their time when both were mainstays on the PGA Tour, but by the 2010s, Andrade and Faxon were having trouble attracting top talent. "D.J., J.T., Spieth—we tried hard, but we never got those guys," says Andrade. "We understood. It's a long way to go, and they're not getting paid. The tournament was winding down by 2018. We really needed a headliner and we didn't have one. We were getting desperate, so I walked up to Rory at the Seminole Pro-Member and made my pitch. He had a lot going on, as always, and said he'd get back to me. Well, the next week was Bay Hill when he started working with Faxon, and Rory made every putt he looked at. I told Fax, 'I went seven innings, now you gotta be the closer.' Unfortunately, Fax is a gigantic pussy. He was afraid to say anything because he now had this professional relationship with Rory. So Augusta comes, and since Fax hasn't closed the deal, I tell him I'm gonna approach Rory again. He says, 'Are you crazy?! It's Masters week, he's locked in—you can't bother him!' Settle down, bro. It's Tuesday. It'll take thirty seconds. He begs me not to do it. Fine, I back off. Long story short, Faxon finally worked up the courage to ask Rory, and he made a big effort to come to the tournament. He was awesome—so charming, so giving. And you know what? People around Rhode Island still talk about Rory McIlroy."

THAT MCILROY WOULD FIND the time to play in the Seminole Pro-Member was not a surprise given his partner: his father, Gerry, who became a member of the club in late 2017. Seminole is a suntan-and-loafers version of Augusta National, a place where golf's ruling class gathers. Among the members are Fred Perpall, the most recent USGA president; Mike Davis, former CEO of the USGA; Seth Waugh, the former CEO of the PGA of America; Pete Bevacqua, Waugh's predecessor at the PGA; and Jimmy Dunne and Ed Herlihy, who will be remembered as the two most impactful members of the PGA Tour's board of directors—for better and for worse.

Dunne still runs herd at Seminole as the club president. Like many Augusta National members, Dunne also volunteers his services during Masters week. He could have had any front-facing job he wants, including chairman, but is content to preside over the caddie shack. Dunne grew up on Long Island in a large Irish family, the son of a shirt salesman. At the age of eleven, he began caddying at Southward Ho Country Club, helping to pay for his ensuing education at Notre Dame. Dunne was rejected from the five law schools to which he applied. He pursued a career on Wall Street, making his considerable fortune as a cofounder of Sandler O'Neill & Partners, a leading investment banking firm. He is a revered figure in the golf world, the quintessential insider who is reputed to be the first man to attain membership at Seminole, Augusta National, Cypress Point, and Pine Valley, the four leading private golf clubs in the United States. Dunne could play unlimited golf on Mondays at Southward Ho, and he turned himself into a heckuva stick: he once shot 63 at Shinnecock Hills (where he is also a member). Golf probably saved his life. On September 11, 2001, he was attempting to qualify for the U.S. Mid-Amateur Championship instead of sitting in his office on the 104th floor of the South Tower of the World Trade Center. Sandler O'Neill lost sixty-six of its eighty-three New York City employees on that dark day. Dunne insisted that the company pay ten years of salary to the family of each victim and cover the college tuition of the seventy-six children who had been left behind. Decades later, he was still known to weep when discussing 9/11 with friends.

Dunne first met McIlroy in 2012, when he received a text out of the blue from what he calls "some Irish kid" who used to caddie at Shinnecock Hills, asking for help in arranging a game at the fabled U.S. Open venue. Dunne didn't recognize the name but said yes anyway, agreeing to play host. "I have a soft spot for caddies," he says. Sean O'Flaherty was the Irish kid. He'd said he would bring two friends but did not name them, and they turned out to be McIlroy and his caddie, J. P. Fitzgerald. McIlroy shot 65 at Shinny, and he and Dunne hit it off famously. The Wall Street sage quickly became a friend and confidant.

One day, Dunne was playing golf at Augusta National when a caddie made an offhand, derogatory remark about McIlroy. Dunne debriefed him after the round, and the caddie said that Rory had stiffed him years earlier during a visit to the club in advance of the Masters. This didn't really make sense, because guests do not pay the caddies at Augusta National; the host member notifies the pro shop how much to give the loopers, and they are paid out of the shop. Nevertheless, Dunne found the caddie the next day and said he'd spoken to McIlroy, who was very upset and insisted that Dunne give him a huge wad of cash to rectify the misunderstanding. This was a ruse; Dunne hadn't bothered to check with McIlroy, he just paid off the caddie out of his own pocket because, he says, "you always stick up for your friends." He later mentioned the story to O'Flaherty, who said, according to Dunne, "Jimmy, whatever you do, please don't tell Gerry about this. If you tell him that Rory was somehow involved with a waiter or a caddie not being treated with generosity, he will rip his head off." Says Dunne, "That was very telling to me. I liked Gerry immediately, because I would do the same thing." At PGA Tour events it is customary for the players to tip the clubhouse staff; most players peel off a Benjamin at the end of the week. Two hundred dollars is considered generous. Rory started tipping $1,000 a week.

Jimmy and Gerry began spending time together, including very spirited matches on the golf course. They are about the same age and play with no strokes given; Dunne says McIlroy wins about 60 percent of the time. "I used to always argue with Gerry about parenting," says Dunne, a father of three. "I would say that I think raising children properly is much easier if you have very little than if you have a lot. He'd disagree and insist it's much tougher. Not to diminish the challenges of trying to make ends meet, but if you're trying to instill values in your kid, if you want them to have guts, grit, heart, drive—I always thought that comes easier if you grow up without money. Then one day, Gerry told me a story from when Rory was a kid. Gerry was working different jobs, Rosie was working the graveyard shift, and yet they were barely getting by. Gerry had made a vow he wouldn't borrow any more money. So it's a beautiful Sunday over there, and Rory wants to go to the driving range. Gerry is not getting paid until Tuesday, and he's flat broke. They go to the range, and Gerry takes the last few quid out of his wallet and puts them in the ball machine. It's not enough even for a full bucket. He brings the balls over to Rory, who is maybe nine years old. He's disappointed because he wants to hit five buckets. But even at that age, Rory has the good sense not to complain too much. Gerry gets down on one knee so they're eyeball to eyeball. He says, 'Son, I've worked hard, your mother has worked hard, but all we have left is in that bucket. I want you to hit every shot like winning the Open Championship depends on it.' I thought, *Wow, what a terrific life lesson.* That told me so much about Rory, about Gerry, about their bond, and the way he and Rosie raised their son."

As Dunne came to know and admire Gerry, he decided he would make an excellent addition to Seminole. It's highly doubtful that any other members cleaned toilets and tended bar for a living, as Gerry once did. Did the club president get any blowback on this unexpected new member? "I will never, ever tell who it is," says Dunne, "but one guy came up to me and said, 'Jimmy, I see Gerry McIlroy is on the membership list. I just want to make sure you understand what Gerry did for his occupation.' I said yes, I certainly did, but if it made him feel any better, he should just pretend that Gerry was the CEO of an Irish insurance company. And oh, by the way, this guy wasn't even a member at Seminole!"

Dunne says Gerry is now "the most popular member in the club." He adds with a laugh, "That drives Rory crazy. He hates it when I say that because he thinks it goes to his father's head, which it doesn't. It's true that Gerry likes to talk about the skins games and wears shirts with the logo and wears the club blazer, but he's not showing off—he just has a real appreciation and gratitude for being a member."

And why shouldn't he? Gerry lost an uncle to the Troubles and, as a Catholic living in Northern Ireland, was imbued with an unshakable sense of otherness. Being made a member at Seminole is the ultimate measure of belonging. It is the American dream.

•

JAMAL KHASHOGGI LONG HELD a unique place in Saudi Arabian society: a celebrated journalist in a country that brutally stifles the press and any public dissent by its citizens. He came from a famous family. In addition to his uncle Adnan, the playboy arms dealer, Khashoggi's first cousin was Dodi Fayed, the Egyptian film producer who, in 1997, died in a Paris tunnel alongside his girlfriend, Princess Diana. Khashoggi's grandfather was the personal physician of Ibn Saud, who in 1932 united the warring tribes of the Arabian Peninsula and created the modern nation-state of Saudi Arabia. Six years later, oceans of oil were discovered beneath the Saudi desert, altering geopolitics forever.

Khashoggi had an enduring love for his country. In addition to his high-profile work as a writer and editor at various media outlets throughout the Middle East, he served as an official in the Saudi embassy in Washington, D.C., and reputedly aided the Saudi Arabian intelligence community. His deep connections and immense personal charm kept him in good graces with the royal family even as he occasionally published things that would have landed other journalists in jail, or worse.

Khashoggi was an early supporter of Crown Prince Mohammed bin Salman, who seized power in 2015. The journalist was impressed by MBS's efforts to modernize Saudi Arabian society, which would include reopening movie cinemas and ordering the removal of the cinder-block walls that separated the sexes in restaurants. (These efforts got a lot of attention in the Western media, but MBS continued a bloody crackdown on dissent within Saudi Arabia.) Khashoggi subsequently criticized in print the Saudi bombing of Yemen in 2015 and the blockade of Qatar two years later, earning back-channel warnings from the royal court. Unlike previous rulers, who had tolerated Khashoggi as a kind of distant family member who occasionally said impertinent things around the dinner table, MBS had zero tolerance for criticism. When more than a dozen Saudi public figures were arrested in one fell swoop in September 2017—including a prominent economist, Essam Al-Zamil, who had merely tweeted a critique of the IPO of Aramco, the state oil company—Khashoggi registered his disgust in an interview with *The New York Times*, calling the crackdown "absurd." Friends and colleagues beseeched him to be more careful. In late 2017, just as the Saudi government was about to ban him from leaving the country, Khashoggi fled to the United States. He signed on as a columnist with *The Washington Post*. His first piece, published September 18, 2017, carried an incendiary headline: "Saudi Arabia Wasn't Always This Repressive. Now It's Unbearable." He wrote, "We Saudis deserve better." MBS was incensed. He ordered one of his top lieutenants to bring Khashoggi home or "make arrangements," according to a later CIA assessment.

Despite Khashoggi's withering critiques, MBS became a darling of the ruling class as his oil reserves powered the global economy and his $750 billion Public Investment Fund (PIF) reshaped industries. In 2018, he was received as a head of state in the United Kingdom, where he met the queen, and Rupert Murdoch hosted a dinner for him in his home. When MBS continued his charm offensive in the United States, he hobnobbed with Mark Zuckerberg, Bill Gates, Sergey Brin, Tim Cook, Oprah Winfrey, and the CEOs of Disney, Uber, and Lockheed Martin. The PIF bought $2 billion worth of Tesla stock shortly after MBS's meeting of the minds with Elon Musk. At the White House, President Trump said publicly, "It is an honor to have the crown prince of Saudi Arabia with us. The relationship is probably the strongest it's ever been—we understand each other."

Meanwhile, Saudi security forces planted spyware on the phone of dissident blogger Omar Abdulaziz, who had fled to Canada. In text messages with his old friend Khashoggi, they discussed ways to organize MBS's critics into a previously unfathomable unified opposition.

In September 2018, Khashoggi, fifty-nine, went to the Saudi embassy in Istanbul to fill out the paperwork necessary to wed a Turkish native, Hatice Cengiz. He was told to return in a couple of weeks to retrieve the completed documents. Unbeknownst to Khashoggi, his surprise visit to the embassy led to a phone call to intelligence officials in Riyadh, setting a deadly plan into motion. By the time he returned to pick up his documents, Saudi agents had swept the building for electronic listening devices—they missed many—and dispatched the Rapid Intervention Force, a special forces unit that reports directly to MBS. Among the assembled men was Lieutenant Colonel Salah Mohammed Al-Tubaigy, a doctor with the Ministry of Interior. As they waited inside the embassy for Khashoggi to arrive, the fifteen-man kill squad chatted freely, unaware that their every utterance was being recorded by the Turkish government. "Has the sacrificial animal arrived yet?" one goon asked. Al-Tubaigy casually mentioned that he liked to listen to music and drink coffee while cutting up corpses. The Saudi workers at the embassy had been told to stay home that day, and upon arrival, Khashoggi was taken to the consul general's office, where the Saudi agents had gathered. A needle was plunged into his neck, flooding his body with sedatives. Then he was strangled. Six minutes later, the whirring of a bone saw could be heard through the recording devices as Al-Tubaigy began dismembering the corpse. The body of Saudi Arabia's most famous public intellectual was wheeled out of the embassy in two suitcases and flown home in a private jet owned by the Public Investment Fund.

Just a few weeks after Khashoggi's murder became public, thanks to leaks by the Turkish government, the second annual Future Investment Initiative, aka Davos in the Desert, was held in Riyadh. MBS, once the darling of the international business community, had suddenly become so radioactive that Jeff Bezos canceled his appearance, Hollywood super-agent Ari Emanuel backed out of a $400 million investment from the PIF that he had been chasing for years, and Richard Branson pulled out of a $1 billion deal for his space travel company. Referencing Khashoggi's murder, Branson said that it "would clearly change the ability of any of us to do business with the Saudi government."

Golf played an unlikely role in the unfolding geopolitical drama. His Excellency Yasir Al-Rumayyan, the chairman of Aramco and governor of the PIF, had been wooing the European Tour for years, culminating in the launch of the inaugural Saudi International tournament to be played in January 2019 . . . three months after Khashoggi's assassination. At a moment when Saudi leaders were desperate for allies, the European Tour did them a monumental favor by not canceling the tournament.

"We are a global tour that plays all over the world," said Keith Pelley, then the Tour's CEO. "Our board members and players were consistent in expressing the sentiment 'We don't mix politics with sport. You can't be hypocritical and single out one country now.'"

Determined to make its first tournament a smashing success, Golf Saudi earmarked an unprecedented $20 million for appearance fees, with Dustin Johnson and Brooks Koepka each receiving in excess of $1.5 million. Fellow Americans Patrick Reed, the reigning Masters champ, and Bryson DeChambeau also made the trip and spouted the predictable pablum about "growing the game." Reed even made a cringey visit to an elementary school, camera crew in tow, where he got the kids to reenact the finger-to-the-lips shushing gesture that the erstwhile Captain America had used to taunt McIlroy, among others, at the Ryder Cup. Other players were loath to participate in such publicity stunts. McIlroy turned down a reported $2.5 million appearance fee, saying, "One hundred percent, there's a morality to it." The battle had been joined for the soul of professional golf.

BETWEEN THE ROPES, MCILROY had plenty to prove in 2019, as the competition was only growing fiercer. Brooks Koepka was coming off a season during which he won his second straight U.S. Open as well as the PGA Championship, where he held off Woods down the stretch. With three major championship victories, Koepka was now only one behind McIlroy's tally. Dustin Johnson won seven tournaments across the 2017 and '18 seasons and spent sixty-four consecutive weeks at number one in the World Ranking. He and Koepka played the same brand of smashmouth golf as McIlroy but appeared to have far less self-doubt.

The brutal loss to Tiger at the 2018 Tour Championship sent McIlroy on a quest for self-knowledge. He began keeping a journal to jot down the many thoughts in his active mind. Like Don Draper in the finale of *Mad*

Men, McIlroy turned to meditation to try to quell his demons. (In Rory's case, that came at the suggestion of Dr. Clayton Skaggs, his new "performance coach.") McIlroy took up juggling because, he said, it engaged both hemispheres of the brain. His bookshelves began to sag with all the self-help tomes he consumed: *The Greatest Salesman in the World*, by Og Mandino (from 1968!); *Ego Is the Enemy* and *The Obstacle Is the Way: The Timeless Art of Turning Trials into Triumph*, by Ryan Holiday; *Digital Minimalism: Choosing a Focused Life in a Noisy World*, by Cal Newport; *Essentialism: The Disciplined Pursuit of Less*, by Greg McKeown; *Quiet: The Power of Introverts in a World That Can't Stop Talking*, by Susan Cain.

Thanks to the koans of his coach, Brad Faxon, McIlroy had continued to embrace a more natural, organic style on the greens. His putter was evolving from a liability to a weapon. At the 2019 Players Championship, McIlroy rolled the ball beautifully to put himself in position to finally bag the second-biggest tournament missing from his résumé. McIlroy meditated for twenty minutes before the final round and then went out and stepped on his opponents' necks, birdieing five of the last ten holes. With the win, he joined Jack Nicklaus and Tiger Woods as the only players to take fifteen Tour events and four major championships before turning thirty. Even as McIlroy kept making history, the most striking aspect of his victory at the Players was the celebration on the final green . . . or lack thereof. He barely smiled, part of his new commitment to not being wholly defined by golf. "I think the big thing is: I am not my score. I am not my results," McIlroy said.

As always, the Masters—conducted three weeks after the Players—loomed as the ultimate test. This would be McIlroy's fifth attempt to complete the career Grand Slam. He arrived playing, statistically, the best golf of his career. But he made a head-scratching six bogies during the first round, shooting a buzzkill 73 that guaranteed another lost Masters. McIlroy's struggles became an afterthought when Woods won his fifth Masters and fifteenth major championship. His joyous hug with son Charlie behind the eighteenth green came in nearly the same spot where, twenty-two years earlier, Tiger shared a moving embrace with his father, Earl. His comeback from the depths riveted the sports world. Eight years earlier, the baby-faced McIlroy won the U.S. Open in a blowout while a woebegone Woods was still trying to piece his life back together. Their ebbs and flows ever since were a vivid reminder that Hall of Fame golf careers are rarely linear.

A month after the Masters, McIlroy turned up for the PGA Championship at Bethpage Black, a big ballpark that seemed to favor him. Alas, two rounds into the tournament he trailed Koepka by fifteen strokes. Koepka went on to outduel Dustin Johnson on the back nine on Sunday to win his fourth major championship. McIlroy's haul of majors had always been his trump card in the debate about the best players of his era. Now he could no longer claim that superiority. Koepka ascended to world number one a few months after Bethpage, leading him to disrespect McIlroy with breathtaking frankness. "I've been out here for, what, five years?" Koepka said. "Rory hasn't won a major since I've been on the PGA Tour. So I just don't view it as a rivalry. I'm not looking at anybody behind me. I'm No. 1 in the world. I've got open road in front of me. I'm not looking in the rearview mirror, so I don't see it as a rivalry."

McIlroy, the onetime boy wonder, had turned thirty a couple of weeks before Bethpage. (He'd already been around so long it felt like his age should be measured in dog years.) Was it possible he'd peaked during his go-go twenties? McIlroy offered a strong rebuttal at the Canadian Open, shooting a final-round 61 to win by seven strokes. But the golf world no longer cared about McIlroy winning a second-tier Tour event against a mediocre field; he needed another major championship to change the narrative. He had the ultimate opportunity with the Open Championship returning to Royal Portrush for the first time since 1951. It would be the biggest sporting event ever to visit Northern Ireland and a ringing endorsement of the progress McIlroy's homeland had made in the two decades since the signing of the Good Friday Agreement, which ended the Troubles.

The homegrown heroes put the heart into that Open. Darren Clarke was granted the honor of hitting the opening tee shot, at 6:35 a.m. Thursday morning. The packed grandstand roared when he striped one down the middle. Graeme McDowell was so moved to play an Open in his hometown he shed a tear on the first tee. But all eyes were on McIlroy, the prodigal son returning to where he began his legend with a course record 61 at age sixteen. "Everywhere you went in the town, everyone was talking about Rory," says Iain Carter, BBC golf correspondent. "I popped into a chippy and there were pictures of him all over the walls and one coffee shop was selling Rory Macachinos."

The crowd was in full throat on Thursday morning as McIlroy arrived on the first tee. The opening hole at Portrush is an uphill par-4 that would be benign but for the out-of-bounds on both sides of the fairway—controversial gerrymandering for a links course. McIlroy had sliced his driver OB right during his practice round the day before, so, to begin his Open, he was not in attack mode; he held a 2-iron in his hands. McIlroy had spent a lifetime waiting to hit this shot, but he badly underestimated the emotion of the moment. "The way they do it at the Open almost feels like a ring walk for a boxer," he says. "People are cheering. You come down the steps and through a tunnel and onto the tee box, and there's this massive ovation. And I'm like, 'Woah!' That was the first time I felt it, 'Jesus, this is huge!' And I hadn't prepared myself for it. I had prepared for the golf, and the golf course, but I hadn't prepared for that feeling. And I don't know if I could have prepared for that feeling. I was overwhelmed by the support. I looked up and just thought, 'Holy shit!' So that was the moment, and then nervous, real nervous." At impact, he was a little flippy with the right hand, and the crowd hushed as McIlroy's ball rode the wind toward the OB. McIlroy plaintively yelled, "Sit!" Then he did it five more times, to no avail. "To see it sailing left, that was tough," says Gary Woodland, McIlroy's playing partner that day. "I was deflated for him, the crowd was deflated. You had to feel for him."

McIlroy's ball pegged a spectator and broke her phone. It came to rest out-of-bounds by half a dozen paces. He tugged the reload into the thick left rough, barely advanced his fourth shot, and then had to take an unplayable lie from the weeds. When the hole mercifully ended, McIlroy had made a quadruple bogey 8, tying the worst single-hole score of his career. He started the round as a 6–1 favorite at Ladbrokes and was downgraded to 33–1 by the time he reached the second tee box. "It was extraordinary," says John McLaren, who was caddying in the group for Paul Casey. "Like I said, I wasn't too shocked, as Rory is quite prone to nerves, otherwise he'd have probably won a lot more majors really. That's where he differs to Tiger. He gets hyped up."

McIlroy rallied to play the next fourteen holes in 2-under to keep himself in the tournament. But he missed a six-foot par putt on the sixteenth hole and then rushed the tap-in, missing again from ten inches. The crowd audibly gasped. Then McIlroy triple-bogeyed eighteen. "I want to punch myself in the face," he said afterward. His 79 left him 150th in a 156-man field. How did McIlroy regroup that evening? "Opened a bottle of wine," he said, "finished a bottle of wine . . ."

But McIlroy played with fire in his belly during the second round. By the time he birdied the twelfth hole, he was –5 for the day, and the entire island of Ireland appeared to be following his group, cheering with gusto. "It was the most electric Friday atmosphere I've seen in my time on Tour," says Woodland. "It was a crazy change in emotion from Thursday to Friday." McIlroy erased a bogey at thirteen with a birdie on fourteen and then drilled a twelve-footer at the sixteenth hole to reach –6 for the day. He needed one more birdie on the final two holes to improbably make the cut. Having teed off at 3:10 p.m. local time, McIlroy was playing his way through prime time. From Belfast to Dublin, Londonderry to Limerick, Nobber to Doodys Bottoms, Bastardstown to Fannystown, McIlroy's quest for redemption riveted the entire island. (Yes, these are real places.) But he missed a midrange birdie putt on seventeen and then, at the last, pulled his approach left of the green, dooming himself to a par. McIlroy's 65 established a new course record for the reconfigured Portrush—Shane Lowry would lower it to 63 the next day—but Rory missed the cut by one stroke, the second monumental letdown in as many days. Asked afterward what emotions he was feeling, a choked-up McIlroy said, "There's a lot of them. Disappointed not to be here for the weekend. Unbelievably proud of how I handled myself today, coming back after what was a very challenging day yesterday. And just full of gratitude toward every single one of the people who followed me to the very end and were willing me on. As much as I came here at the start of the week saying I wanted to do it for me, you know, by the end of the round there today I was doing it just as much for them as I was for me." He called his furious rally "one of the most fun rounds of golf I've ever played." This expat Floridian with an American wife noted how rarely he'd been back to Northern Ireland in the preceding decade and said, "The last week has been an eye-opener for me. Sometimes you're so far away and you forget about all the people that are cheering you on back home. Then you come and play in front of them. It definitely hit me like a ton of bricks today." McIlroy's raw emotion endeared him, again, to the golf world. As always, his heartbreak was as riveting as any of his triumphs.

As much as his clubhead speed, McIlroy's resilience has been the defining characteristic of his professional career. "His ability to pick himself off the mat time and time again and just keep moving forward, honestly, I'm in awe of it," says Brad Faxon. A month after Portrush, McIlroy rode a hot putter to win the Tour Championship, joining Woods as the only two-time FedEx Cup champion. (For the season, McIlroy would finish twenty-fourth in strokes gained putting, by far the best showing of his career to date.) Then he took the WGC-HSBC Champions, his fourth victory in the span of four months. For the 2018–19 wraparound season, McIlroy had fourteen top-ten finishes in nineteen starts. He gained 2.22 strokes per round, making it the twenty-first best season since 1999. History may remember only the major championships, but McIlroy's colleagues were wowed by his week-to-week consistency and voted him the PGA Tour player of the year. One number may have loomed largest: $25.4 million. That's how much McIlroy made in tournament winnings and bonuses on the PGA Tour, a monster wage in a sport suddenly obsessed with money.

EMBOLDENED BY THE SUCCESS of the initial Saudi International, Yasir Al-Rumayyan spent the rest of 2019 looking for ways to further invest in a sport that was willing to turn a blind eye to the atrocities of his boss, the crown prince. Al-Rumayyan's baby, Golf Saudi, pledged $500 million to Andy Gardiner's PGL and began helping to recruit players to the cause. In January 2020, Golf Saudi paid a seven-figure appearance fee for Phil Mickelson to play in the Saudi International. (Previously, Lefty had always hated to compete overseas.) In the tournament pro-am, Mickelson played alongside Gardiner; Al-Rumayyan's top lieutenant, Majed Al-Sorour; and Colin Neville of the Raine Group, which had also pledged $500 million to help launch the PGL. Back in Florida, PGA Tour commissioner Jay Monahan fumed as these pieces moved on the chessboard. He sent a strongly worded letter to his players affirming the Tour's commitment to "strict enforcement of the Conflicting Event and Media Rights/Release rules." He wrote that if the PGL were to get off the ground, "our members will have to decide whether they want to continue to be a member of the PGA Tour or play on a new series." When news of the letter inevitably leaked, GolfChannel.com summed up the Tour's stance nicely in one headline: "Monahan to Players Regarding Premier Golf League: Us or Them."

In February 2020, the PGL rented a big house near Riviera Country Club in Pacific Palisades, California, and held an informational meeting with players and agents during the week of the Los Angeles Open. Al-Rumayyan and Al-Sorour attended but did not speak, underscoring their role as silent investors; their half a billion spoke loudly enough. In the wake of that meeting, the PGL made its first formal contract offers: $200 million to Tiger Woods and $50 million each to McIlroy, Mickelson, Koepka, Spieth, Dustin Johnson, Justin Thomas, and Rickie Fowler. Those eight players were envisioned as captains of PGL's four-man teams, with the other four squads to be cocaptained by less noteworthy players.

The PGA Tour called a Player Advisory Council meeting at the Los Angeles Open to address the gathering storm. McIlroy, a member of the PAC, stood up and announced, "This is easy, either you are about money or you are about legacy." That would become Monahan's rallying cry. The following week, at the WGC-Mexico Championship, McIlroy expanded on his thoughts to reporters: "Money is cheap. Money is the easy part. That shouldn't be the driving factor. The more I've thought about [the PGL], the more I don't like it. The one thing as a professional golfer in my position that I value is that I have autonomy and freedom over everything I do. If you go and play this other golf league, you're not going to have that choice." McIlroy also referenced Arnold Palmer renouncing Greg Norman's attempts to launch a big-money world tour in 1994 that would have been funded by the Shark's fellow Australian iconoclast, Rupert Murdoch. McIlroy said that, like Palmer, he wanted "to be on the right side of history." Norman had been courting Al-Rumayyan for years; he served as the keynote speaker at the golf summit at the tainted 2019 Saudi International, which was played just three months after Jamaal Khashoggi's assassination. Norman saw all that oil money as a way to launch his world tour three decades after the idea had been crushed and he was turned into a pariah by Monahan's predecessor, Tim Finchem. Still bitter after all these years, Norman fired off a pithy text message to McIlroy upon reading the Palmer reference. Said McIlroy, "We had a pretty testy back-and-forth and he was very condescending. 'Maybe one day you'll understand' and all this shite."

Their war of words would only intensify. McIlroy had spent the 2010s merely winning and losing golf tournaments. Now he was taking on a far more fraught role: ambassador for the PGA Tour and, to many, the entire sport.

15.

When COVID shut down the world in March 2020, Rory McIlroy was happy to hunker down at home in Florida with his wife, Erica. It was a precious time in their lives because Erica was pregnant with their first child. Instead of being a road warrior, Rory was able to dote on his wife around the house and help with all the preparations for the baby.

Tournament golf resumed in June 2020. As a perennial fan favorite, McIlroy felt flat and disengaged playing without crowds. He finally found a spark at the U.S. Open in September, opening with a 67 to put himself in a tie for fifth, only two strokes off Justin Thomas's lead. But McIlroy blew up on Friday with a 76, ending his chances at victory. Adam Scott, his playing partner for the first two rounds at Winged Foot Golf Club, saw a larger pattern in the wild swings in McIlroy's scores at the major championships, where the course setups are more exacting and there is a steeper toll for mistakes. "To play at the top level, you live right on the edge," Scott says, "especially with his style of play. When Rory's on, no one's beating that. And then if he's a bit off, he pays a big price because of the speed he generates—just a little bit off and the ball is gone. At the U.S. Open, the penalty is extra severe. But it's a worthwhile trade-off, because it's his aggression and his speed that have allowed him to win so much."

Pádraig Harrington makes a similar point in his imitable way: "Think of penalty kicks in football, or what you people call soccer. I would choose five players to take those penalties who want to score over five players who don't want to miss. It's a different mentality. No doubt, there is risk involved; the players who aren't afraid to score might very well miss the target completely, but they are also the ones who are going to win you the game. The problem is, in a high-pressure situation, if a player misses the goal, he's the one who's hung out in the papers the next day. Whereas if another player hits an average penalty kick and it's saved, he doesn't get hung out—we celebrate the keeper! So it's safer to try an average kick than to try to be extraordinary, but you're going to win a lot less. I think it's pretty obvious which personality Rory is."

Okay, but after all these years, shouldn't McIlroy have learned how to throttle back on his off days and turn that 76 at Winged Foot into a 72 and keep himself in the tournament?

"Yeah, but very few guys are given it all, right?" says Scott. "Tiger was kind of that guy, although maybe it's unfair to say he was given it all—he was given so much and then he worked on all the rest. And maybe Rory hasn't worked on all the other departments to be a force like Tiger was. It could be an issue of course management or, you know, people criticize his wedges at times. For all of us, and even Rory, there's always something that is holding you back when you're not winning."

At Winged Foot, yet another young stud arrived. (A month earlier, twenty-two-year-old Collin Morikawa prevailed at the PGA Championship at Harding Park.) Bryson DeChambeau, twenty-seven, had spent the quarantine months consuming ungodly amounts of calories; a typical day of grazing included a half dozen eggs, a heaping serving of bacon, six to eight pieces of toast, a few peanut-butter-and-jelly sandwiches, a handful of granola bars, an enormous steak, a bag of potatoes, eight protein shakes, and various snacks. He also put in countless hours in the gym. He emerged as a bloated menace and then dominated the U.S. Open by utterly overpowering Winged Foot, which previously had been considered a monster. McIlroy was unmoored by DeChambeau's game-changing bomb-and-gouge style of play. "It's the complete opposite of what you think a U.S. Open champion does," he said. "It's kind of hard to wrap my head around it."

McIlroy was still trying to steady himself when he arrived at the November Masters. Even with the date change, he continued his long-standing tradition of first-round self-immolations. "I honestly have been playing so good coming in here," McIlroy said, "and then I go into the first round and I shoot 75, and I'm like, *Where the hell did that come from?*" His long-hitting playing partner over the first two rounds, Dustin Johnson, torched Augusta National to the tune of 20-under to nab the green jacket, the culmination of a four-year run during which D.J. won fourteen tournaments and spent 134 weeks atop the World Ranking, where McIlroy used to dwell.

After his winless 2020, McIlroy resolved to chase distance gains à la DeChambeau (though it would be months before he admitted publicly that the beefy Bryson influenced him). Throughout his career, McIlroy had changed caddies, agents, houses, kits, hairdos, irons, drivers, putters, putting coaches, and significant others . . . but he always had the good sense not to mess with the gift from the gods that was his golf swing. At McIlroy's Open Championship debut in 2007, when he was still an amateur, Sir Michael Bonallack came out to watch him play a few holes. Bonallack was himself a decorated amateur who served as both the secretary and captain of the R&A. Drawing on a lifetime of being around high-level golf, he sought out McIlroy's swing coach, Michael Bannon, and delivered a stern message: "Don't let anyone change him. Ever." Yes, McIlroy and Bannon made little tweaks and refinements through the years, but both love to say that Rory has had the same swing since he was a teen. Now, with his drought in the major championships having reached six long years, McIlroy, thirty-one, was desperate for reinvention. His length off the tee had always been his superpower, but that advantage had eroded with the arrival of a new generation of ball-bashers. McIlroy seized on a simple formula: a faster backswing led to a faster downswing, which led to longer drives. He spent the run-up to the 2021 season ingraining more violence in his transition. It worked, as he picked up some ten yards off the tee. But he also fell into the bad habit of taking the club too far to the inside on the backswing, which would lead to it getting trapped behind his body on the downswing. The result was wilder misses with the driver and more inconsistency with his irons. McIlroy finished tenth at the 2021 Arnold Palmer Invitational but sounded lost afterward, saying, "There were some good parts this week, some stuff that I don't know how to describe." He admitted to being "just a little dejected." Then he went to the Players Championship and reached the first of a few breaking points. After a first-round 79, McIlroy retreated to the driving range searching for answers. Bannon had been marooned in Ireland due to COVID-related travel restrictions. McIlroy spied on the Bay Hill Club range another swing coach, Pete Cowen, whom he had known since he was thirteen. He beseeched Cowen to give him a lifeline. They spent the next two days hitting mountains of practice balls, working on stabilizing the clubface and finding a more consistent ball flight. A week later, *The Daily Telegraph* had the scoop that Cowen was McIlroy's new swing coach, which came as news to Bannon. "It wasn't handled well," says McIlroy. "It got out before I spoke to Michael, which is pretty shite actually . . . I felt ashamed that I was going down this other path and didn't want to confront that part of it. I basically didn't have the balls to ring Michael and say, 'Look, this is what I'm doing.' That's what it came down to. And thankfully, he's a good man and he understood, but it was a weird period . . . It was a difficult conversation, like telling your wife you want to live in different houses for a bit."

McIlroy's next start came at the WGC Match Play in Austin, where he lost his first-round match. "Yeah, I was beaten by Poulter—fucking hell!" says McIlroy. "That was a low point." But not the nadir; next time out, he shot 76-74 to miss the cut at the Masters. McIlroy kept scuffling. He broke par only once in four rounds at the 2021 Open Championship, finishing a ho-hum forty-sixth. That left him fifteen shots behind Morikawa, who outdueled Jordan Spieth to win his second major championship in six tries. Since McIlroy had won his last major, he had witnessed the rise of Spieth, Koepka, D.J., DeChambeau, Justin Thomas (who won the '21 Players Championship, his thirteenth win in the span of four years), Jon Rahm (who reached world number one *before* winning the '21 U.S. Open), and now Morikawa. In the locker room at St. George's, McIlroy finally voiced to his manager, Sean O'Flaherty, his deepest, darkest fear: "Maybe I'm just not that good anymore and the competition has got better."

A month after the Open, McIlroy suffered a high-profile disappointment when he lost a playoff for the bronze medal at the Tokyo Olympics. (Along the way, he had yet another change of heart, saying, "I've never tried so hard to finish third.") McIlroy's confidence was at an all-time low as he arrived at the 2021 Ryder Cup at Whistling Straits. He spent the practice rounds grinding on mechanics with Cowen, which only left him feeling more bewildered. In the Friday morning foursomes, McIlroy and Ian Poulter got smoked 5 and 3 by Xander Schauffele and Patrick Cantlay. That afternoon, Rory was given the responsibility of shepherding Ryder rookie Shane Lowry, with whom he had a bond dating back to their teenage years with the Golfing Union of Ireland. But McIlroy struggled badly in a 4 and 3 loss to the inferior duo of Tony Finau and Harris English. Rory felt like he had let down the entire Irish island, to say nothing of the rest of the continent. In an act of mercy, European captain Pádraig Harrington sat McIlroy for the Saturday morning foursomes—the first time in five Ryder Cups he had been benched for a session. The vanishing act of their team leader further demoralized the Europeans: they lost three of four points in the session as the U.S. extended its lead to 9–3. Then McIlroy and Poulter got trashed again in the afternoon four-balls, 4 and 3, to Morikawa and Dustin Johnson. Along the way, the player who had screamed his head off versus Patrick Reed looked strangely flat and disengaged. Europe trailed 11–5 heading into singles, and McIlroy had hit rock bottom.

It took a couple of Irishmen to change everything.

Harrington sent out McIlroy first in singles, an audacious showing of confidence. "He needed a spark and the team needed a spark," says Harrington. "I needed him to know I still believed in him. That the whole team did." Before the singles matches began, Lowry sought out his old comrade in the locker room. Their friendship had come a long way in the preceding two years. One of the reasons McIlroy jilted his agent Chubby Chandler in 2011 and went to Conor Ridge's Horizon Sports was the lure of being stablemates with Lowry (and Graeme McDowell). Lowry got caught in the cross fire once McIlroy and Ridge started suing each other; an old friendship nearly died. But two months before the '19 Ryder Cup, Lowry had united the Irish island by winning the Open Championship at Royal Portrush. A celebratory couples dinner ensued; Erica McIlroy and Wendy Lowry hit it off so famously that their hubbies were forced to become chummy again. Now, at the Ryder Cup, Shane was there for Rory when he needed him most, with a pep talk for the ages: "You just need to remember who you are. You're Rory McIlroy. You're one of the greatest players of all time and you're not even close to being finished yet."

In his singles match versus Schauffele, McIlroy let go of any technical thoughts and finally accessed his genius. He rolled to a 3 and 2 victory, but it wasn't nearly enough as Europe lost the Ryder Cup. When it was over, McIlroy broke down in tears in interviews with the BBC and NBC, crushed from having let down his teammates (and the accumulated strain of the season). "I'm incredibly proud to be part of this team," he said on the NBC telecast between sniffles. "The more and more I play in this event, I realize it's the best event in golf, bar none. I don't think there's any greater privilege than to be part of one of these teams. I've gotten to do this six times, and they've always been the greatest experiences of my career. I have never really cried or gotten emotional over what I've done as an individual. I couldn't give a shit. But this team . . . is phenomenal, and I'm so happy to be part of it." He ended the interview by apologizing for his profanity.

Whistling Straits marked the end of the Cowen experiment. McIlroy and Bannon reunited and immediately went back to the basics. "Michael does a great job in keeping Rory grounded," says Paul Gray, the general manager at Holywood Golf Club during McIlroy's teen years. "He is brilliant at that. Everybody sees Michael as Rory's swing coach but he is actually a coach in the most holistic sense of the word. You had someone like David Leadbetter with Nick Faldo, very focused on technique and that would probably be the extent of his coaching. With Michael it is very much also about life, what Rory needs to focus on in his life to make it good."

Gerry McIlroy goes even further, saying, "He knows Rory's whole personality, his golf game, inside out. I would even say Michael knows Rory as well as I do."

Three weeks after the Ryder Cup, McIlroy turned up at the Tour stop in Las Vegas with only one swing thought: to have no swing thoughts. He played with a clear mind and his old freedom, and the birdies inexorably followed. His 62-65 weekend carried McIlroy to his twentieth PGA Tour victory. That is a monumental number: only thirty-nine players in the long history of the Tour have won twenty or more times, and only two from the post-Tiger generation: McIlroy and Dustin Johnson. With all the young talent dominating the headlines, McIlroy's milestone win served as a needed reminder of his tremendous body of work. He wasn't back, exactly—he had never gone away. But Whistling Straits/Vegas was the fulcrum on which the second act of McIlroy's career turned.

Of course, with Rory there will always be melodrama. McIlroy took a one-stroke lead into the final round of the European Tour's season-ending event, putting him in prime position to win the Race to Dubai for a fourth time. But he bogeyed three of the final four holes to gift the tournament to Morikawa, who became the first American to win the Race to Dubai. McIlroy was so frustrated with his sloppy play that he tried to tear his polo off his torso in the scoring tent as if he were Magic Mike. Photos of the aftermath went around the world, with McIlroy still wearing his tattered shirt, one nipple on full display. It was funny and ridiculous, but also meaningful. McIlroy had been mostly flatlined for the better part of two seasons. Hey, good to know he still cared!

•

THE BUSINESS OF PROFESSIONAL golf was being reshaped throughout 2021, even if few people knew it. The Saudis were working both sides of the street, trying to partner with both the PGA Tour and the European Tour. In April 2021, Golf Saudi's Majed Al-Sorour sent an enigmatic letter to PGA Tour commissioner Jay Monahan, writing, "I want to introduce you to our proposition and outline its value as a prospective partner of the PGA Tour. We are proposing an innovative league featuring twelve 'teams' of top talent competing head-to-head over 14 weeks, creating a new dimension for sports and stakeholders . . . It is possible that the league should be operated on a schedule that is largely complementary to the PGA Tour. With the positive responses we have received, we have chartered our course to launch in 2022." The formal language did not disguise the inherent threat: *We are doing this with or without you.* Monahan never responded to Al-Sorour, creating one of golf's all-time what-ifs. But the commish, a former college hockey player, did not take kindly to the Saudis' threat. He raised the stakes in a subsequent Tour board meeting, declaring, "We are at war. We do not negotiate with another entity that is trying to put us out of business. We do not negotiate with people who are trying to ruin the golf ecosystem."

Simultaneously, the European Tour's leadership spent months examining and debating a bid to merge with the PGL to create a supertour funded in part by the Saudis. That would have offered real competition to the PGA Tour, but Monahan swooped in to kill the deal. "Jay came in heavy," says Paul McGinley, then a member of the Euro Tour's board of directors. "He showed us the color of his eyes." Afraid of being aced out of the new world order, the PGL's Andy Gardiner pivoted to wooing the PGA Tour. In October 2021, Gardiner sent a letter to McIlroy, the chairman of the Player Advisory Council who was about to join the Tour's board of directors. (The PAC has no real authority but builds consensus and makes recommendations to the board, which sets policy in concert with the commissioner.) The PGL proposed a partnership in which it would commit 75 percent of its equity to become co-sanctioned as part of a redesigned PGA Tour schedule, with 50 percent of the equity being distributed to PGA Tour players, 7.5 percent to Korn Ferry Tour members, and 2.5 percent to European Tour players. The proposal optimistically stated that the PGL would generate $10 billion of equity value by 2030, which would mean roughly $20 million to each of the two hundred or so PGA Tour members and $3 million to all the Korn Ferry Tour dreamers living on the margins of professional golf. More immediately, the PGL offered to pay a cash advance of $460 million—thanks, Yasir!—upon the launch of the PGL, equating to $2 million for each PGA Tour player and $300,000 for the approximately two hundred Korn Ferry Tour members.

McIlroy was all ears.

"In my role as PAC chairman and now on the Policy Board, I have to think of those guys that are down at the bottom, right?" he said in late 2021. "I'm not doing a good job for the players if I don't bring that to the attention of the Tour and be like, *Just sit down and listen to this guy, do something* . . . If someone comes along and says I think I can create this amount of revenue and distribute it among every player, you have to listen to that, right? Because again, that's my responsibility to all the players who voted me into this position."

In November 2021, Monahan forged a "strategic alliance" with the European Tour. The PGA Tour paid $100 million in cash to buy 15 percent of European Tour Productions, a quiet moneymaker that produces tournament coverage for more than two hundred countries. The PGL was dead in the water, which seemed like a spectacular political victory for Monahan. But this reshaping of the golf landscape had an unintended and far-reaching consequence: Al-Rumayyan realized that earning a seat at the table would not be possible through partnership or compromise. No, the Saudis would have to buy it with the crushing weight of their money.

McIlroy's rebirth culminated, surprisingly, in a tournament he did not win: the 2022 Masters. This marked his eighth attempt to consummate the career Grand Slam, a storyline that had grown increasingly tiresome for all involved, particularly McIlroy. He downplayed the quest for the Slam, saying, "I'm maybe at a different stage of my life where back then golf was everything." What McIlroy was most looking forward to this time around was his daughter, Poppy, taking part in her first Par 3 Contest on the eve of the tournament proper. As for the golf itself, McIlroy sounded ready to finally capitulate and play more cautiously: "It feels like playing very negatively, playing away from trouble, not firing at flagsticks, not being aggressive. It feels like a negative game plan, but it's not. It's just a smart game plan. It's playing the percentages. You just have to stay as disciplined as possible. To me, yeah, that goes against my nature a little bit, so it is something I have to really work hard on. That's what this place is all about. It's as much of a chess game as anything else, and it's just about putting yourself in the right positions and being disciplined and being patient."

Alas, McIlroy got off to his usual sluggish start (73-73), which left him ten strokes behind leader Scottie Scheffler. The good news was that Rory had his struggles in each round but always battled back. On Friday, he pulled an approach shot into the pond on the eleventh hole, leading to a double bogey, but rallied with two subsequent birdies. The larger perspective that came with fatherhood had its limits; asked if post-round hugs from his daughter made such gaffes less painful, McIlroy showed a refreshing honesty: "I'd like to say yes, but no. I'd like to say, *Yeah, it's lovely.* No, I'm still playing with Poppy and thinking about the 6-iron on eleven. So I'd love to say yes, but no."

McIlroy shot 71 during a frigid, windy third round, a score bettered by only two players. That propelled him into a tie for ninth, but he was still ten strokes adrift of Scheffler, who entered 2022 winless on Tour but was riding a surge of confidence from his stellar play at the Ryder Cup at Whistling Straits. Scheffler busted loose for three victories in the run-up to the Masters, and his precise iron play and unflappable demeanor were tailor-made for Augusta National. McIlroy's audacious goal for the final round was to shoot 63 and put a scare into Scheffler. McIlroy hit it to eight feet on the first hole for an auspicious birdie. He drove it to the edge of the green on three and two-putted for another bird. A big-breaking thirty-footer on seven was followed by a nifty wedge on eight. McIlroy had surged into third place, and the crowd was with him. Then he chipped in on ten. And flagged a mid-iron into thirteen. When that eagle putt dropped, McIlroy couldn't hold back a fist pump. He was only four strokes back with Scheffler about to face the eleventh and twelfth holes, the scariest ones on the golf course. But Scheffler parred them both and then birdied the fourteenth and fifteenth holes, sealing the deal. As McIlroy walked up the eighteenth fairway, the fans still rose as one to salute his spirited play. From the greenside bunker, he played a shot to the top of the ridge that bisected the green, feeding his ball down the slope. The crowd roared as it trickled toward the hole. When the ball disappeared into the hole, McIlroy flung his club and did an awkward two-armed celebration that looked a little like Michael Phelps performing the butterfly. McIlroy's 64 was one shot off the course record held by Greg Norman, among others. He was practically giddy afterward, saying, "It's what you dream about, right? You dream about getting yourself in position. I wasn't quite close enough to the lead, I don't think. To play as well as I did today and then to finish like this, I mean, it's just absolutely incredible. This tournament never ceases to amaze. Yeah, that's as happy as I've ever been on a golf course right there."

McIlroy's solo second was his best finish in a major championship in eight years. It was the first time he had mattered on a Grand Slam Sunday since the 2018 Open Championship. He would later admit that this fallow stretch was a kind of self-protection. "At a certain point in someone's life, someone doesn't want to fall in love because they don't want to get their heart broken," McIlroy said. "I think instinctually, as human beings, we hold back sometimes because of the fear of getting hurt, whether that's a conscious decision or subconscious decision, and I think I was doing that on the golf course a little bit for a few years. But I think once you go through that, once you go through those heartbreaks, as I call them, or disappointments, you get to a place where you remember how it feels, and you wake up the next day and you're like, *Yeah, life goes on, it's not as bad as I thought it was going to be.* You dust yourself off and you go again." Wise words . . . but he had no way of knowing the anguish that awaited.

16.

Having been rebuffed by the PGA and European Tours, Yasir Al-Rumayyan decided to start his own golf circuit to compete with the old guard, essentially cutting and pasting all the details of the PGL. In October 2021, Al-Rumayyan hired Greg Norman to serve as the front man of the nascent LIV Golf, a provocative choice given that the Shark had been a pariah ever since trying to launch a world tour to compete against the PGA Tour in the early '90s. "What Norman did with the world tour amounted to insurrection," says former PGA Tour commissioner Deane Beman. "The PGA Tour gave him a platform to become an international star and make more money than he ever dreamed of, and he tried to tear it down. Those of us who love the Tour, who helped build it; the players who supported it and benefited from it all these years—we will never forget, and we will never forgive." Making Norman the figurehead of whatever the Saudis were scheming wasn't merely a hiring; it was a declaration of war. "They could not possibly have selected a more divisive, controversial, or, frankly, disliked figure than Greg Norman," says Beman. "It was a very clear signal that they did not want to work within the existing structures of professional golf."

Throughout late 2021 and early 2022, the Saudis began secretly wooing top players with barrels of money. Phil Mickelson was in the middle of everything, as always. He had been helping Al-Rumayyan organize his new tour while simultaneously trying to gain concessions from PGA Tour commissioner Jay Monahan, just in case Mickelson spurned the Saudis.

Phil the Thrill had spent his career jousting with Tour leadership—mostly being rebuffed—and now he was pushing for sweeping change, demanding more money for the players and that they be given more control over their media rights and Tour governance. In February 2022, during the week of the Los Angeles Open, an excerpt dropped from *Phil*, my biography of Mickelson. Just before I sent the manuscript to the publisher, Lefty had called me and laid out the state of play with breathtaking candor. He admitted that the new Saudi circuit was nothing more than what he called "sportswashing" by a brutally repressive regime. "They're scary motherfuckers to get involved with," Mickelson said. "We know they killed [Jamal] Khashoggi and have a horrible record on human rights. They execute people over there for being gay. Knowing all of this, why would I even consider it? Because this is a once-in-a-lifetime opportunity to reshape how the PGA Tour operates. They've been able to get by with manipulative, coercive, strong-arm tactics because we, the players, had no recourse. As nice a guy as [Monahan] comes across as, unless you have leverage, he won't do what's right. And the Saudi money has finally given us that leverage. I'm not sure I even want [LIV Golf] to succeed, but just the idea of it is allowing us to get things done with the Tour."

Was Mickelson really willing to blow up the PGA Tour if he didn't get his way? "I know twenty guys who want to do this," he said of the Saudis' breakaway league, "and if the Tour doesn't do the right thing, there is a high likelihood it's going to happen."

Mickelson's quotes rocked the sports world. Among all the players at the L.A. Open, it was McIlroy who offered the most forceful response. "I don't want to kick someone while he's down," he said, winding up like David Beckham, "but I thought they were naive, selfish, egotistical, ignorant—a lot of words to describe that interaction he had with Shipnuck. It was just very surprising and disappointing. Sad."

Amid the blowback, top players who had been in deep negotiations with the Saudis—including Dustin Johnson, Brooks Koepka, and

Bryson DeChambeau—offered very public repudiations. McIlroy captured the prevailing feeling at Riviera Country Club when he asked, "Who's left? Who's left to go? I mean, there's no one. It's dead in the water, in my opinion. I just can't see any reason why anyone would go. I mean, Greg Norman would have to tee it up to fill the field. Like, I mean, seriously? I mean, who else is going to do it? I don't think they could get forty-eight guys." This was hardly the last time McIlroy would be wildly off the mark when it came to LIV Golf.

Al-Rumayyan did, in fact, purchase the services of forty-eight players, and LIV launched to much fanfare in June 2022, during the week of the Canadian Open. Former Masters champ Charl Schwartzel won the inaugural LIV Golf London and its $4 million first-place check. In Canada, McIlroy and Justin Thomas offered a rousing rebuttal with four-plus hours of riveting golf as they battled for an old, proud national championship. The winner would earn less than a third of Schwartzel's haul, but Rory and J.T. radiated a palpable hunger to put on a good show for their embattled tour. After McIlroy dropped a 62 to surge to victory, he couldn't resist taking a shot at Norman, telling the world, "The guy that's spearheading that other tour has twenty wins on the PGA Tour, and I was tied with him and I wanted to get one ahead of him. And I did."

The feud had heated up that spring, after McIlroy watched a documentary about the Shark's collapse at the 1996 Masters. Fifteen years later, McIlroy blew his own big lead on Sunday at Augusta. In the days after, Norman had reached McIlroy by phone and offered a heartfelt pep talk. Those good feelings were rekindled as McIlroy watched the documentary, after which he sent Norman a text: "Hopefully it reminds everyone of what a great golfer you were. Watching it reminded me of how you reached out to me in 2011, and I just want to say that I'll always appreciate it. It meant a lot. I know our opinion on the game of golf right now is very different, but I just wanted you to know that and wish you all the best."

Norman replied, "I really think golf can be a force for good around the world. I know our opinions are not aligned, but I'm just trying to create more opportunities for every golfer around the world."

"Fine. Really nice," McIlroy says, picking up the tale. "Then, a couple of weeks later, he does an interview with *The Washington Post* and says I've been 'brainwashed by the PGA Tour.' We've had this really nice back-and-forth, and he says that about me. I thought, 'You know what? I'm going to make it my business now to be as much of a pain in his arse as possible.'" It is amusing and telling that McIlroy's relentless campaign against LIV and Norman stemmed from a fit of pique.

A month after his triumph at the Canadian Open, McIlroy rolled into St. Andrews. There was much fanfare around the 150th playing of the Open Championship, and it had even more resonance for McIlroy, given that he had missed the previous Open on the Old Course after injuring himself playing soccer. On the eve of the tournament, the R&A hosted the "Celebration of Champions," in which past winners at St. Andrews played a four-hole exhibition. "Tiger and I knew we wanted to play together," says McIlroy, "so we were like, 'Who do we get to play with us?' I mean, how cool was that? You know, to get to know your childhood hero pretty intimately; to be awarded honorary membership of the oldest golf club in the world at the same time; to be standing on the first tee at St. Andrews with Trevino and Jack Nicklaus and [2018 Women's British Open champ] Georgia Hall . . . I was like, 'Fuck me! This is my life! This is so cool.'"

Inevitably, the ill feelings created by LIV seeped into Open week. Norman, a two-time winner of the Claret Jug, was pointedly not invited to the Celebration of Champions. Mickelson, the 2013 Open champ, was made to feel so unwelcome that he chose not to play. Even more hurtful to Phil was his snub from a private dinner for Open winners held in the R&A clubhouse. Tiger Woods orchestrated that. "He talked to a handful of other [past champions] to get their blessing and then went to the R&A and told them, basically, no one wanted Phil there and it would make the night weird and awkward," says one of the men at the dinner. "Whose side were they going to take, Tiger's or Phil's? That's an easy choice."

The rumors grew louder throughout Open week as to which players would be next to jump to LIV. One name kept coming up: Cameron Smith, the vastly talented twenty-eight-year-old Aussie who four months earlier had won the PGA Tour's flagship event, the Players Championship. Smith didn't exactly quell the loose talk when, during one of the practice rounds, he jogged across the first fairway to crash a photo op of LIV players on the Swilcan Bridge. He remained the center of attention after a first-round 67, tying him for third, four shots behind the leader, Cameron Young, a young slugger from New York. McIlroy was alone in second with a 66.

McIlroy followed with a 68 and then during the third round shot a scintillating 66, including a hole-out from the greenside bunker on the par-4 tenth hole for an eagle that gave him the outright lead. It was a highlight moment that felt destined to go down as the keynote shot of the championship. Through fifty-four holes, McIlroy was tied for the lead at 16-under with young Viktor Hovland, four strokes clear of their nearest pursuers. In one fell swoop, McIlroy was going to win the 150th Open Championship, end his brutal eight-year drought in the majors, and singlehandedly thwart the Saudis. He could not shy away from the magnitude of the moment. "It's what dreams are made of," McIlroy said. "And I'm going to try to make a dream come true tomorrow."

On Saturday night at the Rusacks St. Andrews hotel, McIlroy's father, Gerry, ducked into an elevator carrying a pizza. "He's playing beautifully," a reporter said to him. "It would be good to see him finish this off."

"Aye, it would be good for the game," Gerry replied, neatly summarizing the larger storyline.

The magnitude could be felt the next afternoon on the first tee. Rory's expression was impassive, but as he played his opening drive, a baby-faced standard-bearer stood at the edge of the tee box, struggling to keep his sign steady. It wasn't the wind. "My hands were shaking," the kid said a few minutes later. "I don't know why I'm so nervous, but I am." The whole golf world was equally aflutter. Rarely had a man and a moment seemed so perfectly aligned. Following McIlroy's group, in tartan pants, was Jamie Weir, the Sky Sports reporter from Northern Ireland whose sister had gone to school with McIlroy. He did not try to hide his partisan interest. "In my entire life, I've never wanted any outcome at any sporting event as much as I want Rory to win this," Weir said. He had nothing on the kid in the gallery carrying a handmade sign that said RORY, I'M NAMED AFTER YOU!

But across the front nine, McIlroy looked tense and edgy, and his discomfort showed on the greens as he squandered numerous scoring chances. Hovland retreated, ceding the chase to the two Camerons playing in the group ahead: Young, who wields his driver like a sledgehammer, and Smith, the relentless Aussie whose genius with the wedge and putter threw into sharp relief McIlroy's shortcomings. While Rory was sizing up a hundred-foot eagle putt on the tenth hole, Smith was rolling in a sixteen-footer on eleven for a birdie that momentarily sliced the lead to a lone stroke. But McIlroy deftly cozied his putt to tap-in distance for a much-needed birdie, pushing to 18-under. The crowd released two hours of bottled-up tension with the loudest roar of the day.

"I never let myself believe until a brief moment on Sunday," McIlroy says. "Then I birdied the 10th and I've a [2-shot] lead. That was the moment: 'Don't do anything stupid and you've got this.'" McIlroy had yet to miss a green in regulation and still had two very short par-4s (holes twelve and eighteen) and a par-5 (fourteen) coming. It felt as though he already had one hand on the Claret Jug. At the farthest point from town, the mood was festive, trending toward giddy. But Smith just kept coming, raining in birdies on ten, eleven, and twelve to slice the lead to one stroke. McIlroy drove just short of the green at the twelfth but was a touch timid with his pitch. His twelve-footer was never on line, squandering a prime birdie chance. Smith made another birdie on thirteen to snatch a share of the lead. Then he birdied fourteen to go up by one stroke. A mediocre pitch saddled McIlroy with a par at fourteen, one of only two par-5s on the Old Course. As he reached the fifteenth tee, there were the familiar cries of "Let's go, Rory!"—but the tone had curdled. It was now plaintive, even desperate. Sitting cross-legged under the rope line on the fifteenth tee were a half dozen little boys. Their eyes never left McIlroy. His drive peeled toward the left rough, and the crowd murmured its concern. In the quiet, one of the boys said softly, "You can do it, Rory." It was touching in its tenderness. McIlroy slashed his ball out of the long grass, but it trickled forty feet too far. He missed the birdie putt and was now running out of holes.

After a sloppy wedge at sixteen, McIlroy was doomed to another par when he was desperate for a birdie. McIlroy stuffed his approach to eight feet on the Road Hole. The massive grandstand let out a roar that echoed throughout Fife. It would have been instantly iconic had McIlroy birdied the Road Hole and gone on to win . . . but he made a tentative stroke and missed the putt. He trudged to the eighteenth tee and watched in the distance as the Camerons putted on the final green. Whistling and buzzing accompanied Young's eagle, which momentarily tied him with Smith, one shot ahead of McIlroy. From a thousand feet away, it was hard to tell how short Smith's birdie attempt was, but the ball rolled for only a split second before disappearing. The denouement was stunning in its swiftness. Seven holes earlier, McIlroy had led by two strokes. Now he was down two and needed a miracle at eighteen, which would not come. Smith had shot 64—including a back-nine 30—while McIlroy had made only two birdies and labored to a 70 in ideal scoring conditions.

Afterward, he put on a good show for the cameras. McIlroy had hit all eighteen greens in regulation but, in hindsight, he said he had been too conservative in his game plan and timid with the flatstick—he took thirty-six putts in the final round. He rued his inability to execute a handful of crucial up-and-downs. He offered the big-picture perspective that, if he kept putting himself in position to win at the biggest tournaments, he would certainly break through soon. It was a brave performance.

After the media obligations mercifully ended, McIlroy slid into the second row of a golf cart, next to his wife. As they drove into the night, he buried his face in Erica's shoulder and wept.

ONCE AGAIN, MCILROY KEPT marching forward despite the crushing disappointment. A month after the Open, during the first round of the Tour Championship, he triple-bogeyed the first hole and bogeyed the second. Two holes into the tournament, he was ten strokes behind Scottie Scheffler due to the tournament's weighted leaderboard. But McIlroy kept grinding and, by Sunday, he had played his way into the final group, though he was still six shots back of Scheffler. After a flawless start, he had reeled in Scheffler by the eighth tee. Then McIlroy landed a knockout blow with a thirty-two-foot birdie on the fifteenth hole. When the putt dropped, McIlroy pumped his fist and screamed, "Come on!"

The lustiness of the celebration was a far cry from the stoicism McIlroy had embraced a few years earlier as a form of self-protection. McIlroy had recommitted to working with Bob Rotella throughout 2022, because, says Rotella, "he wanted to do what he had dreamed of always doing." Rotella encouraged McIlroy to be more emotive on the golf course. "Being stoic is almost like not being human," says Rotella. "When you want something badly, the emotions can be so powerful—you need to learn to harness them, not shut them off. Because Rory is so darn good at golf, his tendency when he hit a great shot was to have no reaction, because, in his mind, that's what he's supposed to do. Anything less than great, he would get upset and frustrated. That's backward of what it should be. You have to enjoy the good ones and have no reaction to the bad ones."

McIlroy locked up the Tour Championship victory with a crucial par save of eight feet on the sixteenth hole, punctuating a week of superb work on the greens: he made 116 feet of putts during the final round and, for the tournament, was second in strokes gained putting (and first in driving distance, a potent combination). McIlroy became the only player to win the FedEx Cup three times. "It's in some ways fitting that I was able to get this done today to sort of round off a year that has been very, very challenging and different," he said. "I know that my best stuff is good enough to win any tournament against anybody on any golf course. That's something I can take away from today."

The challenges McIlroy alluded to were partly of his own making, as he had gleefully emerged as the leading troll of LIV Golf. In addition to his high-profile sniping with Greg Norman, McIlroy called Brooks Koepka "duplicitous" for going to LIV after having previously disavowed it. During the week of the Tour Championship, with the cameras rolling for the docuseries *Full Swing*, McIlroy had this to say about Monsieur Mickelson: "Fuck you, Phil." This made the rounds in golf circles long before it was broadcast on Netflix. McIlroy had served as a groomsman in Sergio García's wedding, but the hot-blooded Spaniard grew tired of his friend's criticism of LIV and told him as much in a text message around the time of the U.S. Open. "I was pretty offended," says McIlroy, "and sent him back a couple of daggers, and that was it." A fifteen-year friendship was kaput. The antipathy toward McIlroy from LIV Golf was summed up by one of the tour's senior executives, who described Rory to me as "that little bitch." Says David Feherty, the Northern Irish TV commentator who went to LIV in July '22, "People were mad at him. I won't lie, I felt awkward about it. I want to defend him always, but it hasn't been easy. I don't know why he made it so personal." McIlroy was well aware of this juju, and it helped explain his superb play throughout 2022. "I had dinner with him," says Adam Scott, "and asked how he was playing so well with these distractions, and he said all the controversy is motivating him to play his best. He feels like he has put his reputation on the line, and the most effective way to defend himself is to win golf tournaments."

McIlroy's impact was felt on and off the course throughout the summer of '22. The highfalutin rhetoric about legacy versus leverage, and Jay Monahan's villainizing of the Saudis, did nothing to stanch the exodus of high-profile players from the PGA Tour to LIV Golf. If the Tour was going to fend off LIV's incursion, it would need to fight dollars with dollars. In June 2022, at the J. P. McManus Pro-Am (which draws top players for an exhibition due to the golfers' affection for the host), McIlroy and Tiger Woods called a pair of meetings with their colleagues to plot a reshaping of the Tour's business model. A consensus began to build: the Tour's leading men needed more money, of course, but the product would have to be refreshed. A bedrock principle in the Premier Golf League proposal, which LIV had put in practice, was that every player would compete in every tournament, ensuring more head-to-head clashes among the top talent. The bloated PGA Tour schedule made that impossible, but what if certain tournaments were structured with wildly elevated purses to be shared among a smaller pool of players? In exchange, all the top stars would be compelled to show up for each one, ensuring box office. "Obviously, it was big-idea stuff and pie in the sky, and not all the details were fleshed out," says McIlroy, "but at least it created a framework that we could work from."

McIlroy brought in an adviser, Colin Neville, the boardroom Zelig from Raine Group who led the Premier Golf League's unsuccessful negotiations with the European Tour. Because Raine had not lost any money when the PGL deal collapsed, Neville was happy to jump back into the fray, albeit for a different team. McIlroy, Woods, and Neville began having long phone calls to flesh out the details. Six weeks after the McManus Pro-Am, McIlroy and Woods convened a meeting of twenty-three top players at the BMW Championship to present their new vision for the Tour. There were sixty-eight players in the field at Wilmington Country Club in Delaware; two-thirds of them were not invited to the gathering. The FOMO raged. "Other players were texting me and asking if I was in the meeting and whatnot, and I didn't even know what they were talking about," says Tom Hoge. "It was a weird deal. It was kind of like high school, when the popular people throw a party and you're not invited."

McIlroy and Woods's plan formalized the notion of small-field, no-cut, guaranteed-money tournaments (sounds suspiciously like LIV, no?). The $20 million purses were a monumental pay raise: at that moment, the Tour conducted only four events with purses exceeding $12 million, and three-quarters of the tourneys were offering less than $9 million. (The PGA Tour does not operate the major championships.) There was an obvious downside to cleaving the Tour into the haves and have-mores: the non-elevated tournaments would wither and perhaps have difficulty attracting corporate sponsorship. But that was a concern for another day. To slow the momentum of LIV Golf, the PGA Tour needed to placate its most important players, and McIlroy helped forge the path forward. A week after the Delaware meeting, at the Tour Championship, Jay Monahan formally announced the creation of eight Signature Events with $20 million purses.

That wasn't the only big news to come out of that Tour Championship: McIlroy and Woods also publicly unveiled their Tomorrow's Golf League (TGL), in which teams of Tour players would compete on simulators in front of a live audience in an indoor arena in Orlando. The new concept had the full backing of the PGA Tour, which held a minority equity interest in TGL and was receiving a media release fee for its members' services. Whether the TGL succeeded as an entertainment product didn't really matter to the Tour; in the context of battling LIV, it was just another way to funnel money to the top players. With Tiger and Rory as cofounders, the TGL further intertwined their business interests with each other and the Tour.

Reshaping the future of professional golf together was a milestone in the McIlroy-Woods bromance. "What Rory has said and done is what leaders do," Tiger said. "Rory is a true leader out here on Tour. The fact that he's actually able to get the things he said out in the public eye, be so clear-minded with it and so eloquent with it, and to go out there and win golf tournaments on top of that? People have no idea how hard that is to do, to be able to separate those two things. Everyone respects him, and they respect him because of the person he is."

"I'm drawn to him, yeah," McIlroy says of Woods. "He's an intriguing character because you could spend two hours in his company and see four different sides to him. He's thoughtful. He's smart. He can't sleep so that's all he does—he reads stuff and educates himself on everything. But he struggles to sleep, which I think is an effect of overtraining, so I tell him to calm down sometimes. He'd be texting me at four o'clock in the morning: 'Up lifting. What are you doing?' Erica actually got pissed off with it. He was texting me in the middle of the night and I was like, 'Tiger is in the gym.'"

Their friendship had deepened in the wake of Woods's single-car crash in February 2021. He was in Southern California, having just served as the ceremonial host of the Genesis Invitational at Riviera Country Club while recovering from yet another back surgery. On that fateful Tuesday morning, Woods had to be up early to film content for *Golf Digest* at Rolling Hills Country Club. He was traveling east on a hilly, winding portion of Hawthorne Boulevard in Palos Verdes; the street curved right, but he went dead straight, plowing through the median, careening across the two oncoming lanes of traffic, hopping a curb, knocking down a wooden sign, plunging down an embankment, and smashing into a tree. "There were several rollovers during that process," said Los Angeles County Sheriff Alex Villanueva. Two days earlier, Woods had made a cameo in CBS's eighteenth-hole tower, sending shock waves through Golf Twitter with his glassy eyes, bloated face, and slurred speech—particularly troubling signs given his previous treatment for an addiction to painkillers. In the wake of the crash, Woods steadfastly refused to fill in any details, batting away questions by saying, "It's all in the police report." Indeed, it was: at the time of the crash, he was traveling an estimated eighty-four to eighty-seven miles per hour, more than double the speed limit in the residential area. The most troubling detail? The car's black box revealed that Woods had kept stepping on the accelerator throughout the crash and that the pressure applied to the pedal remained at 99 percent. That could not have happened if he had fallen asleep at the wheel or been momentarily distracted by his phone.

We will never know what darkness visited Woods in the moments before and during the car crash. But the ramifications were clear: having powderized the bones in his right foot, Woods, then forty-six, would never again be a serious contender. Rory visited Tiger while he was recuperating, the first time McIlroy had been inside his hero's home. Their reshaping of the Tour together gave Woods a purpose and the human connection he needed on the road back.

"Tiger has realized that he needs the Tour as much as it needs him," says Adam Scott. "As the game has been taken away from him [as a competitor], he needs new roles to play. It's nice to see that evolution, to be perfectly honest. Having played against him for my entire career, when he was this dominant force, you didn't know whether you'd get a hello out of the guy at times. You know what I mean? But what's nice to see is that Tiger obviously cares a lot about the PGA Tour and all of his fellow players. We've seen a more human side of the guy. That's kind of a relief, because he was a machine for so long."

Their status as cofounders of the TGL cemented the fact that McIlroy was now Woods's peer in every way, but even he's not immune to Tiger's cult of personality: "It's funny," McIlroy said, "I never in a million years thought that I would be in this position in particular, and in this position doing this stuff with Tiger Woods. I said to him the other day, I remember the first golf shot I ever saw him hit live [when I was fifteen]. It was the fifth hole at [the 2004 World Golf Championship at] Mount Juliet with my dad, and I watched him hit a drive off the fifth tee and a long iron into the middle of the green, a par-5. Tiger was my idol ever since I watched him play the 1996 U.S. Amateur. He has been an idol and a hero of mine over the years, and I feel pretty lucky that I've gotten to know him more intimately than some. And he is so passionate about what we're doing. He realizes that the PGA Tour gave him a platform to build his brand and let him be who he is, and he has tremendous respect for the people who have come before us. Having his influence and having his counsel, not just myself but all of the players on the PGA Tour, he's a great advocate to have, and it's awesome to be doing these things with him. I have to pinch myself pretty much every day that I'm in this position."

As Rory and Tiger emerged as the faces and voices of the Tour, they evoked the activism of Jack and Arnie as they led the 1968 rebellion to break away from the clueless bureaucracy of the PGA of America and form the modern Tour. There is more than a passing resemblance between these linked pairs of legends. Nicklaus and Palmer were born a decade apart, while Woods is thirteen years McIlroy's senior. On the golf course, Jack was tactical and Arnie daring, just as Tiger is a plodding strategist compared with the freewheeling Rory. The charismatic Palmer connected intensely with the fans in the same way McIlroy does, whereas Nicklaus and Woods have always been more remote figures. Tiger and Rory spent two years putting together TGL. A third cofounder, Mike McCarley, the former president of golf at NBC Sports Group, observed them closely and says this about the dynamic: "There is a mutual respect there. Tiger values Rory, and he listens to him. He certainly doesn't treat him like a little brother. Maybe a nephew."

Woods needed McIlroy, and he knew it. Tiger was rarely on Tour anymore, and the younger players barely knew him. Rory was more accessible to his peers and more personable. It was McIlroy's position on the Tour's board of directors that helped facilitate their shared vision for the revamped Tour.

Rory further flexed his muscle in late 2022 by recruiting his close friend Jimmy Dunne to join the Tour's board as an independent director. (Dunne was the ultimate insider who turned Gerry McIlroy into a made man by granting him membership at Seminole Golf Club.) Dunne seemed likely to further Rory's agenda and consolidate his influence. No doubt he would keep McIlroy in the loop on any clandestine dealings with the Saudis.

McIlroy ended his 2022 season in—where else?—the oil-rich Middle East for the European Tour's finale in Dubai. He continued his war of words with Greg Norman in a pretournament press conference. "I think Greg needs to go," McIlroy said. "I think he just needs to exit stage left. He's made his mark, but I think now is the right time to say, *Look, you've got this thing off the ground, but no one is going to talk unless there's an adult in the room that can actually try to mend fences.*" These remarks went viral, of course, and Joe Molloy, one of the most popular podcasters in Ireland, couldn't contain his glee that night on his *Off the Ball* podcast. "Oh my god!" Molloy enthused. "He drove over him, reversed back over him, and drove over him a few more times."

McIlroy made more headlines a few days later by winning the Race to Dubai for a fourth time. That was worth a $2 million bonus on top of his €5.55 million in official earnings. (Don't get me started on the Euro Tour's use of different currencies.) He also made $8.6 million between the ropes on the PGA Tour and a whopping $31.7 million in bonuses (FedEx Cup, Player Impact Program, Comcast Business Tour Top 10). McIlroy would later say he played so hard because he wanted to win as much money as possible to prove a point to the LIV defectors.

McIlroy's continued fidelity to the European Tour helped keep the Tour going through the twin crises of COVID and numerous stars leaving for LIV. "He is the heart and soul of the tour," says Keith Pelley, the Euro Tour's CEO from 2015 to '24. "He is the greatest global ambassador golf has and it's not even close. He is loved everywhere he goes, and his presence elevates a tournament in ways that can't be measured. If Rory had gone to LIV, it would have been catastrophic. If he chose to play only on the PGA Tour, it would have been devastating. A lot of great players who came up alongside him turned their back on the [European] Tour. But Rory just gives and gives. Whenever he came back for a tournament, he always said, 'What do you need? What can I do to help?' Every time he tees it up, every other player in the field should go up and shake his hand and say thank you." (In 2025, the Euro Tour enshrined this legacy by creating the Rory McIlroy Award, to be given annually to the player who performs the best across the major championships.)

The Tour wars became increasingly personal when McIlroy was served a subpoena on Christmas Eve by Patrick Reed's mad-dog lawyer Larry Klayman, who had filed a class action lawsuit against the Official World Golf Ranking for denying ranking points to LIV. The Southern Poverty Law Center describes Klayman as "pathologically litigious," "thin-skinned and paranoid," and a "sanctimonious conspiracist." Among those Klayman has sued in his long and rancorous career: his own mother, the FBI, Hillary Clinton, Iran's supreme leader, George Soros, Mark Zuckerberg, OPEC, President Obama, and the Republic of China (for $20 trillion for the "creation and release" of COVID-19). Klayman was behind Reed's rash of lawsuits against numerous members of the golf media, all of which were eventually laughed out of court. McIlroy was still steamed about the subpoena when Reed approached him on the driving range to exchange pleasantries at the Dubai Desert Classic in January 2023. Rory pointedly ignored him. Just to be a brat, Reed flicked a tee in McIlroy's direction while walking away. "Patrick came up to say hello, and I didn't really want him to," Rory said. "I was subpoenaed by his lawyer on Christmas Eve. Trying to have a nice time with my family and someone shows up on your doorstep and delivers that, you're not going to take that well. I'm living in reality. I don't know where he's living." By the end of the tournament, McIlroy was living rent-free in Reed's head: Rory birdied the last two holes to beat his old antagonist by one stroke and win the Desert Classic for the third time. "This is probably sweeter than it should be or needs to be," he said.

The arrival of LIV Golf had made McIlroy wealthier, more powerful, more vindictive, and more focused. The only question was: How long could he sustain this fever pitch?

17.

On June 6, 2023—362 days after the first round of LIV's first tournament—the golf world awoke to the most flummoxing sight imaginable: Jay Monahan and Yasir Al-Rumayyan sitting elbow to elbow on CNBC as they announced that the war was over and the PGA Tour and the Saudi Public Investment Fund had agreed on a framework agreement to reunify the game. LIV Golf's lawsuit against the Tour, and vice versa, would be terminated immediately with prejudice, meaning the litigation could never be refiled. Only a handful of top players and key sponsors were alerted to the breaking news in the minutes before Monahan and Al-Rumayyan went on air; every other stakeholder on both sides of golf's great divide found out in real time.

"I turned on CNBC and saw Jay and Yasir, and it was like, *Did I accidentally take an edible?*" said one LIV executive.

Reached in the frenzied aftermath of the announcement, PGA Tour board member Peter Malnati was all but speechless, saying, "I'm too stunned to opine."

Furious Tour players took to Twitter to rip Monahan for his duplicity. Yet from a certain point of view, he had just cut the best deal in golf history, potentially tapping into an unlimited source of money to secure the Tour's long-term future without having to give up anything—except his reputation and maybe his soul. That could be hailed as the most selfless kind of leadership, but that was not the prevailing mood in a conference room at the Canadian Open, where more than a hundred players gathered for a closed-door meeting with the commissioner, who flew there straight from the CNBC studio. "The voices got very loud at times," says U.S. Open champion Geoff Ogilvy.

Grayson Murray, a twenty-nine-year-old with one career victory, became an unlikely central character. Murray had long been a polarizing figure on Tour. The early years of his playing career were marred by wide-ranging bad behavior that he later attributed to a drinking problem. He got sober but retained an edge, writing in a social media post that he "hates everything to do with the PGA Tour life." He continued: "The pga tour didn't force me to drink. but the pga tour never gave me help. In my 5 years of experience of being on tour not once have i ever had a request been acknowledged by the commissioner or the [Player Advisory Council] other than 'we will get back to you.'"

Now Murray unloaded on Monahan, shouting, "We don't trust you, Jay! You should resign right now! You lied to our face!"

Rory McIlroy, the Canadian Open's two-time defending champ, had heard enough. He shot back, "Just play better, Grayson." That did not go over well with the Tour's middle class crowding the room, the kind of players who had been excluded from McIlroy's reshaping of the sport. Played the week before the U.S. Open, the Canadian Open struggles to attract most top players, its field filled by kids trying to find their way on to the Tour and journeymen clawing to stay there. The exodus of stars to LIV opened up jobs for those grinders, but the new Signature Events had marginalized the lesser Tour pros and imperiled the tournaments where they plied their trade, including the Canadian Open. Now cataclysmic change was coming again, and the collective jitters were distilled into the two words Murray offered McIlroy in rebuttal: "Fuck off!"

The next day, McIlroy held his previously scheduled press conference. He called it "the most uncomfortable I've felt in the last twelve months." He admitted to feeling like a "sacrificial lamb," and no wonder—while Monahan hid out in the Tour's new $75 million headquarters, refusing to meet with reporters, McIlroy had been on the firing line every time he teed it up, forced to defend the Tour with his words and his golf clubs. He summoned an admirably broad perspective in his press conference in Canada, saying, "Ultimately, when I try to remove myself from the situation and I look at the bigger picture and I look at ten years down the line, I think this is going to be good for the game of professional golf. I think it unifies it and it secures its financial future. All I've wanted to do is to protect the future of the PGA Tour and protect the aspirational nature of what the PGA Tour stands for."

As for the Saudis' encroaching influence in professional golf, he said, "I've come to terms with it. I see what's happened in other sports. I see what's happened in other businesses. And, honestly, I've just resigned myself to the fact that this is what's going to happen. It's very hard to keep up with people who have more money than anyone else. And again, if they want to put that money into the game of golf, then why don't we partner with them and make sure that it's done in the right way? And that's sort of where my head's at ... Whether you like it or not, the PIF and the Saudis want to spend money in the game of golf. And they weren't going to stop."

McIlroy's measured diplomacy faltered only when pressed on one topic. "I hate LIV," he said. "Like, I hope it goes away. And I would fully expect that it does." That would prove to be little more than wishcasting.

McIlroy's status as the tragic hero of the tour wars was cemented when word got out that his close friend Jimmy Dunne had laid the groundwork for the deal with the Saudis. For months, Dunne had engaged in secret correspondence with Yasir Al-Rumayyan and his confederates. He then flew to London to play golf with His Excellency and begin the dialogue that led to the framework agreement. Dunne kept McIlroy, a fellow member of the Tour's board, in the dark throughout all of this, an epic bit of tradecraft. "While I did not have specific conversations with Rory about meeting with Yasir," says Dunne, "I knew he was of the belief that we should be talking to him. Rory knows me well enough, and we've talked business enough, for him to know my opinion that every deal has a spiritual leader. It's usually the guy with the money. And in my opinion, it's all horseshit until you talk to the guy with the money. When I came on the [PGA Tour] board, there was zero contact with Yasir. I said to them, 'I don't understand what you guys are doing. We have to engage with this guy.' Rory absolutely knew that would be my point of view. We both understood at some point I was gonna get that done or I was gonna leave."

On the freighted morning of June 6, Dunne called McIlroy a few minutes before Monahan and Al-Rumayyan went on CNBC. "We never had one minute of pain between us, because Rory understood immediately how favorable the deal was—or could have been—for the Tour," says Dunne. "I told him we settled the lawsuits and they can never be refiled, putting us in a position of strength going forward. 'That's good, Jimmy.' I said we were going to save $60 million a year in legal fees. 'That's great, Jimmy.' That [the Public Investment Fund] was going to come in as a minority investor, but the PGA Tour would still have total control of operations, which, by the way, was crucial, because Yasir is a brilliant man and a brilliant investor, but he doesn't know shit about golf. Rory asked if we were obligated to do anything at all with them, and I said no, this is just the framework for future discussions. He said, 'This is awesome! Good work!'"

Then came the media rollout, which Dunne calls "as bad as can be. In the history of business, what was worse? New Coke? People started talking about a merger, which it never was. The LIV guys were beating their chests, saying they'd won the war. And the Tour players were pissed. They were mad that they weren't involved. It was like, *How dare you do something good without me?* Before we signed the framework, I said to the commissioner [Monahan], 'I can get a deal done with this guy that will be very good for the PGA Tour, but you gotta know one thing, and it's something Jimmy Hoffa said: *You can break a two-by-four over a man's head and he will forgive you, but if you slight him, he will take it to his grave. And we will be dangerously close to slighting these people.'* He said he would tell the players at the appropriate time." That turned out to be far too late.

The week after the Tour-PIF bombshell dropped, McIlroy turned up at the U.S. Open at Los Angeles Country Club, wary but unburdened. For the preceding year and a half, he had been the white knight of the PGA Tour, gallantly battling the bad guys who went to LIV (at least, that's how it was often framed in the golf media). Now it was time to put down his lance. It wouldn't become official for months, but he was already on the way to resigning from the Tour's board of directors. His new mantra became: *I'm just going to worry about myself.*

Still, McIlroy brought some baggage to the U.S. Open. The month before, the PGA Championship had been played at Oak Hill, near his wife's hometown in upstate New York. The McIlroys are members of the club, but he enjoyed no homefield advantage at the PGA, finishing tied for seventh, seven shots back of Brooks Koepka, who won his fifth major championship to surpass McIlroy. In the locker room afterward, Rory opened a vein to his manager, Sean O'Flaherty, captured by the *Full Swing* cameras: "My technique is nowhere near as good as it used to be. I almost feel like I want to do a complete reboot. It's the only way I feel like I'm going to break through. It feels so far away . . . I feel good enough to fucking top ten in my head, but not good enough to win. Like pull away. Like winning fucking major championships."

McIlroy fulfilled the prophecy at LACC, going 65-67-69 to put himself in third place, one stroke off the lead shared by Wyndham Clark and Rickie Fowler. McIlroy birdied the first hole, Clark bogeyed the second, and just like that, Rory was tied for the lead. But once again, his self-doubt manifested in tentative play, as McIlroy didn't make another birdie. Twelve straight pars kept him within one stroke of Clark as the action moved to the reachable par-5 fourteenth hole. McIlroy may be a generational driver of the golf ball, but his superpower deserted him at a crucial moment, as he hooked his drive far off the fairway, forcing a layup. The swing flaws he lamented at Oak Hill were most glaring with McIlroy's short irons; in 2023, he was 112th on Tour in proximity to the hole from 125 to 150 yards. His full-swing finesse shots had long been a bugaboo: Tiger Woods, tired of watching McIlroy's missed opportunities on TV, had insisted on giving his friend a tutorial the year before. Little changed. On the most important shot of the national championship—McIlroy's third into LACC's fourteenth hole, from 125 yards out—he was indecisive on club selection in a freshening wind. He opted for a three-quarter gap wedge but fanned it toward the front bunker. His ball embedded into the shaggy fescue face just above the sand. McIlroy doubled over in anguish. He received a sweetheart drop into a good lie in the greenside rough but followed with a mediocre chip and then missed the ensuing eight-footer for par.

In the group behind him, Clark split the fairway and mashed his second shot to twenty feet, pin-high. The two-putt birdie put him three strokes ahead with four holes to play. Clark gave McIlroy a chance with bogies at fifteen and sixteen, but Rory could not summon the one key shot or clutch putt he needed. (For the day, his longest make was 4.5 feet.) McIlroy lost by one to Clark, who came into the week considered a vastly talented underachiever, with only one victory in five and a half seasons on Tour. "When I do finally win this next major, it's going to be really, really sweet," McIlroy said afterward. "I would go through a hundred Sundays like this to get my hands on another major championship." Something else he said at LACC resonated: "I feel like I've shown a lot of resilience in my career, a lot of ups and downs, and I keep coming back. And whether that means that I get rewarded or I get punched in the gut, I'll always keep coming back."

No kidding. On the seventy-second hole at the ensuing Scottish Open, McIlroy produced one of the most memorable shots of his long career, a sawed-off 2-iron from 202 yards that tore through a fierce breeze and cozied to eleven feet. He buried the putt to become the first man to win the Scottish Open, Irish Open, and the Open Championship. McIlroy had defeated Scotland's Bob MacIntyre by one stroke, and afterward MacIntyre's father, Dougie, sighed: "No one else but Rory could've done that."

McIlroy's topsy-turvy summer was hardly over. Next up: the Ryder Cup in Rome, where he would be seeking redemption after his poor performance two years earlier. Not exactly the ideal place to regain one's equanimity.

THE STINK CLOUD OF LIV Golf inevitably hovered over the Ryder Cup. U.S. captain Zach Johnson had no choice but to take Brooks Koepka after he won the 2023 PGA Championship, but Captain Johnson gave zero consideration to other LIV players. "I don't know the golf courses they're playing," he said. "Never seen them. It's not fair for me to guess anybody's true form that I can't witness." That was nonsensical; three venues on which LIV conducted tournaments in 2023 ahead of the Ryder Cup—the Greenbrier in West Virginia, El Camaleón at the Mayakoba in Mexico, and the Gallery Golf Club in Arizona—had previously hosted PGA Tour events. Various Americans had competed in the Singapore Open at Sentosa Golf Club, which hosted the LIV event; in fact, Johnson could have walked down the block on Sea Island to ask his neighbor Matt Kuchar about Sentosa, as Kuch won there in 2020. And nothing was stopping Johnson from doing his due diligence by streaming LIV tournaments. But, being a good company man, he was more than happy to snub Bryson DeChambeau, who finished fourth at the '23 PGA Championship and went 61-58 over the closing two rounds to win LIV Greenbrier, and Dustin Johnson, who was 5-0 at the previous Ryder Cup and, in the run-up to Rome, tenth at the U.S. Open and a winner at LIV Tulsa. The animosity between the establishment and LIV hurt the U.S. team but helped Europe. Henrik Stenson had already signed a contract to captain the 2023 team, but he was stripped of the duties when he went to LIV. Team Europe selected Luke Donald as a replacement, and he grew into a stirring leader. Donald might have felt compelled to give a last hurrah to aging European stalwarts Sergio García, Lee Westwood, and Ian Poulter, but their departure to LIV cleared the way for young studs Ludvig Åberg and Nicolai Højgaard and an ascendant Sepp Straka.

Europe was clearly the better team once the Ryder Cup began, taking a 6.5–1.5 lead on day one as McIlroy was the only player to win two full points. Team Europe pretty much ended the Ryder Cup on Saturday morning, taking three more points as McIlroy won again (alongside Tommy Fleetwood as they went a gaudy −5 in alternate shot). The only remaining intrigue in Saturday afternoon four-balls surrounded the cleanup match, McIlroy–Matt Fitzpatrick versus Wyndham Clark–Patrick Cantlay. In the days before the Ryder Cup, Clark, he of two career victories, said, "I have tons of respect for Rory and, because of that respect, I also want to beat him. I like to think I am better than him, and I want to prove that." Woof.

Then there was the Cantlay factor. He and McIlroy had gotten to know each other serving on the PGA Tour board. Per an endorsement deal, Cantlay proudly wore the hat of Goldman Sachs, the vampire squid of late-stage capitalism. He carried himself with the assuredness of a master of the universe and was already becoming an obstructionist as Dunne and others toiled to consummate the framework agreement. Cantlay had turned down a $75 million offer from LIV—now he wanted vengeance, not for both sides to make nice. Another party to the Tour's inner workings describes Cantlay as "a terrific penis." McIlroy would later render a similar but more succinct verdict, calling him a "dick." Cantlay became the center of attention on Ryder Cup Saturday after Jamie Weir of Sky Sports reported that the balding American was refusing to wear the Team USA hat as a protest against not getting paid for his services, a Ryder Cup tradition that dates to 1927. The fans razzed Cantlay mercilessly throughout the match, though he did not really understand why all the sodden Romans were waving their hats at him, as Weir's report had dropped while he was already on the golf course.

The grudge match inevitably came down to the last hole all square. The U.S. had finally shown a little fight in the final partner-play session, winning two of the preceding three matches. In the gloaming, both teams surrounded the eighteenth green at Marco Simone Golf and Country Club. McIlroy hit a strong approach shot to twenty feet. Cantlay was outside of him but, displaying big brass ones, rolled in a forty-three-foot birdie putt. His fiery celebration included tipping an imaginary cap to the crowd. All good—the Ryder Cup encourages theatrics. But then things went off the rails. As McIlroy lined up his do-or-die putt to halve the hole and the match, Cantlay's caddie, Joe LaCava (formerly of Fred Couples and Tiger Woods), ambled toward the center of the green, waving his hat at the crowd. LaCava nearly ran into McIlroy, who was pacing off his putt. Miffed, Rory briefly went nose to nose with the caddie and told him to get the hell out of the way. This immediately raised the ire of his European teammates; Shane Lowry stepped onto the green and bellowed, "Joe, fuck off!" LaCava followed McIlroy for a few steps, barking at him. This was an outrageous breach of etiquette for a caddie, who is supposed to be seen but not heard. The crowd erupted in boos while poor McIlroy was still eyeing his putt. He missed it, giving the U.S. the win. That brought the score to 10.5–5.5. The Americans had a glimmer of hope and their first bit of momentum heading into singles.

As soon as the match ended, Lowry confronted LaCava on the edge of the green. (Lowry comes from a long line of manly men: his father is a Gaelic football legend.) As their animated conversation continued, LaCava's good friend Jim "Bones" Mackay, serving as an announcer for NBC, stepped in and offered a few gentle words, trying to defuse the situation. McIlroy listened in as he walked by but kept going. Both teams retreated to their locker rooms, and emotions were running high among the Europeans. "Shane's passionate, you know?" says Luke Donald. "He was shouting in the locker room—well, I don't want to say shouting. He was raising his voice: 'That was bullshit!' I don't think Rory quite contemplated everything while it was going on there on the green, but once he heard Shane, he was like, 'Yeah, you're right!'" McIlroy felt "the red mist" upon him and told Lowry that he wanted to go into the American team room to sort things out, Dirty Harry style. He got talked out of that. As Rory and Shane left the clubhouse to return to the team hotel, Bones had the misfortune to cross paths with them. He again tried to be conciliatory, but something broke inside of McIlroy. He shouted at Bones, "That can't fucking happen! That's a fucking disgrace!" As Lowry held him back, McIlroy thundered, "I'm going to go in that fucking team room!" Shane ultimately tossed Rory into the back seat of a courtesy car. (He later joked that he was keen to avoid a brawl because he'd have to do all the work.) Video of the confrontation went around the sports world at the speed of light. "That to me was the real Rory," says Paul McGinley. "He's a blue-collar kid from Belfast, and there's a lot of guys from Belfast who would probably handle that the same way. It was a rare look at what's really inside of him, beneath all of the polish."

Back at the hotel, McIlroy and Lowry took cold plunges to cool down their emotions. Rory was still edgy on the car ride to the course on Sunday morning. He decided he needed something to calm his mind, landing on Marcus Aurelius's *Meditations*, which he had read years earlier when he began practicing Stoicism, the philosophy that is organized around living a "well-reasoned life." Says McIlroy, "I don't know why it popped into my head. Rome? Emperor?"

McIlroy fished out his phone and read through the musings of Aurelius, the onetime ruler of the Roman Empire and an ardent adherent of Stoicism.

You have power over your mind, not outside events. Realize this and you will find strength.

Waste no more time arguing what a good man should be—be one.

If you are distressed by anything external, the pain is not due to the thing itself but to your estimate of it; and this you have the power to revoke at any moment.

The nearer a man comes to a calm mind, the closer he is to strength. You shouldn't give circumstances the power to rouse anger, for they don't care at all.

McIlroy would later tell reporter Paul Kimmage that these were the passages that resonated most with him on the way to golf's version of the Colosseum. He was paired against putting wizard Sam Burns in the fourth singles match. McIlroy's game took on a little more significance when Jon Rahm halved in the leadoff spot versus Scottie Scheffler, and Justin Rose lost in the match before McIlroy's (to that prick Cantlay!). Rory played with fire in his eyes, making eight birdies in fifteen holes to torch Burns 3 and 1. His victory pushed the score to 13–7. Shortly thereafter, Europe went on to clinch another Ryder Cup. McIlroy's 4-1 record was the best of his Ryder Cup career. He shed tears when it was over, now a biennial tradition. But these were tears of joy (and relief). At the end of a long, hard, contentious season, during which he made endless headlines, McIlroy couldn't resist stirring the pot one more time in the victors' press conference by looking ahead to the 2025 Ryder Cup. Pounding on the dais for emphasis, he said, "So I've said this for the last probably six or seven years to anyone that will listen: I think one of the biggest accomplishments in golf right now is winning an away Ryder Cup. And that's what we're going to do at Bethpage."

18.

Heading into the 2024 Masters, Rory McIlroy had finished in the top ten in seven of the preceding eight major championships, including two runner-ups and a solo third. He hadn't won one, of course, but every player dreams of contending every time he tees it up in a big event. For years, McIlroy had been repeating ad nauseam that, if he just kept putting himself in position, one of these major championships was bound to fall into his lap. Tiger Woods remained a believer. "No question, he'll do it at some point," Woods said during Masters week of McIlroy's ongoing quest for a green jacket. "Rory's too talented, too good. He's going to be playing this event for a very long time. He'll get it done. It's just a matter of when. I think that Rory will be a great Masters champion one day, and it could be this week. You never know."

A month before the Masters, McIlroy had begun seeing Woods's old swing coach, Butch Harmon, in hopes of finally solving the riddles of Augusta National. "The work I did with him wasn't a tremendous amount of changing what he did," says Harmon, "it was his attitude and the way he played certain shots. From 150 yards and in he made a full swing like he was hitting a driver and I wanted him to make more 3 quarter swings and chop the follow-through off a little. He's a very high ball hitter, but with short irons high balls aren't good, it's hard to control, we wanted to bring the ball flight down."

Harmon is one of golf's great raconteurs, and McIlroy enjoyed soaking up his wisdom. "He's part psychologist, part swing coach," he said. "Like I always joke, you spend four hours with Butch and you go away with two swing tips and thirty stories. But you always go away hitting the ball better than when you came."

McIlroy opened the Masters with a 71. That left him six strokes back of leader Bryson DeChambeau but still constituted progress, given McIlroy's long history of first-round blowups. When a reporter mentioned that his first-round score was encouraging, McIlroy said, "Is it? That's sort of embarrassing if it is. But, yeah, I guess. I kept it together. I stuck to my game plan."

But during a windy second round, McIlroy seemed ill-equipped to answer the questions the course was asking; he didn't make a birdie while shooting a woeful 77. Even more dispiriting was that McIlroy did it in front of coleader Scottie Scheffler, who had emerged as the best player in the game. Scheffler, twenty-seven, had just won his second straight Players Championship, his eighth victory in the span of twenty-five months (including the '22 Masters). Two days after McIlroy's 77, Scheffler won his second green jacket in a command performance, tightening his grip on the top spot in the World Ranking. McIlroy struggled to twenty-second place, fifteen strokes back. In seven PGA Tour events so far in '24, he had finished better than nineteenth only once.

What was wrong with Rory? It has long been an axiom on Tour that it takes a clear mind to play clean golf. One theory being whispered in golf circles was that McIlroy's marriage was in trouble, no doubt exacerbated by Erica's increasing preference to stay home with their daughter, Poppy, rather than join the traveling circus of the Tour. Rory hadn't done himself any favors with a casual comment he made on the *No Laying Up* podcast when, as a newlywed, he was asked with which figure he would most want to trade places? "A couple of years ago I went to Coolmore Stud, they breed some of the best racehorses in the world, and their biggest stallion is a horse called Galileo," McIlroy said. "I wouldn't mind trading places with him for a week. He has a pretty good life, I tell you. He's loving it." Noted, but any loose talk about his marriage was easy to dismiss as nothing more than scurrilous rumors, the type that both Phil Mickelson and Tiger Woods had to navigate in their heyday.

A very harmonious relationship in McIlroy's life was on display at the '24 Zurich Classic, played two weeks after the Masters. He had talked Shane Lowry into being his partner in the event, which features two-man teams. Lowry had become McIlroy's best friend, their bond intensifying when Poppy was born in 2020. The Lowrys have two young daughters, and they have become like older sisters to Poppy, their families being strangers in a strange land . . . South Florida. "You put together two Irishmen anywhere in the world, they're going to get on with each other," says Pádraig Harrington. "That's just the way it is."

Does it matter if one is from the north and one is from the south?

"Not one bit. They're going to talk and they're going to laugh and they might drink."

Lowry flies for free on McIlroy's G-VI. He always brings a couple of bottles of expensive wine to show his gratitude. "He can drink more than me!" says Lowry, who in private often refers to McIlroy as "the little fooker." There are dozens of pros at the Bear's Club, Jack Nicklaus's private playground in South Florida, but McIlroy and Lowry are rarely seen without the other one as a wingman. "When Shane moved over to Palm Beach [in 2015], initially he was out of his depth," says Paul McGinley, the grand old man of Irish golf. "He was a country lad from Ireland trying to make his way on the PGA Tour with a new wife and young kids. Talk about a duck out of water. He was lost, and his performances on the PGA Tour showed that. When the friendship with Rory ignited, so did Shane's game. Being around the greatest player of his generation pushed Shane to make the most of his massive talent."

And yet McIlroy probably gets more out of the relationship. "It can be lonely at the top, and I think it is for Rory," says McGinley. "He doesn't have a lot of really close friends. He's got his team, but outside of that, he's got lots of acquaintances. He doesn't have many close friends on Tour. That's why Shane means so much to him."

In 2023, the McIlroys and Lowrys vacationed together in New York City. Rory chose every restaurant, every bottle of wine, and arranged tickets for the couples to see Bono's one-man show, *Stories of Surrender*. "The girls went shopping and we went to a bar," says Lowry. "I said to my wife afterward, 'I never realized how famous Rory actually is.' Walking through the city of New York, I was like his bodyguard. But he's great, he always has time for people. He'll never blank anyone. He knows how fortunate he is to be in the position he's in, given from where he's from."

The Rory-Shane chemistry was palpable at their first Zurich Classic in April 2024. Lowry was struggling a little bit with his game, but McIlroy carried them into contention. They played with Aaron Rai and David Lipsky in the third round. "It was very lighthearted between them, great banter between shots," says Rai. "You could tell it was a deep bond. When you play amateur golf together, it's a little simpler than professional golf. It's a smaller group, you're all chasing the same things, it creates deep relationships that last." Still, Rai could feel how hard Lowry was trying not to let down his partner. "He was definitely grinding harder than Rory," says Rai. "You could tell Shane wanted to do it more for Rory than himself." Following the third round, McIlroy and Lowry dined at Arnaud's in the French Quarter. As they got up to leave, their fellow diners rose for a standing ovation. Lowry was thunderstruck; for McIlroy, this was just another day in the life. On the final green the next day, in victory, Lowry picked up McIlroy like a schoolboy and shouted in his ear, "Ye little fooker!" They turned up at a tournament party wearing Mardi Gras beads and cradling bottles of beer. As McIlroy belted out Journey's "Don't Stop Believin'," a fan tossed Ireland's tricolor at Lowry's feet.

He's a proud Irishman and in almost any other scenario would have draped himself in the flag. But in deference to McIlroy's complicated identity politics, he left it on the stage floor.

No one close to McIlroy could ever recall seeing him sing. Lowry felt the catharsis in his pal cutting loose. Referencing Rory's marital difficulties, Lowry says, "He was in a tough spot at the time. So, I'll leave it there. I don't want to say anything more."

McIlroy was grateful to have golf, and Lowry, as an anchor in his life. He says of the shared victory in New Orleans, "I think it probably injected a little bit of joy back into golf for me in some way, which I think is really, really important, not to lose that."

McIlroy had spent the preceding ten months becoming further disillusioned by PGA Tour politics. Since the announcement of the framework agreement, Tour board members Tiger Woods and Patrick Cantlay had been actively working to kill the deal; Woods felt the players who went to LIV were traitors who should never be welcomed back, while Cantlay was sore about having turned down LIV's $75 million offer and wanted retribution on those who enjoyed the largesse. Frustrated by the impasse, McIlroy resigned from the board in November 2023. But among Tour players, he was the only one who enjoyed a relationship with Yasir Al-Rumayyan; they had first sat down to talk in 2017, when His Excellency was first trying to ingratiate himself to the establishment. Al-Rumayyan and Jay Monahan knew McIlroy, the game's biggest star, would have to play a role if the sport was going to be reunified. Both began lobbying him to return to the board. McIlroy made various efforts to reach across the aisle, including patching up his friendship with Sergio García. Rory agreed to return to the PGA Tour board in the spring of 2024 but was blackballed by Woods and Cantlay. (That Tiger would turn on his friend was merely the latest example of his ruthlessness.) Jimmy Dunne tendered his resignation from the board around the same time. LIV Golf had broken the sport, and two key figures who could help put it back together again had been disenfranchised. "It got pretty complicated and pretty messy," says McIlroy. "I think with the way it happened, I think it opened some old wounds and scar tissue from some things that happened before."

McIlroy first went public with the backroom drama in May 2024 at Quail Hollow, his first start after New Orleans. It is a testament to his ability to compartmentalize that days later he roared to his fourth career victory at Quail Hollow. As he stepped off the final green, he was interviewed by CBS's Amanda Balionis. They looked cute together in matching pink shirts in honor of Mother's Day. Asked what it meant to win on such a special holiday, McIlroy waxed poetic about Rosie but did not mention the mother of his child, and no wonder: the next day, McIlroy filed for divorce in Palm Beach County, declaring the marriage "irretrievably broken." The news broke almost immediately, thanks to courthouse molls. McIlroy's management team was forced to put out a statement confirming the split. This thunderbolt struck just a few days before the world's golf press gathered in Louisville for the PGA Championship at Valhalla Golf Club; McIlroy was the quasi-defending champ, having won the last PGA to be played on the course, way back in 2014. Incredibly, that remained his last major championship victory. Once tournament week began, McIlroy's manager, Sean O'Flaherty, and various PGA officials made it clear that McIlroy would not be addressing the pending divorce with reporters, but he was pounded throughout the week with carefully worded questions about "distractions" and his "focus." He looked utterly miserable, doing well to finish twelfth.

Naturally, the whole world had an armchair theory about what had gone wrong in the McIlroy marriage. It didn't help that Erica had become a neo–Elin Woods, never doing interviews and remaining unknown to the golf public. "It can't be easy being Rory's wife," says McGinley. "I'm sure it's not easy for her, because she's quiet by nature. Like Caroline Harrington, she would have been perfect as Rory's wife. I mean, she loves Pádraig being a professional golfer more than Pádraig loves being a professional golfer. But Erica is quiet, and she kind of keeps her thoughts to herself. She's had to find where she fits in and where she doesn't. I mean, Rory is superstar status, and he is a big personality. He's gregarious and knows everybody. Rory's a lot more like Gerry than he is his mom. You know, with lots to say."

A long-standing rumor exploded into the mainstream press once McIlroy filed for divorce. The *Daily Mail* ran on its website an extensive story under the headline "Rory McIlroy and CBS Sports Journalist Amanda Balionis Spark Romance Rumors in Wake of His Divorce from Wife Erica Stoll with Flirty TV Interviews After Married Reporter Ditches Her Ring." Balionis's marriage had actually ended a year earlier, but never mind the details. The article was embellished with twelve photos and two videos, to say nothing of breathless prose: "DailyMail.com can reveal, Rory McIlroy's relationship with CBS's 19th Hole reporter Amanda Balionis is the talk of the links and has left many fans wondering just how close the pair have become." The supposed smoking gun in the story—from the unnamed sister of an anonymous source!—was that McIlroy had been spotted in the Crown Point neighborhood of San Diego, where Balionis owns a condo, picking up take-out food under the name Amanda. The *Daily Mail* piece was aggregated everywhere from the *New York Post* to *Us Weekly*. Neither McIlroy nor Balionis has ever commented publicly, and people close to both of them swear the rumor is not true. But it refuses to die: of the many people I told about this book during its creation, the first question from easily 90 percent of them was "Are you going to write about Rory and Amanda?" (Reluctantly, as it turns out.)

As McIlroy plotted his divorce proceedings, the golf world was rocked by the news that Grayson Murray had committed suicide. It had been less than a year since Murray and McIlroy had their testy exchange in the closed-door meeting that followed the announcement of the framework agreement. McIlroy was visibly shaken when speaking about Murray in a press conference at the Canadian Open. "It's incredibly sad, first and foremost, and we're all thinking of Grayson's family and hoping that they're doing okay and getting through this incredibly tough period. It's cliché, but it puts everything in perspective. At the end of the day, golf is golf, and, yeah, we play it for a living, but it pales in comparison to the things that actually matter in life . . . I've had to realize that at times, and I'm still sort of working my way through that in terms of not making golf the be-all and end-all for me. I think it slaps you in the face when something like that happens."

A week later, at the U.S. Open at Pinehurst, McIlroy dropped another bombshell: he and Erica were back together, a month after the divorce paperwork had been filed. Ewan Murray of *The Guardian* had the scoop, with Rory telling him, "There have been rumours about my personal life recently, which is unfortunate. Responding to each rumour is a fool's game. Over the past weeks, Erica and I have realised that our best future was as a family together. Thankfully, we have resolved our differences and look forward to a new beginning." The short-lived divorce proceedings and hasty reconciliation said more about him than her. If you are a fabulously wealthy and internationally famous athlete, it is probably unwise to file for divorce unless you are one million percent certain there is zero chance to save the marriage. But McIlroy's life has been defined by impetuousness, on the golf course and in matters of business and romance. The recklessness is part of what makes him appealing. He's a complicated human, like the rest of us.

With all the tumult in McIlroy's world, it seemed unimaginable that he could prosper at Pinehurst, the most stressful of all U.S. Open venues. But he shot 65-72-69 to surge to a tie for second place, three strokes behind leader Bryson DeChambeau.

How?!

"He's quite good at golf," Lowry said with a smirk. "He's a different animal, Rory. He's mentally very strong, very tough."

The final-round showdown with DeChambeau offered a new dynamic, as McIlroy had spent his entire career as the gallery favorite. This time, the crowd was with Bryson, who had been tearing up LIV Golf while enjoying one of the more unlikely image overhauls in the annals of the game. DeChambeau had bolted from the PGA Tour to LIV because he desperately needed a fresh start. Goofy, obtuse, and strident, he always had trouble connecting with his peers; the iconic eye roll that cameras captured from Brooks Koepka at the 2021 PGA Championship only hinted at the collective irritation Bryson inspired in his colleagues. Feelings curdled at Torrey Pines in 2022, when DeChambeau began launching drives into the caddie parking lot beyond the end of the range. A tournament official beseeched him to aim into the tall nets down the side of the range. He ignored the plea and kept bombing his driver. Two cars were left with smashed windshields. No wonder DeChambeau could never get any traction in his repeated bids to assume a leadership position among his colleagues on the PGA Tour. "A lot of my time out there was difficult," he says. "I was trying to get on the [Player Advisory Committee] for six years, and it never happened. You get voted on to it by the other players, and nobody liked the way I thought. I felt I had an interesting perspective on a lot of issues. I'd love to have been part of it, but they didn't want me."

DeChambeau finally made friends on LIV because, initially, his teammates on the Crushers—Charles Howell III, Paul Casey, Anirban Lahiri—were forced to be nice to their captain. But DeChambeau won them over with his puppy-dog enthusiasm and relentless team-building exercises, which included presenting the fellas with matching Rolexes in Crushers gold and blue. "He thrives with that social environment around him, which maybe doesn't come naturally to him," says Lahiri. "But in this case, it's not a matter of choice. The social element is very good for him. He enjoys the company, he enjoys the hang."

Says DeChambeau, "They're wise individuals—a lot wiser than me. They've taught me how to play certain shots, how to think through certain situations, and little tricks on the greens. Nuances I never knew about. We're able to talk about things freely and openly because we're all in it to win, together. I've learned so much from them."

"Yeah, we've been telling him to stop trying to find a girlfriend on Instagram," says one of DeChambeau's teammates.

As he became more comfortable in his own skin, Bryson reinvented himself as a YouTube content creator, connecting with new generations of fans. For the final round at Pinehurst, DeChambeau was playing in the final twosome, one group behind McIlroy. When they were announced on the first tee, the roar for Bryson was considerably noisier. There is no doubt that Rory lost some fans with his bitchiness throughout the LIV Golf–PGA Tour battle. His subsequent embrace of Saudi money and calls for reunification between the tours—however pragmatic and nuanced his positions might have been—could also be seen as yet another flip-flop on a controversial topic. Still, everyone loves a winner, and the mood in the Pinehurst gallery began to shift as McIlroy decisively outplayed DeChambeau for the first three hours of the final round. Over his preceding decade of vexing futility in the major championships, McIlroy had often been shaky with the putter in crunch time, but now he was pouring in twenty-five-footers like a birthright. On thirteen, McIlroy made his fourth birdie in the span of five holes, reaching 4-under on the day and pushing two clear of the field. Golf Twitter was melting. McIlroy's quest to win a major had transcended sport and passed into melodrama. At the 2022 Open Championship, he was supposed to thwart the Saudis and save the sport at the Home of Golf. By the time of the '23 U.S. Open, he was searching for meaning as a tragic figure who had been sacrificed at the altar by scheming backroom bureaucrats. Now, the embattled McIlroy was straining to claim the national championship on Father's Day as he fought to save his family. You can't make this stuff up.

But DeChambeau refused to go away. He drove the green of the 316-yard par-4 thirteenth hole (with a 3-wood) to close within one stroke. From that moment on, it felt like Bryson was playing to win while Rory had the air of a man trying not to lose. In the Pinehurst parking lot, six-time major champion Nick Faldo diagnosed the problem. In 1996, at age thirty-eight, Faldo had a chance to steal a Masters from Greg Norman, but he hadn't contended in the cauldron of a major championship in years. "The mental demands were exhausting," Faldo said. "On every shot, I had to have these conversations with myself. 'The wheels are falling off.' *No, they aren't.* 'You can't hit this shot.' *Yes, I can.* When I watch Rory trying to win these majors now, I know he is hearing the same voices. When he looks down at the ball, how much doubt is there inside? One percent? Five percent? It doesn't take much to be the difference between winning and losing. It's the dreaded scar tissue. We all wish we could be eighteen again, when we had no fear. But if you fail enough times, the scar tissue builds and builds."

Pressure can manifest in decision-making, too. On the par-3 fifteenth hole, McIlroy pulled the wrong club and nuked his tee shot over the back of the green. Bogey. Tie ballgame. DeChambeau suffered his first three-putt of the tournament as McIlroy was playing number sixteen. After two stellar shots and a good lag on a long, tough hole, McIlroy faced a thirty-inch par putt to preserve his one-stroke lead. Up until that moment, he was 496-for-496 inside of three feet on the season. Waiting for his turn to brush in the gimme (while that cock Cantlay took his sweet time!), McIlroy admits to feeling "uneasy." He stood over the putt a second or two longer than usual and then flat-out yanked it, his ball spinning out of the hole. Two straight bogies with the U.S. Open hanging in the balance. The ghosts stirred.

The tie at the top of the leaderboard remained as McIlroy arrived at the tee of the uphill, doglegged, 449-yard par-4 eighteenth. With its canted terrain, the fairway plays as the narrowest on the course. Rory could have employed a variety of different clubs to find the all-important short grass. As he mulled the decision, DeChambeau hit a superb tee shot into the green of the par-3 seventeenth, which is just steps from the eighteenth tee. McIlroy waited for the cascading roar to subside before playing his most consequential tee shot in years. He shrank from the moment, pulling his drive into the scrubby native area, the ball settling into a shallow depression hard against a clump of wire grass. McIlroy heard the crowd groan when DeChambeau missed his birdie putt on seventeen, and he got another emotional boost when his mishit approach shot narrowly avoided a fairway bunker fifty yards short of the green and trundled to a welcoming spot just short of the putting surface. On the NBC broadcast, Brandel Chamblee described McIlroy's upcoming pitch as "straightforward."

His frazzled colleague Brad Faxon, serving as both a commentator and McIlroy's putting coach, blurted out, "Is anything straightforward at this point?!"

With the pin in the back of the green, perched on a precarious slope, the one thing McIlroy couldn't do was play his pitch long, above the hole. He played his pitch long, above the hole. It was a catastrophic mistake, leaving a glassy downhill putt of three feet nine inches. Behind him, DeChambeau rope-hooked his drive into the same native area McIlroy had just visited, and this weighed on Rory as he sized up a putt that was like an X-ray of the soul. "It was a really tricky putt," he says. "And I was very aware of where Bryson was off the tee. I knew I had to hit it really soft. If the one coming back didn't matter, I would have hit it firmer. But because I was sort of in two minds—I didn't know whether Bryson was going to make a par or not—it was one of those ones where I had to make sure that, if the putt didn't go in, that it wasn't going ten feet by, which it very easily could have. Thinking back, yeah, maybe I was a little too aware of where Bryson was and what he was doing."

NBC's roving announcer Smylie Kaufman read the putt as left-center. That's at a normal pace. The more McIlroy babied the putt, the sharper it would break. He played it two cups outside left! "There was a lot of swing to it, especially with how easy I was hitting it," he says.

"I just sort of wanted to make sure that, if there was still a chance at a playoff, that it was at least going to be that."

Tiger Woods would not have been thinking about the comebacker. Jack Nicklaus would not have been thinking about the comebacker. Neither would Ben Hogan, Tom Watson, Lee Trevino, Hale Irwin, Ray Floyd, nor Payne Stewart. You want to win the U.S. Motherfucking Open, you need to bury that putt. But McIlroy made a jittery stroke, striking the ball well above its equator. His ball dribbled to the low side and lipped out of the hole. A smattering of overserved yahoos in the grandstand began chanting "U-S-A! U-S-A!" McIlroy's blunder took its place among the most ignominious short misses in golf history, alongside the cock-ups of Doug Sanders (Old Course), Scott Hoch (Augusta National), Davis Love III (Oakland Hills), Stewart Cink (Southern Hills), and Dustin Johnson (Chambers Bay). DeChambeau followed by summoning the best shot of his life, a fifty-five-yarder from the bunker that cozied to within four feet of the hole. Crucially, he left himself an uphill putt.

The cameras found McIlroy in the scoring area, slumped against a table, hat askew, wearing a grim expression as he awaited his fate. DeChambeau drilled the putt for an all-time up-and-down that won him the U.S. Open. McIlroy peeled out of the Pinehurst parking lot without congratulating DeChambeau or speaking to reporters, which was a bad precedent and a tactical mistake. From Greg Norman at Augusta to Phil Mickelson at Winged Foot to Tom Watson at Turnberry, the gruesome losses are leavened by the humanity of the vanquished. It would not serve McIlroy (or golf fans) if he turned to stone during the tough times. DeChambeau was gracious in the champion's press conference, saying, "I'm sure it will fuel Rory's fire even more. He's a strong-minded individual. Rory is going to [win another major championship]. I'd love to have a lot more battles with him. It would be a lot of fun. But, yeah, Rory's going to do it at some point."

McIlroy fled to New York City to be by himself for a couple of days. Hat and sunglasses on, earphones in, he crisscrossed Manhattan on foot, losing himself in the crowds and hustle-bustle. McIlroy enjoyed the anonymity of the city and the perspective that came with realizing that the millions of other denizens on the island didn't care one bit about his woes.

But then McIlroy suffered another disaster at the Paris Olympics. After birdieing the fourteenth hole of the final round, he was only one stroke off the lead and dreaming about gold. On the next hole, McIlroy dumped a wedge into the pond fronting the green, leading to a double bogey that ultimately left him two strokes from the podium.

Going back to the 2022 Open Championship at St. Andrews, McIlroy had been the game's most compelling figure even as he missed out on the biggest trophies. After his latest disappointment in Paris, McIlroy succinctly summed up his tortured place in the game, saying, "I feel like I've been golf's Nearly Man for the last three years." Only one thing could make him whole. Hint: He would have to find it in Augusta, Georgia.

19.

When Rory McIlroy turned pro in 2007, Tiger Woods was squarely in his prime, while Phil Mickelson and Vijay Singh remained week-to-week forces. Other winners on the PGA Tour that year included Fred Funk, Mark Calcavecchia, Scott Verplank, Rory Sabbatini, Chad Campbell, Mike Weir, and Stephen Ames. McIlroy has been so good for so long that he's had to battle two subsequent generations of talent. As thrilling as Bryson DeChambeau's U.S. Open victory may have been, his 2024 season paled in comparison to that of Xander Schauffele, who prevailed at the Open and PGA Championships, or Scottie Scheffler, who won seven Tour events and enjoyed the round of the year in golf, a 62 to steal the gold medal at the Paris Olympics. McIlroy closed '24 by winning the European Tour's season finale and taking the Race to Dubai for a sixth time—insert golf clap here—but it would take another reinvention if he was ever going to return to the mountaintop.

In his decade-long quest to complete the Grand Slam, McIlroy had tried everything to peak for the Masters: play the week before, rest the week before; arrive in Augusta early, arrive in Augusta late; play the course weeks ahead of time, skip the extra preparation. The one thing he had never done was treat November and December as if the Masters were imminent. "Rory's plan for Augusta started in the offseason," says Bob Rotella, his sports psychologist. "He won four times in 2024; he was playing at such a high level, the plan for the offseason was to treat it like it wasn't the offseason. He stayed very active, playing and practicing and working on targeted things."

McIlroy spent a lot of time on his chipping and pitching, having suffered what he called "some stinkers" around the greens in '24. He did a deep dive on his statistics and identified ten-to-twenty-foot putts as a weakness; that became the point of emphasis with putting coach Brad Faxon. Most of all, McIlroy dedicated himself to becoming more effective with his short irons and wedges. Both Tiger Woods and Butch Harmon had harped on McIlroy to address this long-standing weakness in the preceding two years, but now, finally, he was ready to hear it. "That's just how I am: I have to make things my own idea," he says knowingly. This resistance to outside counsel can be found in other vastly talented feel players—makes sense, since safeguarding their gift is part of what makes them who they are. Mickelson didn't win his first major championship until he was thirty-three, having finally accepted what everyone else already knew: he needed to abandon his crashing draw off the tee and embrace a gentler fade. Dustin Johnson did not become dominant until his early thirties, when he began spending the bulk of his practice time dialing in precise distances on his wedges, as various folks had long beseeched him to do. So, as 2024 turned into 2025, McIlroy grinded on different shot shapes and trajectories with his shortest clubs, allowing him to lower the height and spin rate of his shots and giving himself a more varied arsenal, including a baby cut that would serve him well off the hook lies at Augusta National. "Rory is a golf swing nerd, and we have talked swing a lot," says Golf Channel analyst Brandel Chamblee. "I showed him some old videos from 2012 and '14 and said, 'Can you not get down the line with a cupped left wrist like you had back then?' That guy was winning majors by eight shots. He had gotten too deep on the backswing and across the line at the top, with a flat left wrist. Where he was a decade ago was a qualitatively better spot to play iron shots from. The numbers don't lie, he was a better iron player then. He was not going to beat Scottie [Scheffler] if he didn't hit his irons better."

McIlroy is a member at Michael Jordan's Grove XXIII, and during some long practice sessions there, in January '25, he began experimenting with a different model of TaylorMade ball, the TP5. McIlroy found that it launched lower with his short irons—a good thing, given his tendency to send his ball to the heavens—but spun more, allowing for greater control. (Woods had always employed the spinniest ball on Tour to maximize his shotmaking skills.) McIlroy decided to put the new ball in play. Says Faxon, "You gotta respect that a guy who has had so much success and has all the money in the world still turns over every stone looking for the tiniest ways to improve."

No doubt McIlroy's fire had been stoked by Scheffler's dominance. "Scottie has been the best player on the PGA Tour the last two seasons," Rory said. "I feel like I'm close but just not quite there. That is motivating—to get the most out of myself."

Throughout the long offseason, Chamblee could see McIlroy's swing going back to the future. "At the end of 2024, he was posting swing videos online and the technical improvement was obvious," says Chamblee. "At the top [of his swing], he looked more like the Rory of old. Once he got his swing in a better place, he could let go of every mechanical thought. That gave him the clarity to come out and play with more grit, more mettle, more determination."

All of this was on display at McIlroy's 2025 PGA Tour debut at the Crosby Clambake. He arrived at Pebble Beach looking rested and refreshed, a much different energy from his pinched, puckered visage throughout the preceding season's marital drama. McIlroy is a golf romantic; he stirred his soul the day before the Clambake began by playing Cypress Point for the first time. (He shot 67.) McIlroy began the tournament proper on the back nine at Spyglass Hill. The fifteenth hole is a short, steeply downhill par-3 that demands precise distance control. All McIlroy did was fly his ball straight into the hole for a slam-dunk ace, keying his bogeyless round of 66. Nothing like some positive feedback to validate all the hard work.

An ensuing 70 left McIlroy in eleventh place, five strokes behind Sepp Straka. Some vintage Crosby weather blew in on Saturday, and McIlroy rose to the challenge with a dazzling display of shotmaking into Pebble's tiny greens. He set up birdies with a three-quarter wedge on fifteen and then an off-speed 9-iron at sixteen, to say nothing of a 346-yard drive on eighteen. His 65 was his second bogey-free round in the span of three days, and it shot McIlroy into the lead. "This is as complete as I've seen Rory look, tee through the green, around the green, on the green," enthused CBS's Trevor Immelman.

On Sunday, having fought his way to a two-stroke lead through thirteen holes, McIlroy launched from the fourteenth tee one of the more memorable drives in the recent history of Pebble Beach, a 339-yard moon shot that touched 190 miles per hour of ball speed and 168 feet at its apex. He followed with a towering 7-iron from 201 yards that left him twenty-seven feet for eagle. He gutted the putt. Game over.

Sixteen years earlier, McIlroy had defeated Justin Rose in Dubai for his first professional victory. They were paired again on Sunday at Pebble Beach, and Rose was impressed that McIlroy continued to evolve at age thirty-five. "He did all the right things," said Rose, who tied for third. "He had control of his wedges. He was controlling all of his distances quite nicely. It was a very professional round of golf." Rose's smirk betrayed that McIlroy had, in the past, been prone to schoolboy errors. Rory didn't exactly disagree. "I finally feel my game can travel to any sort of golf course in any conditions in any setup, really," he said after his first victory in California. "I feel like I'm now a very well-rounded golfer and can adapt to whatever I need to adapt to." When I asked him to clarify when he had *finally* arrived, he turned philosophical. "Maybe not finally," McIlroy said. "I don't know if any of us should define ourselves as complete because that means there's nowhere left to go, no improvement left, and that's certainly not the case."

It's admirable that McIlroy was still looking ahead, given all that he had already accomplished: his twenty-seventh Tour victory moved him within one of Paul "Little Poison" Runyan and Leo Diegel for twentieth on the all-time list. Within striking distance were legends Lee Trevino (29 wins), Horton Smith (30), and Jimmy Demaret (31). Getting to thirty-one victories would make McIlroy among the fifteen most prolific winners in the history of the PGA Tour, to say nothing of his victories on the Euro Tour (ten and counting circa Pebble Beach, not including the major championships and WGCs, which were already included in his PGA Tour total). Yet McIlroy noted that the Pebble win was so special because it came on one of golf's "cathedrals." Only Augusta National and the Old Course can match Pebble's grandeur. "And I had a big fat zero on all of those going in here," McIlroy said. "So to knock one off [at] Pebble is very cool."

Rotella loved hearing McIlroy talk that way. "I thought that was brilliant on his part," he says. "He embraced the bigness of the moment. What a great word—'cathedral.'" McIlroy didn't mention it, but Augusta National has long carried an overwrought nickname: "the Cathedral in the Pines."

•

THE ROAD TO THE Masters ran through the Players Championship. McIlroy describes Sawgrass's Stadium Course as "fiddly," as it largely demands finesse over raw power, negating some of his advantage. Pete Dye's house of horrors is a test of McIlroy's patience as much as his skill. In the early part of 2025, he often referenced Scheffler as an inspiration, saying he aspired to similarly reduce his on-course miscues. "I'm a big admirer of Scottie's for a lot of different reasons," he said. "Every time I play with him, I watch how he plays, how disciplined he is—it's a really cool thing to watch. Honestly, I'm just trying to take a leaf out of his book." McIlroy admitted that playing the Scheffler way required a different mindset. "There are impulses on the course I have that he doesn't," he said with a laugh. "I have to rein those in and be more disciplined about it." And what does that look like? "Strategy and picking more conservative targets at times and more conservative clubs off the tee."

McIlroy struggled with his ball-striking during the practice rounds at the Players. His edginess came through in comments to the press, when he disparaged the Senior Tour ("Something will have gone terribly wrong if I have to compete at golf at fifty") and expressed disdain for "YouTube golf," which has become a kind of cult in the golf world. During a practice round, a punk college kid heckled McIlroy about Pinehurst, apparently filming it for online clout. (The end of the world is nigh.) McIlroy walked over to the rope line and confiscated the phone, a satisfying bit of vigilante justice. (Embarrassingly, the kid turned out to be a member of the Texas golf team; the phone was eventually returned and the chastened Longhorn issued an apology.)

Rotella labored to turn McIlroy's poor practice-round form into a positive for his frustrated client. "We said, *Hey, this is a great opportunity to win in a different way,*" says Rotella. "We know that when Rory is playing his best, he can run away from the field. But wouldn't it be satisfying to win ugly on that course?" Paired with Scheffler in the first round, McIlroy hit only four fairways but scrambled so adroitly he enjoyed nearly 3.5 strokes gained with his approach play, including a brilliant punch-cut from the pine straw on eighteen that cozied to within eight feet of the hole for a birdie. McIlroy kept scrapping from there, with a 68 followed by a 73 that was blighted by a trio of three-putts. That left him tied for fifth, four strokes behind leader J. J. Spaun, a late bloomer with one of the prettiest swings in the game.

McIlroy wasted no time asserting himself in the final round, starting birdie-eagle to slice Spaun's lead to one stroke. A superb up-and-down on the par-5 eleventh hole gave McIlroy the lead, and then play was suspended for four hours due to thunderstorms. When the final round resumed, McIlroy struggled with the slower greens and reading putts in the encroaching darkness, playing the final six holes in 1-over. Spaun caught him with a birdie on the sixteenth hole, forcing a three-hole aggregate playoff that would be played on Monday morning. "He loves to think of himself as a complete player, to prove that he is one," says Faxon. "He wants to win in other ways than just outdriving everyone. That whole final round was a testament to that. He drove it poorly and his irons were off, but he was resilient enough to win by putting great and chipping great." Instead of ruing having lost the lead on the back nine, McIlroy was all business, looking ahead to how he would execute in the impending playoff. "You've got to make five good swings," he said of Sawgrass's treacherous, watery closing holes. "That's all it is. So try to get up there, make five good swings tomorrow morning, and get this thing done."

McIlroy had struggled all week with his driver, but he began the playoff, on the par-5 sixteenth hole, with a missile that carried 322 yards and split the fairway. A gorgeous approach shot left him pin-high, the carry distance perfectly executed despite a strong wind at his back. The two-putt birdie put him one stroke ahead of Spaun. McIlroy had indeed produced two very good swings on sixteen, but now came the do-or-die seventeenth hole, with its island green. The hole was playing 130 yards, into the fan. In the old days—like 2024—McIlroy might have nuked a pitching wedge, sending his ball to the heavens. This time he selected a 9-iron, which he can easily carry 165 yards. This was the moment of truth for McIlroy's new finesse game. He played a tricky off-speed shot, propelling his ball through the sticky air. The apex topped out at eighty-three feet, significantly lower than McIlroy's usual 9-iron, and his spinnier TP5 settled safely on the green, just past pin-high. "I have this little three-quarter, three-quarter shot, I call it," he said afterward. "It's a three-quarter backswing with three-quarter speed. It's a shot that I've always had with the wedges, but I've been reluctant to use it with 9-iron, 8-iron, 7-iron down. But this year I've gotten more into using that shot with some of those lower clubs, like the 9-iron on seventeen."

Noting that McIlroy was "easily a club longer than me," Spaun selected an 8-iron, but he lacked his opponent's exquisite distance control: his ball flew the green entirely, kerplunking into the water. Ballgame. McIlroy had won again, just four weeks before the Masters. "Honestly, standing over that tee shot on sixteen this morning is the most nervous I've been in a long time," McIlroy said. "So I think that will stand me in good stead, feeling like that and being able to hit the golf shots that I need while your stomach is sort of not feeling great and your legs are a little shaky and your heart rate is racing. To have to go through that today, it's nice to have that in recent memory for some of the tournaments coming up, for sure."

THE GOLF GODS TAKETH and they giveth. The two keynote players of 2024 had their Masters preparation badly compromised by infirmity. On Christmas, Scheffler suffered a puncture wound from a broken wineglass—he was using the glass to cut dough for homemade ravioli—and he missed a month of action leading into Pebble Beach. Xander Schauffele missed most of January and all of February with a rib injury. Both were winless and on edge heading into Augusta, making McIlroy the undisputed pretournament favorite. "It was his to win or lose, and we had never said that before," says Chamblee. "Scottie's struggles, Xander being off his game, [Collin] Morikawa being a little lost, Bryson [DeChambeau] out of sight out of mind on LIV—all of that freed up Rory mentally. He was the guy. He didn't have to do anything special to win, he just had to play the way he had been playing."

McIlroy certainly projected alpha status on the eve of the tournament. He was leaving the range with his usual wingman, Shane Lowry, when they crossed paths with Spaun, who was on his way to a playoff to determine the winner of the annual Par-3 Tournament. McIlroy caught Spaun with an all-time stray: "Better get the club right this time." Says Spaun, "That hurt. That hit me. Shane Lowry was like, 'Fuckin' hell, Rory.' It was a little too soon [after the Players playoff] to hear that. That wound was not healed yet."

McIlroy brought that same energy to the first tee on Thursday. Through the years, he had uncorked a litany of nervy, wild drives on Augusta National's opening hole; this time, he pounded one to the dead center of the fairway. Then he went flag hunting to a dangerous front-left hole location. McIlroy lipped out the eight-foot birdie putt, but that didn't matter to Chamblee, who says, "Second shot of the tournament, I thought, *It's over!* Because Rory had a hook lie to a left pin, and he cut a wedge in there. He'd never had that shot before." On the third hole, McIlroy nearly drove the green and then pitched to four feet for his first birdie. On eight, he blasted a 343-yard drive over the bunker and reached the green with a mid-iron for a two-putt birdie. Then on nine, he unleashed a 360-yard drive that reached the *uphill*. A nifty wedge to four feet for another birdie sent him flying up the leaderboard. At the thirteenth hole, McIlroy continued his pyrotechnics with a 335-yard drive that set up another two-putt birdie. He was −4 and tied for second place. The energy was cresting at Augusta National.

McIlroy found the fairway at the par-5 fifteenth. From 241 yards out, his approach shot landed next to the front-left pin but skittered across and over the back of the firm green. He now faced an exceedingly delicate chip down a putting surface that sloped toward the pond in front of the green. McIlroy carried his shot too far, and his ball was a goner even before it passed the pin. The crowd audibly gasped as it plunged into the water. McIlroy wanted no part of a do-over after this brutal mistake, so he trudged to the drop area on the other side of the pond. He hit his fifth shot too hard, and the ball ran through the green and almost into the bunker. He did well to two-putt from there for a double bogey. Hard to imagine a bigger buzzkill . . . until the seventeenth hole, when McIlroy flew the green with his approach shot and then three-putted from thirty feet for another double bogey. You could feel the shudder run through Augusta National, Twitter, and the larger golf world. The 72 left him in twenty-seventh place, seven strokes behind Justin Rose's lead. Following the ceremonial first tee shot that morning, Jack Nicklaus had met with reporters, and he all but predicted McIlroy's collapse: "The discipline is what Rory has lacked in my opinion. He's got all the shots. He's got all the game. He certainly is as talented as anybody in the game. But if you go back and see his history the last few years . . . a lot of times an 8 or a 7 pops up, and that keeps him from getting to where he needs to go."

McIlroy had been blessed with the late-early wave, so he was at Augusta National just after dawn on Friday morning, eager to atone for the shaky finish. As he did prior to each round that week, McIlroy met Rotella for a chat in the deluxe caddie shack on the edge of the driving range. Rory needed the reset; he had been so pouty he refused to speak to reporters after the desultory finish the night before. "We wanted to make a couple of adjustments," says Rotella. "It looked like he might have pushed a little too hard at the end of the first round. I kept reminding him he has lots of time. It's only Friday. Either you stay patient or you panic. And if you panic, the course beats you up pretty good.

"We didn't talk about the mistakes [late in the first round], we talked about everything he was doing well. He was playing great. He hit so many good shots on Thursday. The key was: *Don't let the ball own your mind. As soon as the shot is over, it's over. Don't give it any meaning. Just get lost in your own little world. You have a gift and a passion and a commitment to this game, let's get your mind locked in and let your talent flow.*" With a nod to McIlroy's deflating finish on Thursday, Rotella left him with a final thought: "Let's make this a great comeback story."

McIlroy made a textbook birdie on the second hole and followed with a series of quality shots and sound decisions. The birdie putts weren't falling, but he stayed patient and stuck to his game plan, making seven straight pars to close out the front nine. Take that, Jack. "I thought the tournament was won on that front nine on Friday," says Rotella. "Rory showed so much poise." The reward was the back nine of McIlroy's dreams: he flagged approach shots on the tenth and eleventh, two of Augusta National's toughest holes. "Making birdie on ten and eleven is a joke here," said playing partner Akshay Bhatia. On the par-5 thirteenth, McIlroy's drive ran through the fairway onto the pine straw; patience may be a virtue, but no one wins the Masters by playing scared. McIlroy decided to go for the green. He pushed his 4-iron a hair, but his ball carried the creek by three or four yards and settled ten feet from the hole, a putt he buried for eagle. "I don't think it was really a decision to go for it or not," McIlroy said. "But yeah, when the ball was in the air, I was like, *You idiot, what did you do?* . . . I rode my luck a little bit with that second shot." He was fortunate again on fifteen. McIlroy hung his second shot out to the right, but his ball found a safe spot on the very front of the green, a few yards past the water. He two-putted from ninety feet for another birdie. McIlroy's iron play had consistently held him back at the Masters; now, through two rounds, he was second in strokes gained: approach. His 66 was the low round of the day and shot McIlroy to a tie for third, only two shots back of Rose. McIlroy had responded resoundingly to his Thursday stumbles. He was striking the ball with more authority than anyone in the field. The Masters was there for the taking.

The excitement—no, the euphoria—that gripped the golf world was best expressed that evening on the YouTube livestream of the *No Laying Up* podcast, which has become golf's town hall during the major championships. This time, the pod opened with a simulated rave as the hosts gyrated to pulsating techno music. The *NLU* crew had a well-worn bit going back many years, a digital block party that would convene whenever McIlroy was in contention at a major championship. It's been a gathering place for shared optimism, delusion, and ultimately despair. Now the boys were flying high after McIlroy's thrilling second round, which was acknowledged by Phil Landes, the show's resident curmudgeon: "I felt like we were gonna have a trophy ceremony today on [the eighteenth] green to award him . . . I don't know what we were gonna award him."

Neil Schuster tried to put into words why he has always pulled so hard for McIlroy, despite the maddening disappointments: "What it is for Rory with me, he does all the hard stuff really well. He hits these shots I will never dream of hitting. Then he has these typos. *Man, just proofread your work.* Don't chip it into the pond on fifteen from back there. Just don't fucking do it. I find that very relatable. I've had so many rounds where I've done similar stuff. And if he slays the dragon, maybe that gives me a glimmer of hope."

The coronation coverage of McIlroy's second round felt wildly premature, given the many heartbreaks visited upon him at the Masters . . . until Rory began the third round with the most electric golf of his life. He had been charged up even before the round began; the wait until a 2:30 tee time is interminable. McIlroy watched *Zootopia* with his daughter ("Very, very good movie if anyone is interested") and Premier League Football and *still* had time to kill. He was pulsating by the time he arrived at the driving range. "I was [swinging] fast on the range," he says. "Talking about that anxious energy that built up, I was probably three or four miles an hour faster on the range than I have been all week, which is nice. So I knew I didn't have to worry about the bunker on one or two if I just made a good swing."

He pounded a 343-yard drive on the first hole, easily carrying the sand, and then followed with an off-speed wedge to ten feet. Birdie. On two, he mashed a 369-yard drive, but then his second shot carried over the back of the green. Might as well chip that in, which McIlroy did. An adroit pitch on three completed the trifecta: birdie-eagle-birdie. At the fearsome fifth hole, McIlroy drove it 342 yards down the center. He was reducing Augusta National to a pitch-and-putt. After floating his approach shot to eighteen feet, he made that birdie putt, too. Throw in pars at four and six, and he had made six 3s in a row, a first by any Masters competitor to start a round. Unique to McIlroy, his spectacular play couldn't help but conjure concern. Kyle Porter, one of the leading Rory-ologists on the golf beat, tweeted, "We are getting dangerously close to 'he's either going to win the Masters, or it's going to be the most heart-wrenching, soul-sucking defeat in golf history' territory."

Adversity followed, as it inevitably must with McIlroy. He made a mess of the par-5 eighth and then three-putted the tenth for another bogey. By the time he reached thirteen, it had been two hours since McIlroy had made a birdie. But he summoned two superb shots for a crucial two-putt birdie. Then on fifteen, with a 6-iron from 205 yards, he hit a soaring approach to six feet to set up his second eagle of the round. McIlroy's 66 was the lowest score for the second day in a row. He led by two strokes over his Pinehurst antagonist DeChambeau and four over Corey Conners, his Saturday playing partner. "His firepower and his ability to kind of hit the right shot at the right time, kind of get himself on a run, was impressive," Conners said with typical Canadian understatement. No one else was within five shots of McIlroy, including Scheffler, who had been only one back of McIlroy through thirty-six holes but made a series of uncharacteristic mistakes during a 72 that left him seven shots adrift.

McIlroy was in complete control of every aspect of his game. He knew that the challenges of the final round would be metaphysical. "I think I am quite a momentum player," he said. "There is a balance, though. You have to sort of try to ride that momentum as much as you can, but then also temper it with a little bit of, you know, rationale and logic. And so it is a fine dance. I certainly don't want to be a robot out there, but at the same time I don't want to be too animated, either."

DeChambeau, who birdied three of the final four holes to stay on McIlroy's heels, was not in the mood to downplay what was at stake.

"It will be the grandest stage that we've had in a long time, and I'm excited for it," he said.

Masters Sunday dawned with even more excitement than usual but also an undercurrent of dread: there would be no coming back from this if McIlroy blew the Masters. "In the history of golf, no one has ever played with more pressure than Rory on Sunday at Augusta," says Chamblee. "You could say Tiger Woods at the 2001 Masters [when he was trying to complete the Tiger Slam], but I would argue there was such a sense of inevitability that he was impervious to criticism. Maybe Bobby Jones at Merion [in 1930, attempting to complete the Grand Slam], but it was such a different media age, and Bobby Jones had all the reporters in his pocket anyway, so if he didn't win, he would have been celebrated just for giving himself the opportunity. But if Rory didn't win this Masters, he was going to get crucified. The whole world was ready to write his obituary."

McIlroy knew it. "I was unbelievably nervous," he said. "Knot in your stomach, didn't really have much of an appetite all day. Tried to force food down. Your legs feel a little jellylike."

Playing with DeChambeau offered its own challenges. In their battle at Pinehurst, the fans had undeniably tilted toward Bryson, who hammed it up for the crowd like a carnival barker. He tried to rekindle that mojo at staid Augusta National. CBS announcer Dottie Pepper, who followed the group inside the ropes, later described the scene in a *Golf Digest* piece: "When Rory and Bryson arrived at the first tee, their countenances were very different. Bryson made a gladiator entrance, exuberant. He was trying to create an atmosphere he could feed off. Rory was tighter, more serious, a little edgy." It showed in his opening drive. The day before, McIlroy had carried the fairway bunker by twenty yards, but he didn't have the same freedom in his swing on Masters Sunday; his ball fell out of the sky a yard or two too soon and settled in the sand, hard against the lip. He blasted out well short of the green, played his pitch twenty-six feet past the hole, and then rapped his par putt eight feet beyond the hole. McIlroy was fifteen minutes into his final round and nerves were already fraying—his and everyone else's. He missed the putt on the low side, taking his third double bogey of the week. Kyle Porter was locked and loaded with the perfect tweet: "You guys thought this was going to be easy? Straightforward?"

Craig Stadler was the only player in Masters history to make three double bogeys during tournament week and still win. Living his worst nightmare somehow relaxed McIlroy. "I was really nervous going out," he says, "and it was almost as if the double bogey at the first calmed my nerves a bit and sort of got me into it in a funny way." But he drove it into the bunker on number two, the second hole in a row that he failed to fly the sand by the tiniest margin. After laying up, McIlroy played an eighty-eight-yard pitch that was so mediocre he dropped his club in disgust and bent over at the waist in anguish. He had said the night before he didn't want to be too animated; McIlroy already appeared to be coming undone. He doomed himself to a par while DeChambeau holed an eight-foot birdie putt that was so pure it would have gone into a thimble. Bryson had made up three strokes in two holes, seizing the lead. The gravediggers began reaching for their shovels.

CBS's Pepper has had an up-close view of McIlroy for most of his career. Walking off the second green, she says, "I saw a quality in him I'd never seen before: anger—not frustration or fear, just downright anger and defiance. It's not his normal way." McIlroy had planned to lay up off the tee of the short, dangerous par-4 third hole—with a dicey front-left pin, many players were laying back to leave themselves a full wedge shot in. But given McIlroy's red ass, driver became the play. He smoked a tee shot that looked like it would reach the putting surface, but his ball took a hard left turn just short of the green and settled in a deep swale, leaving one of the scariest pitches on the property. Curse you, golf gods! Somehow, some way, with his entire world caving in, McIlroy summoned a perfect shot, bouncing his ball into the hillside and trickling it to within eight feet for birdie. He called it the most important moment of the final round. Big, bad Bryson turned timid off the tee—"I could not believe he laid up," McIlroy said—and then three-putted. When McIlroy made his uphill birdie putt, he had climbed back into the lead. "Where that resilience comes from—it's an interesting question," says Rotella. "Some people may be born with it. A lot of people aren't. Either way, if you want to be great, you have to develop that resilience. It's a skill just like any other."

Ben Hogan, the steely-eyed Hawk who will forever be revered for his toughness, once said, "I feel sorry for rich kids now, I really do. Because I knew tough things, and I had a tough day all my life, and I can handle tough things. They can't." Hogan's father shot himself through the heart while his young son played in the next room. McIlroy was blessed with loving, supportive parents, but they had to scrape and claw to give their son every opportunity. McIlroy observed it all and has modeled their flintiness. "My dad took on three jobs; my mum worked night shifts," he says. "They were doing what they had to do to support their son and never complained or moaned. They just got on with it."

Rory had honors at number four, the 232-yard par-3 that is one of Augusta National's toughest holes. The pin was cut so close to the bunker that, from the tee, it looked like it was in the sand. McIlroy hoisted a sky-high 5-iron, and his ball actually spun back a little on the brick-hard green, stopping nine feet from the hole. "His ability to hit a long iron to the moon is so cool," says Tour veteran Harry Higgs. "Even out here, he's a total outlier. Yeah, I mean, there's not another player who can instruct a golf ball to do the things he makes it do." DeChambeau hooked his tee shot long and left and couldn't get up and down. Then McIlroy drilled his birdie putt, the third straight hole with a two-shot swing. He now led by three strokes. "So much craziness would transpire, but to me the tournament flipped at the fourth hole," says Pepper.

Suddenly, luck was on McIlroy's side: on the long, hard fifth hole, he sliced his drive into a thicket of trees, but his ball found a spot that left him a clean look at the green. He played a strong approach shot just over the back of the putting surface and saved par with a crafty up-and-down. At seven, McIlroy pulled his drive into the trees but again had a window, though it required a daring shot over the pines from a spot where almost anyone else would have taken the safer route under the branches. "If Rory can see it, he can hit it," says Rotella. "A lot of other players say to me, 'How can he see that shot?' It's about having the guts and the mental toughness to take on the shot." After the wild start, McIlroy was now stacking up pars. He began to radiate an icy intensity, and his playing partner could feel the chill. "Didn't talk to me once all day," DeChambeau whined afterward.

Said McIlroy, "I don't know what he was expecting. Like, we were trying to win the Masters, I'm not going to try and be his mate out there."

On nine, a massive drive left Rory with only eighty-five yards in. It was an exacting shot, uphill to a sloping green with a wicked false front. McIlroy played a perfect three-quarter lob wedge to seven feet and then made the putt; even with the opening double bogey, he had toured the front nine in thirty-five strokes. DeChambeau putted next, missing from six feet. He was listing badly and now four behind. Just like that, the fans deserted him. "The rooting interests were fascinating to observe, especially the way they shifted," says Pepper. "Bryson had the 'bro' crowd with him, louder and brash with a lot of chirping. Rory seemed to appeal more to traditionalists. By the ninth hole, after Rory had gotten on track and Bryson wasn't responding, the bro crowd became more subdued. Bryson wasn't out of it by any means, but the sentiment had shifted permanently in Rory's favor."

McIlroy rode that wave on the long walk to the tenth tee. The fans formed a human tunnel of craziness, as much as such a thing is allowed at Augusta National. Fourteen years earlier, he had arrived at the same spot also leading by four strokes. It all came crashing down, beginning with a jittery tee shot to the front door of a cabin way left of the fairway. This time, McIlroy made a languid move with his 3-wood and split the fairway. But from 175 yards out, he toed his approach shot, and the feeling at impact was so unsatisfactory that he dropped the club while completing his follow-through. The ball didn't know it: a tight draw flew at the flag and settled fifteen feet away. The clear views at the green on five and seven, and now this . . . the golf gods were smiling upon McIlroy. He poured in the putt to reach −14 and restore the lead to four strokes over a charging Justin Rose, who had just finished birdieing his way through Amen Corner. McIlroy was not doing a victory lap yet. "The worst I felt on Sunday at Augusta," he says, "was probably when I holed the birdie putt on ten to go four ahead, because I'm like, *Oh, I really can't mess this up now.* There's that pressure. You know that you're not just trying to win another tournament, you're trying to become part of history, and that has a certain weight to it."

At eleven, McIlroy sliced his drive to the edge of the trees but again(!) had a clear path to the green, or, at the very least, to a safe spot just short and right of it, away from the pond left of the green. Back in 2016, during the third round, McIlroy had faced a similar shot and hooked his ball into the water. Now, on the telecast, Pepper intoned gravely, "He really needs to play the responsible shot, conservatively." Instead, McIlroy played a reckless shot, aggressively, and his ball turned toward the pond. As it trickled closer, an audible buzz of concern and disbelief ran through the huge crowd in Amen Corner. McIlroy's shot expired six inches from the abyss, sparing him the most boneheaded mistake imaginable. "Look, I rode my luck all week," McIlroy said afterward. "And again, I think with the things that I've had to endure over the last few years, I think I deserved it." McIlroy failed to get up and down, but a bogey was survivable; up ahead on fourteen, Rose had made bogey after an errant drive, so McIlroy's lead remained four strokes as he stepped to the tee of twelve, the most frightening par-3 in championship golf. He sent a 9-iron to the middle of the skinny green. You could feel the golf world exhale. When McIlroy tapped in for par, he led by four strokes with six holes to play, two of them par-5s he had been devouring all week. He had one arm in the green jacket.

McIlroy employed his 3-wood off the tee at thirteen, playing to the fat part of the fairway. Rose birdied fifteen as Rory flowed down the fairway, slicing the lead to three. McIlroy knew that thanks to the giant scoreboard framing the thirteenth green. From 239 yards out, he made the uncharacteristic decision to lay up, with a 7-iron. "I wanted to take the big number out of play," McIlroy said. He hit a good one. As he walked down the fairway, Rose flagged his tee shot on sixteen. McIlroy heard that; the sixteenth tee is sneaky close to the thirteenth hole. The tension was building, thanks to Rose's spirited play.

McIlroy had laid up to the left edge of the fairway, giving himself the ideal angle to a front-right pin. The creek fronting the green was barely in play, as McIlroy could play his ball deep into the green and feed it down the slope toward the hole; as Gerry McIlroy later put it, his son had all of Georgia left of the flag. Other than tap-in putts, it was probably the easiest shot he faced all day . . . notwithstanding that the Masters was, at long last, within his grasp. The lie did present a slight complication. "[The ball] had gone into a little valley, and it was on the upslope," McIlroy says. "And usually when I hit wedge shots off upslopes, they come out a little bit left on me. I gave myself a couple of yards of room to the right. I wasn't aiming at the creek, but it came out a little weak and a little right."

Translation: McIlroy duffed it into the water.

Given the magnitude of the moment, the absurdity of the outcome, and the potential ramifications, you can make a case that it was the worst shot in golf history. On Sky TV, Sir Nick Faldo spoke for all of us when he blurted out, "That's horrendous! I can't believe it."

A Normanesque collapse now felt like a very real possibility. The emotional stakes had reached a fever pitch. "It was a drama-tragedy playing out before our eyes, and we didn't know if the hero was going to get murdered in the final scene or save the whole world," says Chamblee. "Who wrote this—Stephen King? Shakespeare? Aaron Sorkin?"

McIlroy played a sound pitch from the drop circle but missed the ensuing ten-footer, taking his second double bogey of the day and fourth of the week. At sixteen, Rose made his 4.5-footer for birdie. Bang-bang, three-shot swing. Twenty-nine minutes earlier, when McIlroy birdied the tenth hole, his win probability rose to 95.3 percent, as calculated by the sharpies at Data Golf. Rose's languished at 2.8 percent. Now it was a tie ballgame.

The fans erupted as McIlroy stepped to the fourteenth tee, but this was not a serenade for their hero. No, you could hear the strain in their shouts—anxiousness, even a tinge of desperation. It's exactly how all those Scots had sounded on the back nine at St. Andrews three years earlier. McIlroy's swing looked out of sequence on the fourteenth tee, and he slashed his ball into the pine straw right of the fairway. His approach shot came up well short, but a terrific pitch left him six feet to save par. He made a tentative stroke, his ball expiring on the right edge. Bogey. For the first time since lunch on Friday, McIlroy was not leading the Masters. His win probability dipped to 29.8 percent.

In their chat before the final round, Rotella had told McIlroy, "It's supposed to be hard. It's a game of mistakes. Can you live with those? Can you overcome them?" Rotella expands on the thought, saying, "The tendency for most players is to overreact. But even the player who wins the tournament makes a lot of mistakes across four rounds. Rory has accepted that. He won't ever give in. He's not afraid of making mistakes because he has developed zero doubt that he can survive them."

Rose had shot 75 on Saturday and begun the final round tied for sixth, seven strokes back. It's one thing to la-di-da your way to birdies when you don't really have a chance to win. As soon as Rose took the lead, he gave it right back, missing the fairway and green on seventeen and then a six-footer for par after taking an inordinate amount of time (mis)reading the putt. That created a three-way tie for the lead with

Rose, McIlroy, and young stud Ludvig Åberg, who had been just kinda hanging around until birdies at thirteen and fifteen.

McIlroy's woes seemed to continue at fifteen, when he pulled his drive to the left edge of the fairway, leaving a shaggy pine branch obstructing his path to the green. But the slightly off-line drive turned out to be a blessing. His layup on thirteen had been rational, reasonable, logical, defensible. It was the well-considered play of a man trying to protect a big lead. The tentative deceleration on the ill-fated wedge shot was the same kind of defensive play that had hurt him on the opening two holes. Only when McIlroy lost his lead to DeChambeau did he play with more freedom. Now, in the fifteenth fairway, McIlroy faced another decision: lay up again and greatly reduce the possibility of disaster—which made all the sense in the world given that McIlroy had played the preceding four holes in +4—or go for broke with a slinging hook around the branch to one of the most fraught greens in golf.

McIlroy has more than a passing interest in anatomy; he took up juggling when he discovered it is one of the few activities that engage both hemispheres of the brain simultaneously. His left brain had compelled him to lay up on thirteen. The right brain would unlock his genius. McIlroy and Rotella had discussed this topic plenty of times. Says McIlroy, "He said to me, 'Rory, have you ever been to Disney?' *Yeah, I've been to Disney.* 'Did you ever get one of those caricature artists to draw your face?' *Yeah, I remember that.* He said, 'When they draw, are they looking at your face or are they looking at their hand?' I said my face. He said, 'Exactly, they're not looking at their hand, telling it how to draw your face. They're looking at their target and letting their hand do what it needs to do.' That's the exact same thing as golf. You need the technique. You need to drill the technique at home, on the range, whatever, but when you go and play, the less thought the better."

McIlroy the artist had been presented the ultimate canvas. In the past, he had talked about "painting" shots around Augusta National, a lovely image for the creativity the course encourages. There would be no laying up. From 207 yards out, he made a freewheeling swing with his 7-iron. His ball rocketed past the pine limb, on line with the right edge of the greenside bunker, and then bent left toward the flag. McIlroy stalked after it. The ball was in the air forever. Did any sports fan anywhere take a breath while it was still in orbit? It's not easy to track a small white ball against a cloudless sky. When McIlroy's ball landed on the green, twenty paces from the hole but bouncing and curling to within six feet, Augusta National shook. "The shot of a lifetime!" Jim Nantz enthused on the telecast. Pepper calls the roar that followed "the loudest I've ever heard in my life. It traveled from the green up the hill and hit me like a truck."

In the span of two holes, McIlroy had hit one of the worst shots in Masters history and now one of the best. From inexplicable to unforgettable. McIlroy always wanted to be the next Tiger Woods, but turns out he's more like Phil Mickelson—wildly unpredictable and always entertaining. Just as Mickelson won a green with two different drivers in his bag, McIlroy's open-mindedness proved crucial at this Masters: the new golf ball he embraced at the start of the season curved more and grabbed harder on the greens. He would later say he could not have pulled off the shot on fifteen with his old ball.

McIlroy had six feet for an eagle that would put him in a commanding position to finally win the Masters. After a shot that transcendent, of course he would make the putt. Right?

McIlroy babied the putt and missed it low. Gentle Jim Nantz offered a harsh verdict: "Feeble."

In an interview, Nantz says, "I try to articulate what the moment feels like to the fan and the player. I had just called it the shot of a lifetime. I thought that shot would win him the green jacket, I really did. There was so much risk on that shot—it was so daring. The putt felt like a foregone conclusion, and that would be one of those moments we play back forever. I didn't even realize that's what I said, but in the moment I felt like, *Darn, he just took away what could have been the perfect, defining moment of the whole tournament.*"

Still, the tap-in birdie gave McIlroy a one-stroke lead. Åberg, who missed a twenty-footer on sixteen that would have given him the lead, missed another putt of a similar length on seventeen that would have tied him with McIlroy. At the par-3 sixteenth hole, with the pin back-right in the exact same spot where Jack Nicklaus had made a legendary birdie fifty years earlier, McIlroy floated a lovely 8-iron to nine feet. It felt like he was back in control of the tournament . . . until a minute later when Rose buried a curling twenty-foot birdie putt at eighteen, tying for the lead. It was his sixth birdie of the back nine (along with two bogies). McIlroy heard the roar but couldn't respond, bricking his birdie putt on sixteen. There was no longer any joy in watching McIlroy try to win the Masters—the only feeling left was existential dread.

The seventeenth hole at Augusta National is an artless brute featuring an awkward, uphill, semi-blind drive and a turtleback green that, with nary a tree nearby, is always bone dry and brick hard late in the day. McIlroy's stress had manifested in his putting stroke, but he still looked reasonably confident with the longer clubs; wielding a 3-wood, he hit a high fade to the right edge of the fairway, leaving 184 yards, uphill. McIlroy pulled an 8-iron but had a moment of indecision, saying to caddie Harry Diamond that he needed a little help to get it there. There was indeed a breath of wind, but it was off the left and not really helping. McIlroy stuck with the 8-iron and played a high draw. Well before it reached its apex, he was already begging: "Go! Aww, go. Awwww, go, go, go! Go . . . go . . . go . . ." McIlroy's ball carried the front bunker by maybe three yards and rolled to within two feet of the hole, another shot for the ages. Stats guru Lou Stagner crunched the numbers: the chances that the average Tour pro would hit it as close as McIlroy did from that distance on that hole were 0.37 percent. And this doesn't factor in the crushing weight of a career Grand Slam hanging in the balance. (Throw in the 1.99 percent odds that McIlroy would hit it as tight as he did on fifteen and the 7.91 percent odds for his shot on sixteen and the likelihood that a Tour pro would produce approach shots that good on three consecutive holes was 1 in 28,700.) When McIlroy rattled in the birdie putt on seventeen, he had again wrestled back the lead from Rose. (Åberg three-putted seventeen to end his bid.)

McIlroy did the hard part at eighteen, finding the narrow fairway with a baby cut. He left himself only 125 yards, a perfect little gap wedge, though he was close enough to the shoulder of the bunker that he had a slight hanging lie, with the ball below his feet. By the end of the 2025 FedEx Cup season, McIlroy's upgraded wedge game would place him eighth on the PGA Tour in proximity to the hole from 125 to 150 yards, his average approach shot settling at 20 feet 5 inches. With the pin cut in its usual front location on a two-tiered green, McIlroy had a big backstop to provide even more margin for error. One more decent swing (plus a careful lag putt and a tap-in) and the green jacket would be his. It was the easiest shot he'd faced since, well, the pitch on the thirteenth hole.

Years ago, when Tom Watson blew an Open Championship on the Road Hole, Dan Jenkins described his wayward approach shot as "a semishank, half-flier, out-of-control fade-slice that wanted to go to Edinburgh." Now McIlroy produced something similar, though his ball veered toward Aiken. When it splashed in the greenside bunker, Nantz couldn't hide his incredulity: "Oh my goodness! Wedge play has betrayed him again." McIlroy bent over at the waist in anguish. Minutes earlier, the crowd had been deliriously chanting "Rory! Rory!" As the man himself walked up the hill to meet his fate, he was greeted by tepid applause. Who could cheer at a time like this?

McIlroy now faced a delicate, downhill bunker shot . . . from pretty much the exact spot where he holed out during his breakthrough round on Masters Sunday in 2022. He played another beauty, to 4.5 feet, leaving himself what every boy dreams about until he grows up and has to face it: a putt to win the Masters. A month after blowing short putts on the seventieth and seventy-second holes to lose the 2024 U.S. Open,

McIlroy was asked how much he still thought about those misses. His answer offered rare insight into all the scar tissue he'd built up through the years: "I still think about the short putt that I missed at Crans-sur-Sierre [Switzerland] in 2008 in a playoff. You think about all of them."

As McIlroy waited for DeChambeau to finish off his shaky 75, Rory smacked his lips and licked his gums to no avail; the cotton-mouth wouldn't quit. And no wonder—he had looked tentative and perhaps even a little scared with the putter on crucial misses at fourteen, fifteen, and sixteen. McIlroy's putting coach, Brad Faxon, admits to barely being able to watch his pupil on the final green. "I don't know how the heck you prepare for a putt like that," says Faxon. "He's very aware of golf history and his place in it, which makes all of this a lot harder than it is for a guy who doesn't really care and just goes out and plays. Now he's got a downhill putt on a white-hot green, all those demons and ghosts are swirling around, the whole world is watching . . . it's just tough. He told me later he was really nervous over the ball on the seventy-second hole. Man, I'm nervous now just talking about it!"

As McIlroy stepped into the putt, CBS offered a diabolical chyron: FOR CAREER GRAND SLAM.

McIlroy's ball didn't touch the hole.

All he had needed to win was to shoot even par, but he came home in 73, with only two pars on the final ten holes. Sudden death loomed with Rose.

But before that, it was Diamond's time to shine. The caddie had become an easy punching bag during McIlroy's long drought in the major championships. After costly misclubs coming down the stretch at Pinehurst, Diamond had been ripped publicly by Hank Haney, Tiger Woods's old swing coach, and Smylie Kaufman, the former player turned broadcaster. McIlroy bristled at the critiques, saying, "Hank Haney has never been in that position. Smylie has been in that position once [at the 2016 Masters, when he played in the final group on Sunday and shot 81]. At the end of the day, they are not in the arena. They are not the ones hitting the shots and making the decisions. Someone said to me once, 'If you would never take advice from these people, you would never take their criticisms, either.' Certainly wouldn't go to Hank Haney for advice. I love Smylie, but I think I know what I'm doing, and so does Harry . . . But just because Harry is not as vocal or loud with his words as other caddies, it doesn't mean that he doesn't say anything and that he doesn't do anything. These guys that criticize, they are never there to say Harry did such a great job when I win, but they are always there to criticize when we don't win."

McIlroy's ringing endorsement of Diamond was noteworthy because, says Paul McGinley, "Rory rarely gives praise to anybody around him. He has a very high sense of his value. He feels like, *I'm the guy who does the donkey work out there—nobody else is allowed to take any praise off my back. I'm the guy out there firing the shots and taking the arrows, nobody else.* He's very much like Tiger in that way. The flip side of that, which I much admire about Rory, is that when it goes wrong, he never throws anybody else under the bus. You ever heard him criticize anybody around him? He has ownership of everything that he does, and nobody else is allowed to claim any of that ownership."

Now, in the moments before the playoff, Diamond offered his best friend one simple thought: "Well, pal, we would have taken this on Monday morning." McIlroy told this story to the world during his Sunday evening press conference at Augusta while lavishing praise upon Diamond. After hearing his caddie's succinct pep talk, McIlroy says, "It was an easy reset." That's because he knew Diamond was right. In the preceding four and a half hours, McIlroy had stepped on his dick, shit the bed, screwed the pooch . . . and yet somehow he had vanquished DeChambeau, Åberg, Patrick Reed, Scottie Scheffler, Xander Schauffele, and sundry others. To live his childhood dream, all he had to do now was outlast the battle-scarred Rose, forty-five, whom he had been regularly beating for the last decade and a half. And oh, by the way, Rose's career playoff record on the PGA Tour was 2-4 (including a loss to Sergio García at the 2017 Masters!) while McIlroy's was 4-2.

Rose had the honor when the playoff commenced on the eighteenth hole, by virtue of having completed his final round first. He hit a solid drive down the right side of the fairway. For McIlroy, the chute between the trees suddenly looked that much tighter. His game will always be defined by a spectacular ability to drive the golf ball. Now, when it mattered most, McIlroy unleashed a swing of pure poetry, pounding his ball thirty-two yards past Rose's. Playing first, Rose had the chance to apply a ton of pressure to his foe; he summoned an excellent shot that landed right next to the hole but was a little unlucky when it rolled out to twelve feet. McIlroy had the exact same distance as the last time he played the hole, 125 yards. But now he was in the dead center of the fairway, far enough away from the shoulder of the bunker to have a perfectly flat lie. McIlroy selected a gap wedge again. This time, he played a tight draw over the flag. He carried it deeper into the green than Rose had, using the backstop to feed his ball back toward the hole. It rolled, trickled, and curled to three feet. The roar at Augusta was substantial but not quite delirious. After all that McIlroy had put the fans through, no one believed it was over yet.

Rose putted first, and he understood that he had landed in the Stewart Cink role. "I wanted to be the bad guy today," he said. But his putt was never on line, and Rose cleared the stage. How many three-footers had Rory McIlroy made in his lifetime? Half a million? More? And yet, after all the preceding melodrama, absolutely no one would have been surprised if he missed this one. But he didn't.

McIlroy tossed his putter over his head and collapsed onto his knees, his forehead pressed against the parched putting surface. His body heaved and shook with catharsis. He sat up, tilted his head back and roared. "There wasn't much joy in that reaction," he said. "It was all relief." He rose to his feet, unsteadied by the moment, and fell into a hug with his best friend as they pounded each other on the back. "We've had so many good times together," McIlroy said. "He's been like a big brother to me the whole way through my life. To be able to share this with him after all the close calls that we've had, all the crap that he's had to take from people that don't know anything about the game, yeah, this one is just as much his as it is mine."

McIlroy dapped up Rose and his caddie, Mark Fulcher, both of whom were exceedingly gracious. They left the green, but McIlroy lingered. He spiked his hat to the ground, pumped his fists, and then doubled over again, shaking. Diamond came over and spoke into McIlroy's ear and then guided him off the green, his arm around his boss's back while Rory cried into his shoulder. Incredible scenes. McIlroy ran a gauntlet of gladhanding green jackets and finally arrived on the walkway at the back of the green, the site of so much emotion. It was where Tiger Woods embraced his father, Earl, in 1997 after they had conquered the world together. Twenty-two years later, it's where Tiger came full circle and hugged his son, Charlie, after the sport's ultimate victory lap. It is the same patch of grass where Phil Mickelson embraced Amy after winning the Masters for his cancer-stricken wife in 2010. Now all eyes were on the McIlroys. In the eleven months since her husband filed for divorce and then very publicly changed his mind, Erica had retreated from the public eye. But she was waiting for her man behind Augusta National's eighteenth hole. They melted into each other, faces obscured by the broad brim of her hat. There was a lot of feeling in that hug. As Rory picked up his daughter, a guttural sound escaped him; there was no holding back the rawness of the emotions. He buried his face in Poppy's neck and sobbed. He tenderly planted a kiss on her forehead and stroked her hair. More hugs with his inner circle followed, including with manager Sean O'Flaherty. (McIlroy's parents were back home in Northern Ireland, moving into a new house.) Dottie Pepper was last in the receiving line. Rather than offer a hug, she extended her arm for a handshake, a pro's pro until the end.

Now, finally, McIlroy would walk alone.

It's about 150 yards from the back of the eighteenth green to the scoring area. Fans formed a corridor and carried McIlroy home, chanting his name and cheering. As Rory made his way through the delirium, his handsome face was like a movie screen playing out a lifetime of yearning, toil, heartache, triumph. It was riveting to watch him process the victory in real time. He took long, billowing breaths and covered his face with his hands in disbelief. He ran his fingers through his graying hair, seemingly as incredulous as the rest of us at what had just transpired. In a masterstroke of television directing and self-control by the talent, the CBS announcers stayed silent throughout all of this for five cinematic minutes. Looking back now, Nantz narrates the scene: "That walk was a thirty-year journey for him. That walk turned into a moment that will live forever, that will define him forever. He was walking on a cloud. You could see on his face this dream that fermented three decades ago, just a mom, a dad, a boy, and a crazy dream. Every ball Rory ever struck led to this moment, every lesson, every session putting until the sun set. It sounds like a gift to be a prodigy, to be superhuman. But he had to carry the weight of that his whole life. And then, suddenly, it lifted, and we all got to see that weight come off. He was walking, but he couldn't feel his feet—he was flying. He had just completed something that took thousands of days, tens of thousands of hours. He took those last steps by himself but carried with him the hopes of millions."

As McIlroy neared the clubhouse, his eyes softened and he laughed—even before the camera panned to the left, you knew that Shane Lowry was waiting for his friend. He wrapped the little fooker in a bear hug and swept him off his feet. McIlroy cradled his friend's face while Lowry placed one of his meaty paws on the back of Rory's neck. "You are a legend," Lowry said. "Aww, fucking hell. Nice job. Well done."

McIlroy got a meaningful hug from Tommy Fleetwood and shared a long embrace with Rose's wife, Kate. Then he got pulled into a group of lads from back home. More hugs, more daps. Finally, McIlroy seemed to realize that, amid these very private moments, the world was waiting for a certain ceremony. "I gotta go get a green jacket," he said, taking his leave and setting off raucous cheers.

The emotion was flowing far beyond Augusta National. A hundred folks had packed into the grillroom and spike bar at Holywood Golf Club, living and dying on every shot. "It was unbearable at times," says club member Paula Denvir. "You should have heard all the expletives. We all just sat in there going, 'Seriously, this is what you're putting us through?'" Crusty old pro Billy Andrade was watching on TV back home in Rhode Island. "I just sat there and started crying," he says. "I don't even know why, except I'm a fan of the game and I know the kid a little bit. The pressure that this fucking guy was under for all these years was just enormous. To see the grit and the grind, even as he kept fucking up; to see the all-world talent on some of those shots; for him to overcome all of the mistakes and come through at the end and get it done the way he did; and then seeing him break down like that—oh my gosh, it hit me like a ton of bricks. And I know I'm not alone. I talked to a lot of other golfers who lost it, too." Indeed, Shane Ryan of *Golf Digest* called Masters Sunday "a watershed moment . . . in the realm of dudes crying." He reported that he had polled forty-six male friends and thirty of them admitted to shedding tears over McIlroy's triumph.

On social media, the tributes poured in from everyone from the prime minister of Britain to the president of the United States, Ben Stiller to Adam Sandler, Manchester United to the British royal family, from Jack Nicklaus to Tiger Woods ("Welcome to the club"). Why did McIlroy's victory resonate so deeply? Sure, there was the historic nature of the achievement: McIlroy joined Nicklaus, Woods, Ben Hogan, Gene Sarazen, and Gary Player as the only players to win the career Grand Slam. He cemented his status as the most accomplished European golfer of all time, becoming the first man from the continent to win the Slam while matching Seve Ballesteros's career haul of five major championships. Then there was the lingering thrill of bearing witness to what Chamblee calls "one of the most riveting performances in the history of sport."

"I'm not into overhyping things," says Nantz, who has covered forty Masters, thirty-two Final Fours, seven Super Bowls, and a smattering of Olympic Games and tennis U.S. Opens, "but it really is one of the greatest sports stories ever told. Something so elusive, so coveted, that had brought him so much pain—it all just made the story and the moment more iconic. It touched everybody, whether they were a golf fan or not. Everybody understood the magnitude of what they had witnessed."

It is impossible to be too hyperbolic about what transpired on Sunday afternoon of the eighty-ninth Masters. McIlroy hit three of the greatest shots in tournament history (on fifteen, on seventeen, and in the playoff), definitely the worst (the pitch on thirteen), another all-time stinkeroo (the approach shot into the seventy-second hole), and the shakiest pressure putt this century (the four-footer to win in regulation). Yet he persisted. "If I was ever going to win the Masters," McIlroy said, "it was gonna have to happen that way—an absolute mess of a back nine." It was a nonstop thrill ride that left the sports world exhausted and exhilarated. All of that made McIlroy's win unforgettable, but it's not why the triumph touched so many hearts.

We all have outlandish fantasies and ambitions when we're young, but who is crazy enough to keep chasing them to the brink of middle age? For all of McIlroy's otherworldly talent, in the end, his victory was about much more relatable things: overcoming your fears, believing in yourself, never quitting, refusing to grow up and give in. "My dreams have been made today," McIlroy said during the green jacket ceremony. With his voice cracking, he saluted the small tribe of family and loyalists who were seated among the sport's royalty. "They've been on this journey with me the whole way through, they know the burden that I've carried to come here every year to try and try and try again. And the one thing I'd say to my daughter, Poppy, who's sitting over there: Never give up on your dreams. Never, ever give up on your dreams. Keep coming back and keep working hard, and if you put your mind to it, you can do anything."

20.

"You dream about the final putt going in at the Masters," says Rory McIlroy, "but you don't think about what comes next." In his case, that meant going deep into Augusta National's famous wine cellar in the hours after his life-changing victory. McIlroy shut down the clubhouse on Masters Sunday, toasting the win with his amateur partner at the Pebble Beach Pro-Am, Jeff Rhodes, who has a green jacket of his own. Shane Lowry tagged along, feeling very underdressed. The next day, McIlroy fielded phone calls from two U.S. presidents; it is a measure of his across-the-aisle appeal that both Barack Obama and Donald Trump wanted to chop it up about the Masters win. Not to be outdone, the British postal service cooked up a special postmark that was stamped on every piece of mail across three days in mid-April: *Congratulations, Rory McIlroy, on completing your Grand Slam!*

Gerry and Rosie had skipped the trip to Augusta to move into a new home in Northern Ireland. Their son felt a visceral need to share the win with them, so, in the week after his masterpiece, Rory jumped on his G650 along with Erica and Poppy and returned to the auld sod. The green jacket, in 38 regular, is a little too long for Gerry, and is a bit wide at the shoulders for Rosie, but it belonged to them as much as Rory. The McIlroy family story was part of the warm glow that enveped Rory's Masters win. Parents sacrificing everything for their child is a tale as old as time. Who couldn't get swept up in the journey of a working-class family from a war-torn land nurturing their only child into an all-time legend in the most patrician of sports?

Rory and Erica conducted more family business on the overseas trip, getting their first glimpse of the new house they had built at the Wentworth Estate outside of London. Wentworth is among England's most prestigious addresses, home to Sir Elton John and assorted football and cricket stars, in addition to Ernie Els, Justin Rose, and other golfers. Wentworth Club hosts the European Tour's flagship event, the BMW PGA Championship. McIlroy has also taken membership at Sunningdale, a superior course down the road. On the application form for prospective members, there was a section to list their golf accomplishments. McIlroy modestly left it blank. "I didn't want to take the piss," he told a Sunningdale steward.

Forever overcompensating for having prematurely terminated his schooling at age fifteen, McIlroy has told intimates that he loves the idea of Poppy getting a proper English education. There could be serious repercussions for the PGA Tour as London becomes the McIlroy home base. After running himself ragged in 2024, playing twenty-seven tournaments around the world, he cut back his schedule in '25 and has vowed that, going forward, he will consolidate his travels around proud, old national championships and faraway lands he'd like to show Poppy. (In late 2025, McIlroy turned the Indian Open and Australian Open into must-see TV.)

The New Orleans team event with Lowry has become one of McIlroy's favorite PGA Tour stops, so that's where he chose to make his post-Masters return to competition. "It's been an amazing few days after, to be able to reflect on it and everything that happened and the magnitude of everything," he said. "I think the big thing for me is just how the whole journey resonated with people."

Indeed, Golf Channel's Gary Williams says, "I'm still thinking about it—I'll never stop thinking about it. It was the whole human condition in one afternoon. What could possibly top that?"

But as McIlroy has pointed out with great chagrin, the sports-industrial complex never stops. The machine must be fed, its gaping maw devouring the present while forever looking ahead to what's next. In New Orleans, there was already much talk about what McIlroy could accomplish now that the Kong-sized monkey was off his back. After Phil Mickelson had a similarly cathartic breakthrough victory at the Masters in 2004, he went on to enjoy the best year of his career, contending at all the ensuing major championships and then winning two more across '05 and '06. McIlroy's quest for a calendar Grand Slam would continue two weeks after New Orleans at the PGA Championship at Quail Hollow. With four wins at Quail's annual PGA Tour stop, he had been so dominant there that Jordan Spieth dubbed the place "Rory McIlroy Country Club." But the man himself was already rebelling against the expectations; McIlroy freely admitted that he struggled to find the motivation to practice in the weeks after Augusta and then displayed little fire in New Orleans as he and Lowry finished a distant twelfth in their title defense. McIlroy was definitely not in grind mode once he turned up at the PGA Championship. He closed down the Tuesday night past champions' dinner with Pádraig Harrington. "He was in great spirits and he had his share of wine," says Harrington.

How many glasses?

"I'm not the police, I'm not going to tell you that," Harrington sputtered. "I mean, please. I could never tell you that."

Pádraig was one of the few golfers invited to the McIlroys' wedding. PGA Championship week marked one year since the news blew up about Rory filing for divorce. What had Harrington observed of the marriage since the reconciliation?

"Ha, nice try!" he says. "You're not going to get me to touch that one, either. I will say this: Rory is in a very good place now. He's settled. He's happy."

Maybe in private, but McIlroy was grouchy (and hungover?) at his press conference on the morning after the champions' dinner, offering only curt, perfunctory answers. Then he blew off reporters entirely following his opening round 74, which left him in ninety-eighth place. That was weak sauce. Only one man had the chance to win the calendar Slam in 2025—the golfing public was dying to know where it all went wrong and if McIlroy could regroup. Tiger Woods has his flaws, but he understood the obligations of being golf's keynote player: he spoke to reporters after 99.99 percent of his rounds, even the frustrating ones. As Earl Woods once told me, "Tiger plays the game because he loves it. He gets paid all that money to deal with the other bullshit."

There was much indignation in the press corps about having been spurned by McIlroy, but no one should care about the tender feelings of self-important media folks. Reporters matter only because we represent the fans. We get to ask the questions that they want answered, and in doing so, we help the folks at home feel more invested in the players and tournaments. McIlroy isn't fond of the word "narrative," but these storylines drive interest in the sport (which, to put it crassly, translates into the money that he burns on his jet, mansions, and Ferraris). For pro golfers, talking to the press is as much a part of the job as filling out a correct scorecard, whether the players like it or not.

On Friday of the PGA, news broke that McIlroy's driver had been ruled nonconforming during routine pretournament testing. He was competing at Quail Hollow with his backup, information that would be of keen interest to fans and the many folks who wager on professional golf. A backup driver is the backup for one reason: the player doesn't like it as much as his gamer. Given that McIlroy's big stick is the most potent weapon in the sport, his losing access to the club that conquered Augusta National was a big story. Golf Channel's Williams had heard about the failed test from another reporter on Thursday morning and immediately texted manager Sean O'Flaherty seeking confirmation. Williams got left on read. Professional golf is as gossipy as high school; other reporters quickly caught wind of the story and began sniffing around. The PGA of America refused to comment, since the USGA had overseen the testing (as it does every week on the PGA Tour). The USGA refused to comment, not wanting to rain on the parade of the tournament host, the PGA of America. This was a dereliction of duty by both organizations. Either one could have pointed out that a handful of drivers are ruled nonconforming every week on Tour. It's not a big deal.

Modern drivers are manufactured right up to the allowable limit for coefficient of restitution (COR), which measures how fast a ball comes off the thin titanium face. As a player pounds ball after ball, the driver face gets fractionally thinner, introducing a "springlike" effect that launches balls even faster. A driver that has exceeded the allowable COR might be worth maybe three extra yards. But beyond the old-fashioned notion of following the rules, pros are leery of playing with a too-thin face because it can cave in mid-round. Players don't have access to the sophisticated equipment that measures COR; that's where the USGA comes in. But the results are not made public week to week, owing to the PGA Tour's bizarre obsession with secrecy. With no protocol for releasing the results, silence reigned at Quail Hollow until Friday morning, when Johnson Wagner and Taylor Zarzour broke the news on SiriusXM. This was highly germane information, as McIlroy struggled to keep the ball on the planet during the first two rounds of the PGA, ranking dead last in driving accuracy among the seventy-four players who made the cut. LIV bots immediately began trolling McIlroy on social media, trying to sell the dumb idea that the Masters win was somehow tainted.

Following his second-round 69, McIlroy could have defused the whole situation with a few platitudes about how he would never knowingly employ a driver that had become nonconforming and that such test results are common on Tour. But once again, he stomped past waiting reporters. "The thing about Rory, he's quite stubborn," says Paul McGinley. "And he has a heightened sense of justice. If he feels he has been wronged, he won't give an inch."

McIlroy was indignant that the names of the other players whose drivers failed the COR test were not made public, including Scottie Scheffler. "I didn't want to get up there and say something that I regretted," McIlroy later explained. "I'm trying to protect Scottie. I don't want to mention his name. I'm trying to protect TaylorMade. I'm trying to protect the USGA, PGA of America, myself." (Scheffler would later self-report to the media that his driver had been ruled nonconforming.) McIlroy said he boycotted the press because he was "pissed off" that the putatively confidential information had been "leaked" by the media. This misguided indignation displayed a surprising naivete. Reporters have a responsibility to disseminate information. Giving the public the goods on McIlroy's driver wasn't a nefarious leak, it was the media performing a valuable service. The actual leaker was the USGA or PGA of America official who tipped off the reporters. McIlroy should have been mad at the bureaucrats, not the press.

On Saturday, the PGA of America finally put out a milquetoast statement, not naming McIlroy (or Scheffler) but noting that "finding driver heads that have crept over the line of conformance is not an unusual occurrence, especially for clubs that are hit thousands of times over a long period of time. The results are kept confidential to protect players, who are unaware the club has fallen out of conformance . . . To publicly identify players whose club did not conform can lead to that player being questioned unnecessarily. Neither the USGA nor the PGA of America has any concerns about player intent." Did these words placate McIlroy? Impossible to say, because he again blew off reporters after the third round. This had now become bizarre, especially given that, in the wake of the Masters, he had enjoyed the most over-the-top lovefest in the history of the golf media. Following his final-round 72, which left him in a disappointing forty-seventh place, McIlroy again declined to visit the interview area, proceeding directly to the Quail Hollow locker room to pack up his belongings. A handful of reporters waited for him outside the clubhouse. It was a reasonable gambit—after cooling off a little, and away from the cameras, perhaps McIlroy would offer a few parting thoughts. He didn't. But his father, Gerry, made a point of staring down the reporters and shaking his head in disgust, a wholly inappropriate gesture given that the scribes were just trying to do their job. This was just another reminder that the McIlroys will always remain a fiercely insular tribe.

Rory's petulance did not go over well. He got ripped by the self-styled "fanalysts" at No Laying Up, only one month removed from their delirious Augusta Block Party. Even Kyle Porter, who was employed by McIlroy's TGL during its inaugural season, offered a carefully worded rebuke, calling McIlroy's behavior an "abdication of responsibility." This was akin to LBJ losing Cronkite on Vietnam.

McIlroy's ennui carried into the U.S. Open. He jilted reporters (again!) following his first-round 74. The next day was when he lobbed his f-bombs at me on the driving range and then smashed a tee marker and hurled a club. McIlroy was in danger of missing the cut until he played the final fifteen holes in 2-under. "It's funny, like it's much easier being on the cut line when you don't really care if you're here for the weekend or not," he said when finally addressing reporters following the third round. "I was sort of thinking, *Do I really want two more days here or not?* So it makes it easier to play better when you're in that mindset." The apathy was jarring from a man who had exuded so much passion two months earlier at the Masters.

McIlroy finally offered some insight into his weird headspace, post-Augusta. "It's more a frustration with you guys," he told reporters. "I don't know, I have been totally available for the last few years, and I'm not saying . . . maybe not [frustrated with] you guys, but maybe more just the whole thing." McIlroy had been golf's most emotionally accessible superstar for a decade and a half. At the Masters, he presented the golf world with a memory to last a lifetime. Now, he had nothing left to give, unapologetically. "I feel like I've earned the right to do whatever I want to do," he said.

It surely didn't help McIlroy's mood that his rival Scheffler, twenty-nine, had regained his form. Coming into Oakmont, Scheffler had won three of his last four starts, most notably a stirring performance at the PGA Championship. Then Scheffler went to McIlroy's home turf, Royal

Portrush, and won the Open Championship; Rory played much better than in 2019 but still finished seven strokes back, in a tie for seventh.

Scheffler's victory gave him three legs of the career Grand Slam and four major championship victories, one less than McIlroy's career haul. Coming out of Augusta, Rory seemed destined to win player of the year for the first time since 2019, but in the span of three months, he had been eclipsed again by Scheffler. There was no end in sight for the post-Augusta blues.

IN 2019, MCILROY FOUNDED Symphony Ventures, a venture capital firm based in Dublin. The name was a reminder that golf would always come first, but there was other money to be made in concert with his on-course performance. McIlroy's manager, Sean O'Flaherty, took a 20 percent stake in the firm. Together, they have focused on two sectors: sports performance and the broader wellness space. An early investment was LetsGetChecked, which sends medical tests to a consumer's front door. That business exploded during COVID, as did another investment, Kaia Health, an app that tailors daily at-home workouts for subscribers, particularly those with chronic pain. McIlroy became the first big endorser of Whoop, the fitness tracking system. He took an equity stake when the company had only twelve thousand subscribers. Now, thanks to millions of paid subscribers, McIlroy's piece of the company is worth north of $75 million. To date, Symphony Ventures has made more than two dozen investments, giving McIlroy an extremely profitable hobby.

Cofounding the Tomorrow's Golf League was one of the big bets that has paid off for McIlroy. The whiz-bang simulator league debuted in January 2025 and immediately found a surprisingly big audience. (The timing was carefully considered: What else was there to watch on Monday and Tuesday nights during the winter?) There is an inescapable irony that McIlroy—LIV Golf's most ardent detractor—is now presiding over his own nontraditional, team-oriented golf league that is groping for a younger, cooler audience. But LIV's problem is that it's neither fish nor fowl. It makes a lot of noise about team golf, but most of the purse, and interest, is still focused on the individual leaderboard. LIV wanted to be radical and different but chickened out; ultimately, it's just dudes playing their own ball in stroke play on traditional, mostly uninteresting golf courses ... plus reggaeton. Meanwhile, the TGL is a unique product, with an indoor arena and cutting-edge tech that simulates real golf but adds a new twist. Crucially, it has the good sense not to take itself too seriously.

McIlroy may or may not regret some of his rhetoric, but when it comes to LIV, his wish has been granted: he will be remembered for being on the right side of history. McIlroy's reshaping of the PGA Tour has been a resounding success, as the Signature Events produced glittering champions and huge TV ratings in 2025. With their $20 million purses, the Signatures brought so much new money to the PGA Tour that the exodus of big-name players to LIV ended abruptly. The Tour has retained virtually all its corporate sponsors while becoming a more agile for-profit business led by a new forward-thinking CEO plucked from the NFL's C-suite. (Jay Monahan will conclude a long, tedious farewell tour as commissioner in 2026.) Nearly three years since the framework agreement was announced, neither side has the will to consummate a partnership. LIV muddles along, but the PGA Tour won the war, thanks to McIlroy's star power, Scheffler's brilliance, a pipeline of young talent, and feel-good stories like Tommy Fleetwood breaking through at the 2025 FedEx Cup. And it was McIlroy's conciliatory leadership that paved the way for Brooks Koepka to jilt LIV and return to the PGA Tour in 2026, a hugely symbolic flip-flop. It has always been part of Nicklaus and Palmer's legacy that they birthed the modern Tour with an insurrection in 1968. McIlroy, and to a lesser extent Woods, will similarly be remembered for saving it.

McIlroy continues to grow his off-course empire. In the wake of the Masters win, he announced that he was teaming up with TPG, a leading private equity firm, to create TPG Sports, for which McIlroy and O'Flaherty will serve as operating partners. The intent is to invest in businesses that underpin the sports world, with an emphasis on ticketing, data services, performance technology, and facility operations. None of this is as sexy as buying a franchise, but there is much money to be made, and none of it is exposed to the volatility of competitive results. In December 2025, McIlroy announced that he was getting into showbiz, like Tom Brady, LeBron James, and Steph Curry before him. McIlroy's newly formed Firethorn Productions—the 15th hole at Augusta National is nicknamed Firethorn—will produce documentaries and longform storytelling about "Rory's world and the modern golf lifestyle," according to a breathless press release. Rory McIlroy Inc. has now swelled to thirty employees, from pilots to accountants, publicists to lawyers. The company has quarterly board meetings, presided over by McIlroy himself. It is a moneymaking machine.

In September 2025, *Forbes* cited McIlroy's combined on- and off-course earnings as $87 million in the preceding twelve months . . . and that was before he'd had the chance to fully leverage the Masters win. Is this son of a bartender already a billionaire? Someone in a position to know says, "Not yet, but soon. Very soon."

•

IN HIS POST-AUGUSTA HAZE, McIlroy said, "Look, I climbed my Everest in April, and I think after you do something like that, you've got to make your way back down, and you've got to look for another mountain to climb."

That arrived with September's Irish Open. Other than the Masters, no tournament had brought McIlroy as much heartache as his national open. When he won it in 2016, thanks to an iconic 5-wood into the final green, it seemed like McIlroy would dominate his national championship for decades. But he was oh-for-Ireland ever since.

Everything changed for McIlroy on that Thursday at the K Club. His opening round 71 was nothing special, but what followed gave the entire island goose bumps. The tournament had organized a special event with its prodigal son. Onstage were trophies from McIlroy's victories at the U.S. Open, PGA Championship, and Open Championship. Then McIlroy came out in his green jacket, the first time it had ever been seen in public on the Emerald Isle. Thousands of fans screamed and shouted for McIlroy. "It's absolutely amazing to be able to share that with people," he said. There may be a few crusty buggers left in the Republic of Ireland who will never forgive McIlroy for saying, early in his career, that he feels more British than Irish, but that's ancient history now. There was so much love in the air for McIlroy at the K Club that he couldn't help but be inspired. The day after the jacket ceremony, he shot a bogeyless 66 to roar into contention. Then he followed with a bogey-free 68 to move into a tie for fourth, four strokes back of leader Adrien Saddier.

It felt like all of Dublin turned out to cheer for McIlroy in the final round. He birdied the second hole and then the fourth. The energy began to crest. Then McIlroy birdied the fifth hole. At nine, with an awkward hillside stance and shaggy lie in the rough, he ripped a wedge to ten feet. When McIlroy made the putt, he was in a four-way tie for the lead. *C'mon, Rors!* You could practically hear the pint glasses clinking. On thirteen, McIlroy played a beautiful dead-arm wedge to six feet. His birdie putt did a 360 around the hole, spun out for a split second—"Like it was in slow motion!" McIlroy said—and then tumbled back in, as if kissed by a leprechaun. The birdie gave him the solo lead. It was happening. Sunday at the Masters had been a telenovela; this was a fairy tale. But McIlroy followed with four straight pars, while Sweden's Joakim Lagergren eagled the sixteenth hole and birdied the eighteenth. So McIlroy came to the watery par-5 eighteenth needing an eagle to tie the lead. He mashed a 340-yard drive to the left-center of the fairway and then, from 202 yards out, nuked a downwind 8-iron to 27 feet 10 inches. The make percentage for pros at that distance is less than 8 percent, not factoring in the weight of an entire island on the putter head. After his crunch time misses at Augusta, McIlroy realized, on reflection, that he had been too obsessed with the outcome instead of committing to his process. Now, he as he stepped into another defining putt, he focused on his fundamentals: line up to a spot a couple of feet in front of the ball; soften the right arm; keep the putter head level at impact. That putt was never not going in. Eagle! "Such a cool moment, such a cool feeling," McIlroy said.

Lagergren had only one role to play in sudden death: to lose to McIlroy. He did so on the third extra hole. The champion was visibly emotional afterward in an interview behind the final green, speaking over a delirious crowd that was chanting his first name in the singsong cadence of "*Olé, olé, olé, olé.*" Said McIlroy, "Look, I feel just so lucky that I get to do this, I get to do this in front of these people. The support has been absolutely amazing all week. I thought it was going to be a nice homecoming, obviously coming home with a green jacket and all that, but this has been absolutely incredible. This has exceeded all of my expectations. Just so, so happy I could play the way I did this week for all of them and get the win."

It used to be said that no one could have as much fun being Arnold Palmer as Arnold Palmer did. That's starting to be true of McIlroy. PGA Tour veteran Harry Higgs watched the Irish Open with keen interest—he calls McIlroy "my Tiger." Says Higgs, "This is not an original thought of mine, I saw it on Twitter, where someone said that one of the best things about Rory is that he often seems amazed to be Rory. Like, he takes so much joy in his accomplishments. I think that's so cool."

The post-Augusta swoon was over. McIlroy had found himself by going home again.

It felt right that the defining moment of the Irish Open was delivered by McIlroy's putter. When he won his first PGA Tour title in 2011, 89 percent of McIlroy's strokes gained came off the tee. He was like a pitcher blowing away batters with nothing but a 104-mile-per-hour fastball. At the end of the 2025 FedEx Cup season, McIlroy ranked fourth on the PGA Tour in strokes gained putting, with 39 percent of his total strokes gained coming with his putter and only 43 percent off the tee. He still has the heater—he was second on Tour in driving distance at 323 yards a pop—but he can now paint the corners with a changeup, a curveball, or a slider. That McIlroy continues to evolve at thirty-six helps explain his mind-boggling longevity: he has spent nearly eight hundred consecutive weeks in the top twenty of the World Ranking, dating to March 2012.

The Irish Open was McIlroy's twelfth victory on the European Tour (not counting majors and WGCs) to go with twenty-nine wins on the PGA Tour. Considering his many FedEx Cup and Race to Dubai titles and, most important, the gravitas of the Grand Slam, his career has now surpassed those of Phil Mickelson, Lee Trevino, and Nick Faldo, three legends who each own one more major championship victory than McIlroy but can claim neither the Slam nor his global impact. That makes McIlroy one of the dozen greatest golfers of all time. Jack Nicklaus, Tiger Woods, Bobby Jones, Ben Hogan, and Walter Hagen are my top five, in that order. (We can quibble about this another time.) The next tier comprises Gary Player, Gene Sarazen, Arnold Palmer, Sam Snead, Tom Watson, and Harry Vardon, a deeply important, popularizing figure who won all his big titles before World War I. If McIlroy picks off another major or two, the case can easily be made that he will have surpassed Palmer, Snead, Sarazen, and Watson.

The Irish Open seemed to settle the debate as to how badly Rory wants it as he enters the final act of his career. "Jack [Nicklaus] always said one of the hardest things to do is keep playing well after you win," says Brad Faxon. "That's not a classic definition of resilience, but it's a function of how much a player burns to win. Are they willing to pay the price even when they've already achieved one dream after another? Rory is not slowing down. He's hungry for more. He is a student of history, and that's why he was so overwhelmed with the Masters win—he knows how much it means. And he wants to keep going. He wants to make more history. He knows it won't be easy, and, honestly, I think he kind of likes it that way."

What, exactly, is McIlroy chasing? "I know because I asked him," says Pádraig Harrington. "It was his wedding night, and he had a few drinks in him, so it was a good time to ask. He said nine [major championship victories]. So that's what he's thinking. That's the deep-down thing. So he's just getting started."

Speaking these numbers into existence has a strange power. At the 1995 U.S. Amateur, in the hours after nineteen-year-old Tiger Woods had won it for a second straight year, his father, Earl, his tongue loosened by champagne, said, "I'm going to make a prediction. Before he's through, my son will win 14 major championships." Later in life, Tiger was stuck on fourteen majors for over a decade, before finally picking off his fifteenth and (almost certainly) final one, at the 2019 Masters. McIlroy is going to come up well short of the career haul of his idol, but he is at peace with that. Woods broke his body and smashed up his life, collateral damage in his maniacal quest to be the greatest golfer of all time. In the final analysis, McIlroy wasn't willing to pay that cost, which is the giveaway that he's a healthy, well-adjusted person. He is content with the Slam and to be, as Faldo observed all those years ago, "a whole person." Way back in 2017, Rory said of Tiger, "I've seen it firsthand. I've seen what his life is like in Florida. I've played golf with him and said: 'What are you doing tonight? Do you want to come and have dinner with us?' And he can't. He just can't. And for me that's unfathomable. I could not live like that ... If someone was to say, 'You can have 14 majors and 70 wins but have to deal with that, or nine majors and 40 wins and stay somewhat the same as you are,' I'd take the second option all day."

If McIlroy gets to nine major championship victories, we're moving him past Player and Hagen and into the top five of all time.

A curious thing about discussing the legacies of top players is that, aside from Seve Ballesteros, the Ryder Cup is never mentioned, even though it's often referred to as the biggest event in the sport—golf's Super Bowl! Nonbelievers like to dismiss an individual's accomplishments in the Ryder Cup, saying it's a team event. But everyone knows how many Super Bowls Tom Brady won, and that's a team event, too. McIlroy's Ryder Cup heroics are an important part of his legacy. His 4-1 individual record led Europe to another victory in 2023, the fifth time he had been on the winning side. That's as many champagne showers as Seve, Monty, and Nick Faldo enjoyed and more than venerated U.S. Ryder Cuppers Paul Azinger and Payne Stewart.

McIlroy's win at the Irish Open came three weeks before Bethpage and sent a jolt of confidence through Team Europe. Paul McGinley, a key piece in Europe's cohesive leadership cadre, was never worried about McIlroy, despite his summertime swoon. "When his heart is engaged in something, and it really means something to him, he generally delivers," says McGinley. "And then he goes into these flat periods in his career—he's had lots of them. It's an Irish thing to be melancholy, and he goes into these periods of melancholy, but it's not that he's not caring—it's almost like he's in a slumber. And then, all of a sudden, he ignites. And when that heart goes on fire, that's when he comes out and does something that amazes us. If he has that quiet look of determination combined with that joyfulness of chasing a goal, that's when the magic happens."

Bethpage was always going to be a brutal arena for the Europeans, mostly because New York fans pride themselves on being assholes; they had been abusive toward foreign-born players during the previous jingoistic U.S. Opens at Bethpage. McIlroy had put himself in the crosshairs from the moment he banged on the table in Rome and promised a victory in New York. He smartly tried to turn down the temperature on the eve of the 2025 Ryder Cup. Asked in a press conference by Skratch Golf's Dan Rapaport what his impressions of the U.S. had been as a boy, McIlroy said, "Everyone wanted to make it in America. It's the land of opportunity. And I still believe it's the best country in the world, and if you come here and work hard and dedicate yourself, you can be or do whatever you want. I am unbelievably grateful and lucky that I got to come to America early on. I think success is celebrated here. I think there's a wonderful sense of work ethic. And yeah, I live here. My wife is American. My daughter is American. I have a lot of affinity toward this country, and I think everyone who lives here should have that same affinity because it is a wonderful place." He has always called it America, which makes sense. The United States is a place; America is an idea.

McIlroy set the tone for the Ryder Cup from the opening foursomes session, producing spectacular golf alongside Tommy Fleetwood. At one point, as all four matches were on the back nine, McIlroy and Fleetwood had rung up five birdies while the entire U.S. team had combined for seven. McIlroy and Fleetwood's 5 and 4 win was the largest margin of victory in foursomes for an away pairing since 2004. Asked their secret, Fleetwood said, "That's Rory McIlroy, first. I'm just lucky to play alongside him." McIlroy put another half point on the board in afternoon fourballs, playing with Shane Lowry. Europe led 5.5–2.5. To borrow a phrase from New York icon Yogi Berra, it was getting late early for the U.S.

The fans were obnoxious on day one, but their behavior curdled on Saturday. The tone was set that morning by comedian Heather McMahan, serving as a celebrity MC to hype up the crowd around the first tee. Her grating voice booming over the PA system, she led the crowd in a chant of "Fuck Rory! Fuck Rory!" This was wildly inappropriate coming from someone representing the PGA of America. (McMahan was quickly relieved of her duties on the mic, and the PGA later issued a formal apology.) McIlroy and Fleetwood were sent out in the first match. On every hole, they were greeted with a chorus of "fuck you"s.

One fan called McIlroy a "midget leprechaun," which seemed rather redundant. These were not masters of psychology, the yahoos who were heckling McIlroy. Playing in a low boil, he was brilliant again as he and Fleetwood won five out of seven holes on the front nine to build an insurmountable lead. On the sixteenth hole, as McIlroy addressed his ball in the rough, an overserved douche on the rope line bellowed, à la William Wallace, "Freeeeedom!" Rory backed off, looked in the direction of the offending spectator, and barked, "Shut the fuck up." Then he stuffed his approach shot, icing the 3 and 2 win. It was one of the most macho sequences of his career. How did it feel?

"Very fucking satisfying," McIlroy said.

Asked how he decides when to engage with the fans, he added, "Honestly, I'd say it's just on impulse. Sometimes I do, sometimes I don't. I'm quite an impulsive character, if you haven't noticed. Sometimes I'll engage, and sometimes I'll catch myself and refrain. But I don't really choose when."

Team Europe led 8.5–3.5 by the end of the session. It was crystal clear they were going to become the first Ryder Cup team to win on the road since . . . Europe in 2012, when McIlroy helped lead the Miracle at Medinah. The spectators at Bethpage had paid exorbitant ticket prices and then suffered soul-sucking logistical quagmires to journey to the course. Now the home team was showing no heart on the way to yet another dispiriting defeat. On a hot day, with the alcohol flowing, all that angst fueled the most deplorable crowd behavior in golf history during the afternoon four-balls. McIlroy went out with the fiery Lowry, who caught some strays; if you didn't know better, you might have thought his given name was Shane You Fat Fuck. But as Europe's team leader, the alpha of the entire event, the game's biggest star, a press conference provocateur and a man with more aura than all the American players combined, it was McIlroy who became the target of unprecedented abuse, even though, as he said, "The police out there and the amount of security presence was insane."

The endless profanity was bad enough, but the fans became intensely personal with McIlroy, focusing on his love life. One yelled, "How is your fake marriage going, Rory?" An old rumor was repeatedly excavated: "Hey, Rory, where's Amanda?" "Do it for Amanda, Rory." "Rory, imagine the hole is Amanda and you'll slip right in." Easily three-quarters of the abuse directed at McIlroy involved Amanda. Erica McIlroy was following the match inside the ropes and had to listen to all of this. By the eleventh hole, Lowry was so irate that he started to go after a fan before being held back by his caddie. McIlroy played in a controlled rage, celebrating every birdie with fiery fist pumps and glares at the crowd. Walking off one green, he repeatedly jabbed a finger at the fans, punctuating the gesture by bellowing, "Fuck you!" (Paul Azinger, of all people, would clutch his pearls about this, but in fact McIlroy displayed heroic restraint in the face of unrelenting abuse.) Lowry did most of the work in the match, though his partner's birdie on the sixteenth hole was crucial in allowing them to win 2-up. That pushed McIlroy's individual record to 3-0-1 as Europe became the first road team to take all four partner sessions in a Ryder Cup. In the most hostile arena imaginable, McIlroy had been a towering figure. As soon as the match was over, he fought through the melee behind the eighteenth green to seek out Erica. He knew what she had just been through in the preceding five hours. He squeezed her hard and kissed her harder. His eyes were glistening. McIlroy whispered in his wife's ear, "I love you so much." It was a beautiful, intensely personal moment amid the chaos. It has to be brutally difficult to work on your marriage in the public eye. The McIlroys' embrace was a monument to their love for each other, and to second chances. Alas, the New York fans are not romantics at heart: a few moments later, Erica was pegged by a beer thrown from the crowd.

Rory was exhausted physically and emotionally the next day, but he still took Scheffler to the eighteenth hole before losing 1-up. No matter, he had done more than enough during partner play, and Europe wrapped up the Ryder Cup 15–13, the sixth time McIlroy had been on the winning side. That's the same number as one of Europe's most celebrated warriors, Sergio Garcia. In the history of the modern Ryder Cup—beginning when the Continent joined Great Britain and Ireland in 1979 to form a united Team Europe—only one player has enjoyed more victories than McIlroy: Lee Westwood, with seven. Rory has been the key connector between two eras of European dominance. With 21.5 career Ryder Cup points, he is tied for ninth all time, but only 2.5 points from third on the list. Barring the unforeseen, McIlroy will go down as the most prolific winner in Ryder Cup history. In victory, European captain Luke Donald hailed his leadership, saying, "Rory has made no qualms about how important the Ryder Cup is to him, and I think that's inspiring to me. It's inspiring to his team."

She was not in attendance, but Erica played a starring role in the victors' press conference. Asked about all the personal abuse he and his wife suffered, McIlroy said, "It should be off-limits, but obviously it wasn't this week. Erica is fine. She's a very, very strong woman. You know, she handled everything this week with class and poise and dignity, like she always has. I love her, and we're going to have a good time celebrating tonight." All of Team Europe broke into an ovation. There had been some clucking that, at Augusta, McIlroy never mentioned his wife by name and that the only time he got choked up in the winner's press conference was when discussing . . . his caddie. This tribute to Erica was the most emotion McIlroy had displayed toward her publicly since their marital drama played out a year and a half earlier. A little while later, after being doused in champagne by teammates, he opened up even more. "This is the best year of my career," McIlroy said, with red eyes and a voice thick with emotion. "The best year of my life, on and off the course. I've got so many things to be grateful for and lucky for away from the golf course. Beautiful wife, beautiful daughter, my parents are healthy. I've got a great support group, great friends. And that's the important thing. Like this [victory] is amazing, this is obviously incredible what we're doing here, but when it's all said and done, I'm going to have those really important people in my life, and I feel so lucky for that."

After years of turbulence on and off the golf course, it was moving to see Rory—who once dubbed himself golf's Nearly Man—so content. He doesn't make it easy on himself, but that is a big part of his appeal. For all the controversies and crushing disappointments, McIlroy just keeps marching forward, giving us one unforgettable moment after another. He was once a boy wonder, openly dreaming about changing golf history. The journey has been more fraught than he ever could have imagined. But a prodigy who never falters doesn't make for a good tale. McIlroy has grown into something far more interesting: a man in full.

Notes

Being a biographer can feel like archaeology: You are forever sifting through detritus, looking for meaningful clues. Researching this book once again made me appreciate my colleagues in the typing trade. Special tip of the cap to Brian Keogh, Paul Kimmage, and Ewan Murray, the Jenkins, Wind, and Bamberger of the Rory beat.

Except where noted below, every quote is from my own reporting or taken from press conferences or similarly public utterances. Some material previously appeared, in different forms, on Skratch.Golf and FirePitCollective.com and in *Sports Illustrated* and my book *LIV and Let Die*; it is reprinted here with permission.

FOREWORD

xi *"He's a lovely person"*: Gene Wojciechowski, "Holywood's Adoration Shines on Rory," ESPN, July 11, 2011, https://www.espn.com/espn/columns/story?columnist=wojciechowski_gene&sportCat=golf&page=wojciechowski-110711.

CHAPTER 1

1 *"He was holding a golf club"*: Brian Keogh, "Sky's the Limit for Rory McIlroy," *Irish Golf Desk*, December 6, 2006, https://www.irishgolfdesk.com/news-files/2006/12/6/skys-the-limit-for-rory-mcilroy.html.

2 *"As soon as Rory was able"*: Mark Cannizzaro, "McIlroy Charted Course from His Club in Northern Ireland to Atop the Golf World," *New York Post*, July 11, 2011, https://nypost.com/2011/07/11/mcilroy-charted-course-from-his-club-in-northern-ireland-to-atop-the-golf-world/.

3 *"At seven he had a complete game"*: Ewan Murray, "How Rory McIlroy Was Made in Holywood," *Guardian*, April 4, 2015, https://www.theguardian.com/sport/2015/apr/04/rory-mcilroy-holywood-masters.

3 *"You could see them progressing"*: Michael McHugh, "Juniors Coach Who Gave McIlroy His First Break Receives British Empire Medal," *Belfast Telegram*, October 9, 2020.

3 *"And then he'd fill out his score"*: Wojciechowski, "Holywood's Adoration."

4   "*I watched it all*": Mike Hall, "Rory McIlroy Praises Tiger Woods—'He Was My Inspiration and Hero,'" *Golf Monthly*, March 9, 2022, https://www.golfmonthly.com/news/mcilroy-praises-woods-he-was-my-inspiration-and-hero.

4   "*Ever since then all I*": Harry Latham-Coyle, "'There'll Never Be Another Tiger': Rory McIlroy Opens Up on Relationship with Woods," *Independent*, February 15, 2023, https://www.the-independent.com/sport/golf/tiger-woods-rory-mcilroy-full-swing-b2282748.html.

4   "*I would never stand there*": Michael Bamberger, "Hair Apparent," *Sports Illustrated*, April 7, 2009.

5   "*Bend your knees a wee tiny bit*": Barry Svrluga, "For Rory McIlroy, It's Hooray for Holywood, and Vice Versa," *Washington Post*, July 13, 2011.

5   "*Just like a Seve*": Ibid.

5   "*Sometimes, you might get a bit browned off*": Will Griffee and Malcolm Folley, "Revealed: The Huge Sacrifices Made by Rory McIlroy's Working Class Parents as Their Son Achieves His Masters Dream—Including No Family Holidays for 10 Years and 100-Hour Working Weeks," *Daily Mail*, April 15, 2025, https://www.dailymail.co.uk/sport/golf/article-14614297/Rory-McIlroy-parents-Masters.html.

5   "*They basically never saw each other*": Marty Smith, "Rory McIlroy, and the Chase for That Elusive Green Jacket," ESPN, April 2, 2017, https://www.espn.com/golf/story/_/id/19049821/masters-2017-rory-mcilroy-tries-yet-again-tackle-augusta.

6   "*Rosie would ask how he was doing*": Murray, "How Rory McIlroy Was Made."

7   "*I remember being on the 18th fairway*": Paul Kimmage, "Paul Kimmage Meets Rory McIlroy: The Truth About the Olympics, Close Friendship with Tiger and the Important Things in Life," *Irish Independent*, January 8, 2017, https://www.independent.ie/sport/gaelic-games/paul-kimmage-meets-rory-mcilroy-the-truth-about-the-olympics-close-friendship-with-tiger-and-the-important-things-in-life/35349397.html.

8   "*I cried for days*": Bamberger, "Hair Apparent."

9   "*They called out this big guy*": Cannizzaro, "McIlroy Charted Course."

9   "*His swing is him*": Bamberger, "Hair Apparent."

10   "*He says, 'Rory, come here'*": Keogh, "Sky's the Limit for Rory McIlroy."

10   "*He was always miles behind us*": Cannizzaro, "McIlroy Charted Course."

14   "*There were a lot of talented players*": Brian Keogh, "'It Brings Out the Worst Golf in Rory McIlroy'—Why Holywood Star Must Face His Demons and Shane Lowry Is a Masters Contender," *Irish Independent*, April 4, 2025, https://www.independent.ie/sport/golf/it-brings-out-the-worst-golf-in-rory-mcilroy-why-holywood-star-must-face-his-demons-and-shane-lowry-is-a-masters-contender/a1436270958.html.

15   "*He swung the club better*": Paul Kimmage, "Paul Kimmage Meets Rory McIlroy and Shane Lowry: The Inside Story of the Ryder Cup—and Explosive Row

with US Team," *Belfast Telegraph*, November 12, 2023, https://www.belfasttele graph.co.uk/sport/golf/paul-kimmage-meets-rory-mcilroy-and-shane-lowry-the -inside-story-of-the-ryder-cup-and-explosive-row-with-us-team/a24921842.html.

CHAPTER 2

17 *"And no girl in the U.S."*: Brendan Quinn, "How Did That Guy End Up There? The Odd Stories of European Ryder Cup Golfers at American Colleges," *Athletic*, September 21, 2021, https://www.nytimes.com/athletic/2823912/2021 /09/21/how-did-that-guy-end-up-there-the-odd-stories-of-european-ryder-cup -golfers-at-american-colleges/.

17 *"People think that"*: Eddie Sefko, "Montgomerie Returns to Place That Started It All," *Houston Chronicle*, March 27, 2002, https://www.chron.com/sports/golf /article/montgomerie-returns-to-place-that-started-it-all-2085045.php.

20 *"I was smart but lazy"*: Guy Yocom, "My Shot: Chubby Chandler," *Golf Digest*, January 25, 2012, https://www.golfdigest.com/story/chubby-chandler-interview-yocom.

22 *"Rory, you don't know it yet"*: Michael Smith, "Oakley Taking a Bigger Swing at Golf," *Sports Business Journal*, February 19, 2012, https://www.sportsbusinessjour nal.com/Journal/Issues/2012/02/20/Marketing-and-Sponsorship/Oakley/.

22 *"Rory is a fantastically talented golfer"*: Bernie McGuire, "McIlroy Fails to Fire at Forest," *Irish Independent*, May 12, 2005, https://www.independent.ie/sport/golf /mcilroy-fails-to-fire-at-forest/25984755.html.

22 *"an experience and a learning curve"*: Ibid.

CHAPTER 3

27 *"I was certainly peeved at the time"*: Lawrence Donegan, host, *McKellar Golf Podcast*, episode 43, "Rory McIlroy," May 14, 2020, https://podcasts.apple.com/us/pod cast/mckellar-golf-podcast-43-rory-mcilroy/id1483786770?i=1000474633300.

28 *"Mr. H.S. Colt . . . has thereby built himself"*: Sean Martin, "5 Things to Know About Royal Portrush," PGA Tour, July 15, 2019, https://www.pgatour.com/article/news/latest /2019/07/15/5-things-to-know-about-royal-portrush-the-open-championship.

28 *"Steady enough but nothing special"*: Ewan Murray, "Reliving Rory McIlroy's 'Out-of-Body' Royal Portrush 61 as Open Looms," *Guardian*, July 16, 2019, https://www.theguard ian.com/sport/2019/jul/16/rory-mcilroy-the-open-championship-royal-portrush.

28 *"The crowds were getting bigger"*: Ibid.

28 *"that you can only dream of hitting"*: Ibid.

29 *"You could see the look"*: Ibid.

29 *"A member of the golf club phoned"*: Brentley Romine, "McIlroy Recalls Record 61 at Royal Portrush: 'I Always Think About That Round,'" NBC Sports, July 15, 2019, https://www.nbcsports.com/golf/news/rory-mcilroy-recalls-record- 61-royal-portrush-i-always-think-about-round.

30 "*You hear about the next great thing*": Sean Martin, "The Open Championship: How 16-Year-Old Rory McIlroy Shot 61 at Royal Portrush," PGA Tour, July 14, 2025, https://www.pgatour.com/article/news/latest/2025/07/14/how-16-year-old-rory-mcilroy-shot-61-at-royal-portrush-site-of-the-open-championship.

30 "*Maybe if I had made the team*": Donegan, *McKellar Golf Podcast*, "Rory McIlroy," May 14, 2020.

CHAPTER 4

31 "*All I wanted to do*": Mark Simpson, "Rory Brings US Open Trophy to Sullivan Upper," BBC, June 30, 2011, https://www.bbc.com/news/uk-northern-ireland-13981397.

31 "*Leaving school was a big decision*": Liam Kelly, "Why Rory McIlroy Is the Wrong Role Model for Young Irish Golfers," *Irish Independent*, September 22, 2009, https://www.independent.ie/sport/golf/why-rory-mcilroy-is-the-wrong-role-model-for-young-irish-golfers/26568439.html.

31 "*I was away quite a lot*": Simpson, "Rory Brings US Open Trophy."

31 "*The only thing I regret*": Donegan, *McKellar Golf Podcast*.

32 "*For two years*": Kelly, "Why Rory McIlroy Is the Wrong Role Model."

32 "*I was an only child*": Paul Kimmage, "Rory Revisited: No Question Off Limits, No Subject Out of Bounds as Paul Kimmage Meets Golfer of the Decade," *Irish Independent*, February 2, 2020, https://www.independent.ie/news/rory-revisited-no-question-off-limits-no-subject-out-of-bounds-as-paul-kimmage-meets-golfer-of-the-decade/38918652.html.

33 "*She knows me better*": John O'Sullivan, "Rory McIlroy's Love Life from Meghan Markle 'Fling' to Three-Minute Phone Call Split," *Irish Star*, May 15, 2024, https://www.irishstar.com/sport/golf/rory-mcilroys-love-life-meghan-32816633.

33 "*It was a weird one*": Donegan, *McKellar Golf Podcast*.

33 "*started to punch the window*": Kimmage, "Paul Kimmage Meets Rory McIlroy: The Truth."

33 "*My dad was driving*": Donegan, *McKellar Golf Podcast*.

34 "*The plane is amazing*": Keogh, "Sky's the Limit for Rory McIlroy."

35 "*He was known to us*": Ewan Murray, "How a Young Rory McIlroy Burst on to the Open Scene in 2007," *Guardian*, July 16, 2007, https://www.theguardian.com/sport/2017/jul/16/rory-mcilroy-open-debut-carnoustie.

38 "*He wasn't fazed at all*": Ibid.

38 "*I watched him hit*": Ibid.

40 "*I come out of the bunker*": Colt Knost and Drew Stoltz, hosts, *Subpar*, podcast, "Billy Horschel Interview: Going Head to Head with Rory at the Walker Cup, Winning the Tour Championship," February 9, 2021, https://podcasts.apple.com/us/podcast/billy-horschel-interview-going-head-to-head-with-rory/id1498625027?i=1000508372324.

40 *"That outburst of his"*: John Huggan, "Rory's Story," *Golf Digest*, July 15, 2008, https://www.golfdigest.com/story/britishopen_rory?currentPage=1&printable=true.

40 *"He was letting me know"*: Knost and Stoltz, *Subpar*, "Billy Horschel Interview," February 9, 2021.

CHAPTER 5

41 *"It really could have been a 59"*: Brian Keogh, "McIlroy on Course at Q-School," *Irish Golf Desk*, September 13, 2007, https://www.irishgolfdesk.com/news-files/2007/9/13/mcilroy-on-course-at-q-school.html.

44 *"It shouldn't give you an extra boost"*: *No Laying Up*, podcast, episode 56, "Rory McIlroy," November 1, 2016, https://podcasts.apple.com/us/podcast/56-rory-mcilroy/id880837011?i=1000404998991.

46 *"It's something I'll remember"*: Kevin Van Valkenburg, "Rory McIlroy Doesn't Know What He Wants," ESPN, April 6, 2016, https://www.espn.com/golf/masters16/story/_/id/15130940/rory-mcilroy-knows-needs-find-way-balance-golf-life.

CHAPTER 6

48 *"I had never been to a country"*: Kimmage, "Paul Kimmage Meets Rory McIlroy: The Truth."

54 *"Maybe Tiger Woods was just clearing the stage"*: "Rory McIlroy, 19, Makes Splash at Accenture Match Play Championship," *New York Daily News*, February 27, 2009, https://www.nydailynews.com/2009/02/27/rory-mcilroy-19-makes-splash-at-accenture-match-play-championship/.

54 *"Hi. I thought that was you"*: Bamberger, "Hair Apparent."

55 *"It is often criticised for its steep slopes"*: "Rory McIlroy: Holywood Star Has Hit the Big Time," *Belfast Telegraph*, June 19, 2011, https://www.belfasttelegraph.co.uk/sport/golf/rory-mcilroy-holywood-star-has-hit-the-big-time/28628527.html.

57 *"We've had a couple of five or six week breaks"*: Brian Keogh, "When Holly Met Rory," *Irish Golf Desk*, July 9, 2011, https://www.irishgolfdesk.com/news-files/2011/7/9/when-holly-met-rory.html.

57 *"Being like eighteen, nineteen, twenty"*: *No Laying Up*, podcast, episode 99, "Rory McIlroy, Part II," September 19, 2017, https://podcasts.apple.com/us/podcast/99-rory-mcilroy-part-ii/id880837011?i=1000400979905.

CHAPTER 7

66 *"I felt the pressure of having to perform"*: *No Laying Up*, "Rory McIlroy," November 1, 2016.

CHAPTER 8

73 *"I was literally in a daze"*: Paul Kimmage, "Paul Kimmage Meets Rory McIlroy—Part Two: Ryder Cup Battles, Irish Open Win and His Longing for a Green

Jacket," *Irish Independent*, January 15, 2017, https://www.independent.ie/sport/gaelic-games/paul-kimmage-meets-rory-mcilroy-part-two-ryder-cup-battles-irish-open-win-and-his-longing-for-a-green-jacket/35368195.html.
74 "*I was just gone*": Ibid.
75 "*a lot of begging*": Keogh, "When Holly Met Rory."
76 "*Everyone who's played this game*": Robinson Holloway, "Lovable Loser: A Funny Thing Happened to Greg Norman After His Disaster at the Masters," *Sports Illustrated*, April 29, 1996, https://vault.si.com/vault/1996/04/29/lovable-loser-a-funny-thing-happened-to-greg-norman-after-his-disaster-at-the-masters.
77 "*The best thing is*": Ibid.
77 "*She definitely keeps my feet*": Keogh, "When Holly Met Rory."
81 "*I was thinking about laying up*": Kimmage, "Paul Kimmage Meets Rory McIlroy—Part Two."
85 "*I always suspected*": "Rory McIlroy's Ex-Girlfriend Holly Sweeney Tells of Her Heartbreak at Split," *Daily Mirror*, December 11, 2011, https://www.mirror.co.uk/3am/celebrity-news/rory-mcilroys-ex-girlfriend-holly-sweeney-96377.
85 "*I saw a tweet*": Ibid.
86 "*Yeah, that's what everyone says*": Kimmage, "Paul Kimmage Meets Rory McIlroy: The Truth."
86 "*[Rory] went straight to see the dogs*": "Rory McIlroy's Ex-Girlfriend Holly Sweeney Tells of Her Heartbreak."
86 "*It killed me*": Ibid.

CHAPTER 9

92 "*The young sweethearts*": Paul Oberjuerge, "Love Is All Around for Caroline Wozniacki and Rory McIlroy," *National*, March 18, 2012, https://www.thenational-news.com/love-is-all-around-for-caroline-wozniacki-and-rory-mcilroy-1.453155.
92 "*It's working so well*": Kevin Mitchell, "US Open 2011: Caroline Wozniacki Needs Wins to Match Off-Court Romance," *Guardian*, August 27, 2011, https://www.theguardian.com/sport/2011/aug/27/us-open-2011-caroline-wozniacki.
99 "*It was the first time*": Kimmage, "Paul Kimmage Meets Rory McIlroy—Part Two."

CHAPTER 10

103 "*Tom Watson walked into the office*": Jeff DiVeronica, "Golf Star Rory McIlroy Spotted Here Saturday," *Democrat & Chronicle*, April 19, 2015, https://www.democratandchronicle.com/story/sports/2015/04/19/top-golfer-rory-mcilroy-spotted-rochesters-vine/26035053/.
103 "*Erica that week was always*": Will Gray, "Rory Remembers Medinah RC: 'Hopefully Won't Need [Police Escort]' This Time," NBC Sports, August 13, 2019, https://www.nbcsports.com/golf/news/rory-mcilroy-reminisces-frantic-police-escort-12-ryder-cup-medinah.

| NOTES | 295

104 *"Turnsoutifyoumisstheteetime"*: Gene Wojciechowski and Bob Harig, "A Miracle or Meltdown at Medinah?," ESPN, September 22, 2015, https://www.espn.com/golf/story/_/id/11570807/a-miracle-meltdown-medinah-recollections-2012-ryder-cup-golf.
104 *"I had already told"*: Ibid.
104 *"Rory climbs in"*: Ibid.
112 *"It was a reactive decision"*: Michael Bamberger, "'It Was Not the Right Thing to Do,'" *Sports Illustrated*, March 11, 2013, https://vault.si.com/vault/2013/03/11/it-was-not-the-right-thing-to-do.
112 *"He might be the best athlete ever"*: Ibid.
113 *"McIlroy was shadowed"*: Karen Crouse, "McIlroy, a Native Son, Divides Ireland," *New York Times*, July 13, 2013, https://www.nytimes.com/2013/07/14/sports/golf/mcilroy-a-native-son-divides-ireland.html.
113 *"seen enough lawyers to last a lifetime"*: Kyle Porter, "Rory McIlroy and Oakley Settle Lawsuit," CBS Sports, November 25, 2013, https://www.cbssports.com/golf/news/rory-mcilroy-and-oakley-settle-lawsuit/.

CHAPTER 11

116 *"impersonal, civil-servicey thing"*: John Laverty, "Rory McIlroy's Reverse Ferret Is on a Par with Ian ('Never, Never, Never') Paisley," *Belfast Telegraph*, February 7, 2024, https://www.belfasttelegraph.co.uk/opinion/rory-mcilroys-reverse-ferret-is-on-a-par-with-ian-never-never-never-paisley/a341978441.html.
117 *"At that time"*: Jaime Diaz, "The Story of Rory," *Golf Digest*, March 9, 2015, https://www.golfdigest.com/story/the-story-of-rory-mcilroy-diaz.
117 *"I thought at the time that being"*: Kimmage, "Paul Kimmage Meets Rory McIlroy—Part Two."
117 *"It was the most homesick"*: Kimmage, "Paul Kimmage Meets Rory McIlroy: The Truth."
118 *"What was happening was, little by little"*: Colin Montgomerie, *The Real Monty: The Autobiography of Colin Montgomerie* (Orion, 2003).
118 *"I can see parallels"*: Sally Jenkins, "Starting Over in Golf or in Love, Nick Faldo Is Not Afraid to Begin Anew, No Matter the Consequences," *Sports Illustrated*, March 11, 1996, https://vault.si.com/vault/1996/03/11/starting-over-in-golf-or-in-love-nick-faldo-is-not-afraid-to-begin-anew-no-matter-the-consequences.
118 *"We had one player drop out"*: Ibid.
123 *"Rory's father and his friends"*: Darren Rovell, "Rory McIlroy's Father Wins $171K," ESPN, July 20, 2014, https://www.espn.com/golf/theopen14/story/_/id/11239690/2014-open-championship-rory-mcilroy-father-wins-bet-son.
125 *"I saw them fist-pump"*: Kimmage, "Paul Kimmage Meets Rory McIlroy—Part Two."
126 *"When I realised it was OK"*: Ibid.

129 *"He is a force"*: Ruby Flanagan et al., "Rory McIlroy's Romantic History Explored: From Meghan Markle Rumours to Caroline Wozniacki," *Daily Express*, April 15, 2025, https://www.express.co.uk/news/uk/2042089/rory-mcilroy-s-romantic-history-explored.

129 *"The thing I love about it"*: Kimmage, "Paul Kimmage Meets Rory McIlroy—Part Two."

CHAPTER 12

132 *"It was a shitshow"*: Kimmage, "Paul Kimmage Meets Rory McIlroy and Shane Lowry."

132 *"It was messy"*: Ibid.

132 *"I hate talking about it"*: Ibid.

134 *"tedious and nasty business"*: Derek Lawrenson, "Rory McIlroy Made £8M Offer to Settle 'Nasty Business' Lawsuit with Former Management Company out of Court," *Daily Mail*, February 2, 2015, https://www.dailymail.co.uk/sport/golf/article-2937017/Rory-McIlroy-8m-offer-settle-nasty-business-lawsuit-former-management-company-court.html.

135 *"Rory told me"*: Diaz, "The Story of Rory."

135 *"They love an 'era'"*: Kimmage, "Paul Kimmage Meets Rory McIlroy—Part Two."

136 *"Eras last about six months"*: Kevin Van Valkenburg, "Spieth Deserves Title as Top Dog in Golf," ABC News, August 14, 2015, https://abcnews.go.com/Sports/spieth-deserves-title-top-dog-golf/story?id=33095675.

137 *"It's hugely disappointing"*: "Rory McIlroy to Miss Open Championship with Ankle Injury," ESPN, July 8, 2015, https://www.espn.com/golf/theopen15/story/_/id/13221271/rory-mcilroy-says-miss-open-championship-ankle-injury.

138 *"I don't feel Erica wants to"*: Kimmage, "Paul Kimmage Meets Rory McIlroy—Part Two."

140 *"falling apart like wet cake"*: Scott Murray, "The Masters 2016: Third Round—As It Happened," *Guardian*, April 9, 2016, https://www.theguardian.com/sport/live/2016/apr/09/the-masters-2016-third-round-live.

CHAPTER 13

144 *"I would have taken a rowing boat"*: Julia Limitone, "Gary Player: Pro Golf Should Be Kicked Out of the Olympics," Fox Business, July 14, 2016, https://www.foxbusiness.com/features/gary-player-pro-golf-should-be-kicked-out-of-the-olympics.

144 *"'Justin, if I had been'"*: Kimmage, "Paul Kimmage Meets Rory McIlroy: The Truth."

146 *"I swear, the first five holes"*: *No Laying Up*, "Rory McIlroy," November 1, 2016.

148 *"Holes 5 through 8"*: Megan Schuster, "The Greatest Game Ever Played: Revisiting Patrick Reed and Rory McIlroy's 2016 Ryder Cup Showdown," *Ringer*, September 26, 2018, https://www.theringer.com/2018/09/26/golf/ryder-cup-2016-rory-mcilroy-patrick-reed.

151 *"Twitter and alcohol"*: No Laying Up, "Rory McIlroy, Part II," September 19, 2017.
152 *"Who lives over there?"*: Paul Kimmage, "Paul Kimmage Meets Rory McIlroy: Ryder Cup Rock Bottom, Open Heartbreak and Catching Covid with Tiger Woods," *Irish Independent*, November 26, 2022, https://www.independent.ie/sport/golf/paul-kimmage-meets-rory-mcilroy-ryder-cup-rock-bottom-open-heartbreak-and-catching-covid-with-tiger-woods/42167667.html.
153 *"I wasn't myself on the golf course"*: No Laying Up, "Rory McIlroy, Part II," September 19, 2017.
154 *"You can't tell Rory what to do"*: Kimmage, "Rory Revisited."
158 *"I was very, very tentative"*: Ibid.

CHAPTER 14

159 *"The series sounds eerily similar"*: Andrew Both, "Golf: New World Tour with Massive Prize Money Proposed," Reuters, May 21, 2018, https://www.reuters.com/article/sports/golf-new-world-tour-with-massive-prize-money-proposed-idUSKCN1IM1T5/.
160 *"Funny enough"*: No Laying Up, podcast, episode 498, "Andy Gardiner from the PGL," November 16, 2021, https://podcasts.apple.com/us/podcast/498-andy-gardiner-from-the-pgl/id880837011?i=1000542164088.
163 *"Everyone was like"*: Kimmage, "Rory Revisited."
173 *"I've been out here for"*: Brian Keogh, "Brooks Koepka on Rory McIlroy Rivalry: 'I Want to Be a Little Bit Better Than Him Because He's Arguably One of the Best Ever,'" *Irish Independent*, February 24, 2024, https://www.independent.ie/sport/golf/brooks-koepka-on-rory-mcilroy-rivalry-i-want-to-be-a-little-bit-better-than-him-because-hes-arguably-one-of-the-best-ever/a431611117.html.
174 *"Everywhere you went in the town"*: James Corrigan, "The Day Rory McIlroy Imploded and Said: 'I Want to Punch Myself in the Face,'" *Telegraph*, July 16, 2025, https://www.telegraph.co.uk/golf/2025/07/16/reliving-rory-mcilroy-collapse-open-royal-portrush-2019/.
174 *"The way they do it"*: Kimmage, "Rory Revisited."
175 *"It was extraordinary"*: Corrigan, "The Day Rory McIlroy Imploded."
175 *"I want to punch myself"*: Ibid.
175 *"It was a crazy change in emotion"*: Ibid.
179 *"We had a pretty testy"*: Kimmage, "Paul Kimmage Meets Rory McIlroy—Part Two."

CHAPTER 15

184 *"It wasn't handled well"*: Kimmage, "Paul Kimmage Meets Rory McIlroy: Ryder Cup."
184 *"Yeah, I was beaten by Poulter"*: Ibid.
185 *"Maybe I'm just not that good"*: Ibid.
186 *"You just need to remember"*: Ibid.

187 "*Michael does a great job*": Murray, "How Rory McIlroy Was Made."
187 "*He knows Rory's whole personality*": Alan Bastable, "The Quiet Man," *Golf Magazine*, December 2012.
189 "*In my role as PAC chairman*": No Laying Up, podcast, episode 506, "Rory McIlroy," December 16, 2021, https://podcasts.apple.com/us/podcast/506-rory-mcilroy/id880837011?i=1000545232086.

CHAPTER 16

196 "*Fine. Really nice*": Kimmage, "Paul Kimmage Meets Rory McIlroy—Part Two."
196 "*Tiger and I knew we wanted*": Kimmage, "Paul Kimmage Meets Rory McIlroy: Ryder Cup."
198 "*I never let myself believe*": Ibid.
204 "*I'm drawn to him*": Ibid.
207 "*Oh my god!*" *Molloy enthused*: Ibid.
208 "*pathologically litigious*": "Larry Klayman," Southern Poverty Law Center, https://www.splcenter.org/resources/extremist-files/larry-klayman/.

CHAPTER 17

217 "*No one else but Rory*": Cameron Morfit, "Rory McIlroy Walks Off Genesis Scottish Open with 'Career' 2-Iron," PGA Tour, July 16, 2023, https://www.pgatour.com/article/news/latest/2023/07/16/rory-mcilroy-wins-genesis-scottish-open-the-renaissance-club.
220 "*I don't know why it popped into my head*": Kimmage, "Paul Kimmage Meets Rory McIlroy and Shane Lowry."

CHAPTER 18

223 "*The work I did with him*": Matt Vincenzi, "Butch Harmon Reveals What He Worked On with Rory McIlroy During Visit Earlier This Year," GolfWRX, May 16, 2024, https://www.golfwrx.com/739359/butch-harmon-reveals-what-he-worked-on-with-rory-mcilroy-during-visit-earlier-this-year/.
224 "*A couple of years ago I went to*": No Laying Up, "Rory McIlroy, Part II," September 19, 2017.
227 "*He was in a tough spot*": Paul Kimmage, "Paul Kimmage Talks to Shane Lowry: His Strong Bond with Rory McIlroy, Anger at 'Couch Pundits' and Return to Portrush," *Belfast Telegraph*, April 6, 2025, https://www.belfasttelegraph.co.uk/sport/golf/paul-kimmage-talks-to-shane-lowry-his-strong-bond-with-rory-mcilroy-anger-at-couch-pundits-and-return-to-portrush/a743909745.html?flow=subscribe&registration=success&reg=true.
229 "*DailyMail.com can reveal*": Laura Collins, "Rory McIlroy and CBS Sports Journalist Amanda Balionis Spark Romance Rumors in Wake of His Divorce from Wife Erica Stoll with Flirty TV Interviews After Married Reporter Ditches Her Ring," *Daily Mail*, May 21, 2024, https://www.dailymail.co.uk/sport/golf

/article-13443851/Rory-McIlroy-Amanda-Balionis-romance-rumors-divorce-wife-Erica-Stoll-PGA-golf.html.
230 *"There have been rumours"*: Ewan Murray, "Rory McIlroy's Divorce Off Before US Open as Couple Resolve Differences," *Guardian*, June 11, 2024, https://www.theguardian.com/sport/article/2024/jun/11/golf-us-open-rory-mcilroy-divorce-off.

CHAPTER 19

245 *"That hurt. That hit me"*: Colt Knost and Drew Stoltz, hosts, *Subpar*, podcast, "J.J. Spaun Breaks Down His Incredible U.S. Open Victory, Expectations for the Ryder Cup," July 8, 2025.
250 *"When Rory and Bryson"*: Dottie Pepper, "An Inside-the-Ropes View of Rory McIlroy Making History at the Masters," *Golf Digest*, May 12, 2025, https://www.golfdigest.com/story/inside-the-ropes-view-dottie-pepper-rory-mcilroy-masters-augusta-national-history.
251 *"I saw a quality in him"*: Ibid.
252 *"I could not believe"*: The *Fried Egg* podcast, December 16, 2025.
252 *"My dad took on three jobs"*: Paul Kimmage, "Rory McIlroy—The Full Interview: Read Paul Kimmage's Exclusive Talk with the World's Number 1 Golfer," *Irish Independent*, December 8, 2022, https://www.independent.ie/sport/golf/rory-mcilroy-the-full-interview-read-paul-kimmages-exclusive-talk-with-the-worlds-number-1-golfer/42206232.html.
252 *"So much craziness would transpire"*: Pepper, "An Inside-the-Ropes View."
253 *"The rooting interests were fascinating"*: Ibid.
257 *"He said to me, 'Rory'"*: No Laying Up, "Rory McIlroy," December 16, 2021.
258 *"the loudest I've ever heard in my life"*: Ibid.
266 *"It was unbearable"*: Adam Schupak, "Schupak: I Took the 'Rory McIlroy Tour' and Played His Childhood Course. Here's What I Learned," *Golfweek*, July 14, 2025, https://golfweek.usatoday.com/story/sports/golf/majors/british-open/2025/07/14/schupak-i-took-the-rory-mcilroy-tour-in-holywood-northern-ireland/85191127007/.
266 *"a watershed moment"*: Shane Ryan, "Rory McIlroy's Masters Win Might Have Been the Ultimate 'Dudes Crying' Moment in Golf," *Golf Digest*, April 17, 2025, https://www.golfdigest.com/story/rory-s-masters-win-might-have-been-the-ultimate--dudes-crying--m.

CHAPTER 20

282 *"I'm going to make a prediction"*: Tim Rosaforte, "Encore! Encore! Tiger Woods Unleashed a Full Array of Shots to Win His Second Straight U.S. Amateur Title," *Sports Illustrated*, September 4, 1995, https://vault.si.com/vault/1995/09/04/encore-encore-tiger-woods-unleashed-a-full-array-of-shots-to-win-his-second-straight-us-amateur-title.
282 *"I've seen it firsthand"*: Kimmage, "Paul Kimmage Meets Rory McIlroy: The Truth."

About the Author

ALAN SHIPNUCK is the author of ten books, including the bestsellers *Phil*; *Bud, Sweat & Tees*; and *The Swinger* (with Michael Bamberger). He wrote dozens of cover stories across twenty-five years at *Sports Illustrated* and has received thirteen first-place awards from the Golf Writers Association of America—breaking the record of Dan Jenkins, a member of the World Golf Hall of Fame. Shipnuck lives in Carmel, California, where he is the head coach of Carmel High's varsity girls basketball team.